# ASTRONOMY

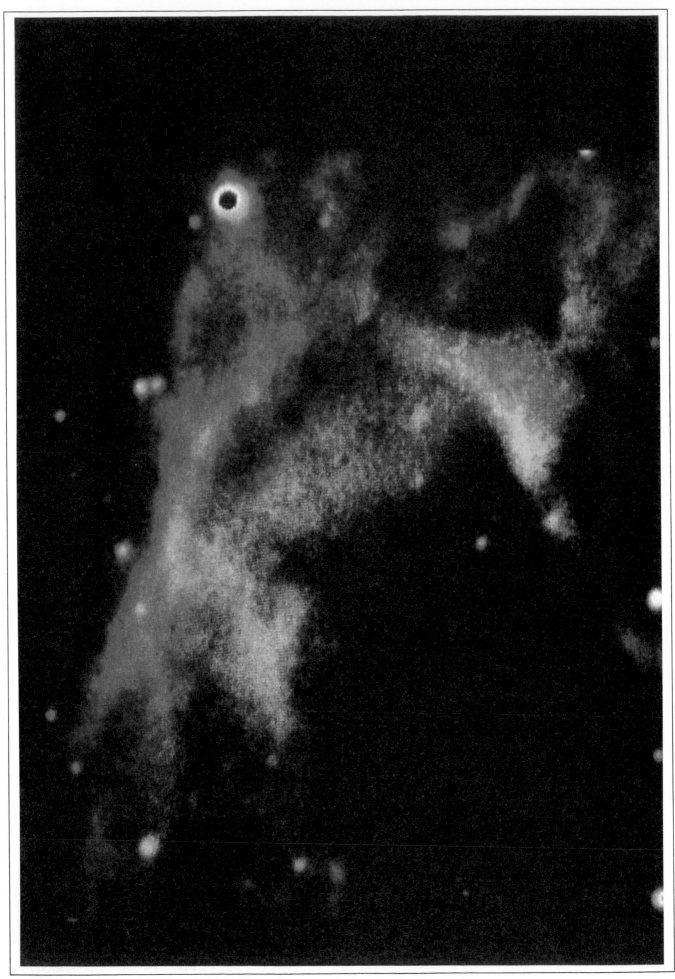

False color enhances an image of galaxy NGC 2359.

THE WORLD BOOK ENCYCLOPEDIA OF SCIENCE
VOLUME 1

# ASTRONOMY

**WORLD BOOK, INC.**
a Scott Fetzer company

CHICAGO LONDON SYDNEY TORONTO

# Staff

**Publisher Emeritus**
William H. Nault

**President**
John E. Frere

**Vice President and
Editor in Chief**
Dick Dell

**Vice President and
Editorial Director/
Product Development**
Michael Ross

## Editorial

**Managing Editor**
Maureen Mostyn Liebenson

**Associate Editors**
Karen Zack Ingebretsen
Patricia Ohlenroth

**Senior Editor**
Melissa Raskovich

**Writers**
Katie Sharp
Rita Vander Meulen

**Permissions Editor**
Janet T. Peterson

**Indexer**
Janet Russell

**Researchers**
Mitchell Bassler
Lynn Durbin
Cheryl Graham
Karen McCormack
Loranne Shields

**Consultant**
April Whitt
Astronomer
Fernbank Science Center

## Art

**Executive Director**
Roberta Dimmer

**Art Director**
Wilma Stevens

**Designer**
Ann Tomasic

**Senior Photographs Editor**
Sandra Dyrlund

**Photographs Editor**
Carol Parden

## Product Production

**Vice President, Production
and Technology**
Daniel N. Bach

**Director of
Manufacturing/Pre-press**
Sandra Van den Broucke

**Manager, Manufacturing**
Barbara Podczerwinski

**Senior Production Manager**
Randi Park

**Production Manager**
Bonny Davidson

**Proofreaders**
Anne Dillon
Karen Lenburg

**Text Processing**
Curley Hunter
Gwendolyn Johnson

World Book, Inc.
525 W. Monroe
Chicago, IL 60661

© 1989, 1984 Verlagsgruppe Bertelsmann International GmbH, Munich.

Library of Congress Catalog Card No. 95-61672
ISBN: 0-7166-3394-9
Printed in the United States of America

18 19 20 21 99 98 97 96

# Contents

# Preface

The quest to understand the universe and describe its creation and subsequent story is nearly as old as mankind. In the Western world, the best known creation story comes from the Bible in the book of Genesis. It tells how God created the earth and all living things. Modern religious thinkers interpret the Biblical story of creation in various ways. Some believe that creation occurred exactly as Genesis describes it. Others think that God's method of creation is revealed through scientific investigation. *Astronomy* describes what most scientists believe to be the unfolding story of the universe.

### The editorial approach

The object of the *Encyclopedia of Science* is to explain for adults and children alike the many aspects of science that are not only fascinating in themselves but are also vitally important for an understanding of the world today. To achieve this, the books in this series are straightforward and concise, accurate in content, and are clearly and attractively presented.

The often forbidding appearance of traditional science publications has been completely avoided in the *Encyclopedia of Science*. Approximately equal proportions of illustrations and text make even the most unfamiliar subjects interesting and attractive. Even more important, all of the drawings have been created specially to complement the text, each explaining a topic that can be difficult to understand through the printed word alone.

The thorough application of these principles has created a publication that covers its subject in an interesting and stimulating way, and that will prove to be an invaluable work of reference and education for many years to come.

### The advance of science

One of the most exciting and challenging aspects of science is that its frontiers are constantly being revised and extended, and new developments are occurring all the time. Its advance depends largely on observation, experimentation, and debate, which generate theories that have to be tested and even then stand only until they are replaced by better concepts. For this reason, it is difficult for any science publication to be completely comprehensive. It is possible, however, to provide a thorough foundation that ensures that any such advances can be comprehended. It is the purpose of each book in this series to create such a foundation, by providing all the basic knowledge in the particular area of science it describes.

### How to use this book

This book can be used in two basic ways.

The first, and more conventional, way is to start at the beginning and to read through to the end, which gives a coherent and thorough picture of the subject and opens a resource of basic information that can be returned to for re-reading and reference.

The second allows the book to be used as a library of information presented subject by subject, which the reader can consult piece by piece as required.

All articles are prepared and presented so that the subject is equally accessible by either method. Topics are arranged in a logical sequence, outlined in the contents list. The index allows access to more specific points.

Within an article, scientific terms are explained in the main text where an understanding of them is central to the understanding of the subject as a whole. There is also an alphabetical glossary of terms at the end of the book, so that the reader's memory can be refreshed and so that the book can be used for quick reference whenever necessary.

Each volume also contains a section on the various careers that pertain to the volume's subject.

The sample two-page article *(right)* shows the important elements of this editorial plan and illustrates the way in which this organization permits maximum flexibility of use.

(A) **Article title** gives the reader an immediate reference point.

(B) **Section title** quickly shows the reader how information is arranged within the article.

(C) **Main text** consists of narrative information set out in a logical manner, avoiding biographical and technical details that might tend to interrupt the story line and hamper the reader's progress.

(D) **Illustrations** include specially commissioned drawings and diagrams and carefully selected photographs, which expand, clarify, and add to the main text.

(E) **Captions** explain the illustrations and make the connection between the textual and the visual elements of the article.

(F) **Labels** help the reader to identify the parts of the illustrations that are referred to in the captions.

(G) **Theme images,** where appropriate, are included in the top left-hand corner of the left-hand page, to emphasize a central element of information or to create a visual link between different but related articles.

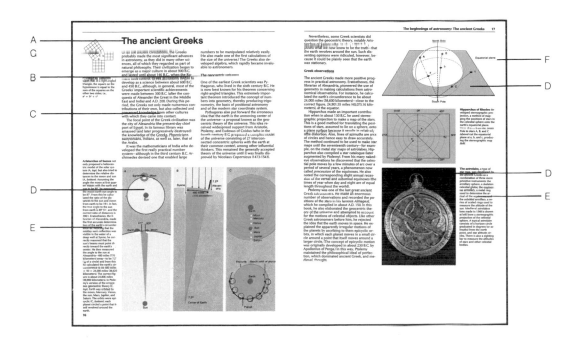

**Astronomers** use a variety of techniques and instruments—like this optical telescope at the Griffith Observatory in Los Angeles—to study the solar system and the universe beyond.

**A**eronautical drafters make mechanical drawings of aircraft, spacecraft, missiles, rockets, helicopters—equipment related to the aerospace industry—and all their components. Aeronautical drafters are also responsible for developing scale drawings of prototype equipment. The mechanical drawings provide the exact information needed to make the equipment, including instructions for manufacturing it. Drafters must draw the equipment precisely to scale and at several different angles, and provide specifications such as dimensions. In the past, aeronautical drafters created the drawings manually. But today, most drafters create their final drawings on a computer using a technique called *computer-aided design and drafting* (CADD).

**A**erospace engineers apply engineering principles and techniques to the design, development, and testing of spacecraft, missiles, and other aircraft. Many kinds of engineers work in the aerospace industry, which is involved in the production of both aircraft and spacecraft. Aerospace *project engineers* direct and coordinate the activities of teams assigned to a particular project. They are responsible for determining the feasibility of a project, as well as its cost and production time. *Aerospace design engineers* develop basic design concepts used in aeronautical and aerospace equipment and systems. *Aerospace test engineers* conduct testing activities on the equipment to ensure it meets established engineering, quality, and safety standards. *Aerospace field-service engineers* investigate and resolve any technical difficulties encountered in aerospace equipment and systems.

**A**erospace physiological technicians use their special knowledge and skills to minimize the physical and physiological stresses of pilots and astronauts in flight. These technicians are responsible for obtaining physiological and medical histories of pilot and astronaut candidates during job interviews to determine if they have any problems that would prevent them from performing their duties. Aerospace physiological technicians also operate a variety of training devices that simulate flying conditions, such as pressure suits, pressure chambers, parasail equipment, and ejection seats. When training a pilot or astronaut in a pressure chamber, these technicians simulate flying conditions through a control panel, adjusting gas and air flow, temperature, and barometric pressure to reflect different altitudes and speeds.

**Astronomers** study the locations and motions of stars, planets, and other heavenly bodies. Most astronomers are also called *astrophysicists* because they use physics and mathematics to examine the physical and chemical processes that occur in the universe.

Today's astronomers spend little time observing the heavens through a telescope. Instead, they use photographic and electronic equipment, computers, and satellites to see far into space. Most astronomers specialize in a particular area, such as *stellar astronomy,* the study of stars; *solar astronomy,* the study of the sun; or *planetary astronomy,* the study of conditions on the planets. Astronomers who study the history and structure of the universe as a whole are called *cosmologists.*

**Preparing for a space mission,** astronaut F. Story Musgrave *(right)* is assisted by a team of aerospace technicians at Johnson Space Center. This team tested tools that were used in the Hubble Space Telescope repair mission in 1993.

**An astronaut prepares** for a practice session in Johnson Space Center's Weightless Environment Training Facility. By carrying out tasks under water, astronauts learn to maneuver during space walks.

**Aerospace technicians** assist engineers in projects involving the design, development, testing, and production of aircraft and spacecraft. Important members of the engineering team, they do the routine work that allows the team's scientists and engineers to focus on issues that require more advanced training. This work may include creating detailed drawings or scale models of a particular kind of vehicle, collecting data, conducting laboratory experiments, or making cost and production estimates. Aerospace technicians must be skilled in using computers, slide rules, and other technical equipment.

**Astronauts** operate spacecraft and space stations, launch and recapture satellites, and conduct experiments in space. On the ground, astronauts participate in space-mission work, and often assist in the design of spacecraft. *Pilot astronauts* command and pilot spacecraft. *Mission specialist astronauts* conduct experiments, launch satellites, and perform spacewalks. They also maintain the spacecraft and its equipment. *Payload specialists* carry out scientific experiments connected with the *payload* (cargo) on the spacecraft. Most astronauts work for NASA and receive extensive training at the Lyndon B. Johnson Space Center in Houston, Texas, where they also live. They attend classes conducted by experts in aerodynamics, physics, physiology, and other subjects. They also receive flight training in T-38 jet aircraft.

**F**light surgeons are medical doctors who study the effects of flight on human health. These doctors specialize in *aviation medicine,* which involves the care of airplane crews and passengers. Aviation medicine and *space medicine,* which focuses on the care of astronauts, are the two major areas in the field of *aerospace medicine.* Flight surgeons help design equipment and develop crew selection and training programs that protect the health and safety of airplane crews and passengers. They also investigate airplane accidents, train flight crews for survival after accidents, and transport sick or injured people by air. Researchers who specialize in space medicine study the effects of space travel on humans. For example, they investigate ways to reduce the bone and muscle loss caused by weightlessness, through diet, exercise, and drug therapy. These scientists also study the effects of radiation on space travelers and the psychological effects of long space missions.

**F**light test data acquisition technicians are specialists in obtaining and analyzing flight test data. These technicians use their knowledge of electronic theory and the operation of computer systems to set up, operate, and monitor the computer systems and devices used to record and analyze the data. Their job begins as soon as a flight test is planned, since they must know which data will be required for post-flight analysis. They discuss all the requirements with members of the flight engineering team to ensure that the correct data will be recorded. Once that step is completed, the technicians set up the equipment and design the computer programs that will be used to capture the data during the flight test. They input the necessary information into the computer program, modifying it as necessary for additional or revised test requirements.

**A planetarium technician** works on the projection equipment at the Jodrell Bank radio observatory.

**P**lanetarium technicians combine their knowledge of astronomy with their technical expertise to plan and coordinate planetarium presentations. A planetarium is a device that shows the changing positions of the heavenly bodies by projecting lights onto the inside of a dome. A planetarium technician performs a variety of "behind the scenes" duties to ensure that all the technical aspects of a presentation work together smoothly and effectively. These specialists install, operate, and maintain sound and projection equipment, making any necessary modifications to create the desired effects. In addition, planetarium technicians make sure that the background music is synchronized with the visual display and commentary, often selecting the music themselves. They also use their knowledge of electrooptic equipment and systems to create and install special effects that enhance the educational and entertainment value of the presentation.

**R**esearch mechanics, also known as laboratory test mechanics, assist aerospace engineers in uncovering design or production flaws when testing new aircraft parts and assemblies. They are responsible for creating, assembling, and testing these parts according to the specifications called for by the design engineers. In addition, research mechanics operate the test equipment and devices, gathering vital information on the performance of each component under various flight and operational conditions. Once they have performed the necessary tests, research mechanics record and interpret all the results, reporting their findings to the design engineering team.

**S**atellite systems engineers are involved in the many facets of designing, producing, maintaining, and monitoring artificial satellite systems. Artificial satellites are manufactured objects that continuously orbit the earth or some other body in space. They provide important information about other planets and solar systems, as well as our own planet's weather patterns. Satellites also serve an important role in worldwide telecommunications by transmitting calls, computer data, and radio signals across the oceans. In addition to planning and designing these complex and highly technical systems, satellite systems engineers are responsible for ensuring that they operate properly at all times. These specialists work in ground control centers situated in remote locations around the world. The engineers are part of a team of specialists who monitor the satellite's position, send instructions to its computers, and retrieve the information collected by the satellite.

**S**tress analysts are responsible for ensuring that the structural components of an aircraft or spacecraft can withstand the stress imposed during its operation. In addition, stress analysts formulate mathematical models, design computer simulation systems, and develop new methods for testing and analyzing stress. To evaluate a component, stress analysts perform tests on *prototype* equipment and systems. Prototypes are specially made, one-of-a-kind models upon which all future production is based. Throughout their testing procedures, stress analysts look at the strength and bending characteristics of each part and assembly, as well as its entire framework. They also review preliminary design concepts and specifications with other members of the engineering team.

**Satellite systems engineers** prepare to send a Solar and Heliospheric Observatory satellite into space.

# The beginnings of astronomy

**Stonehenge,** situated on Salisbury Plain in southern England, is one of the finest examples of a prehistoric stone circle in the world. Considering the primitive state of European technology at the time it was built (between about 2200 B.C. and 1600 B.C.), this megalithic "observatory" is an impressive achievement. About 80 large stones (some weighing more than 25 tons) were transported from Marlborough Downs, a distance of more than 19 miles (30 kilometers). Many of the smaller stones (called bluestones) were taken from southwest Wales, even farther away. Moreover, many of the stones were shaped, dressed smooth, and carefully positioned to mark important astronomical events, such as the rising and setting of the sun and moon.

## Prehistoric astronomy

The ancient astronomers of prehistoric megalithic cultures had a surprisingly good understanding of the motions of the celestial bodies and of practical geometry. Evidence that they possessed these skills comes from the mysterious groups of large standing stones, or megaliths (some weighing more than 25 tons), arranged in regular geometric patterns that are found in many parts of the world. Some of these stone circles found in Europe (Stonehenge in Britain and Carnac in France, for example) were so arranged that they mark the rising and setting of the sun and moon at specific times throughout the year. In particular, they mark the eight extreme positions of the

From the dawn of civilization, when people first began to contemplate the heavens, the sun, moon, stars, planets, comets, and meteors have been objects of wonder, mystery, and awe. Later, but still early in the development of human civilization, people began to study the heavens in a more scientific way. This was an important step toward understanding the natural world and using this knowledge to modify it to advantage. Then, as astronomical knowledge increased (helped by, and also helping, progress in other areas of study) our comprehension and mastery of nature also increased. This knowledge eventually led to the huge body of learning and the sophisticated technology of our modern world. Despite these prodigious advances, however, we still have much to discover about the heavenly bodies and the phenomena that can be observed in the universe.

Imagine what our way of life would have been like if we had been unable to see the sky because it was permanently overcast with clouds. There would probably have been no way of telling the time, for which the sun is invaluable, nor are we likely to have developed calendars. Calendars were essential for determining the best time to plant crops, for hunting and moving animal herds, and for organizing community life. Similarly, the development of navigation—notably the concepts of latitude and longitude—and the exploration of the earth would, at the very least, have been greatly retarded. Moreover, these are only the more obvious of the probable results of a world without astronomical knowledge; the full implications are much more complex and far-reaching. Nevertheless, it is probably a justifiable simplification to postulate that human beings would not have developed far beyond the stage of the Paleolithic cave dwellers, depending for food on what they could hunt or find growing naturally, if they had not studied the heavens and made practical use of the knowledge gained from them.

moon during its changes in declination in the 29.5-day cycle from one full moon to the next.

Stonehenge is probably the best known and finest example of the many prehistoric stone circle "observatories." It was constructed in several phases over a period of approximately 600 years, between about 2200 B.C. and 1600 B.C., and most of the individual stones were sited in relation to the sun and moon rather than the positions of the stars. This plan was probably adopted because the declinations and positions of the stars in the sky change gradually and unpredictably—an effect that would be noticeable over the many centuries it took to build Stonehenge. Whereas, the declinations of the sun and moon change in predictable cycles. Stonehenge was built on the 51st degree of latitude and took account of the fact that the angle between the point at which the sun rises above the horizon at the summer solstice (approximately June 21, when the sun reaches its greatest declination) and the southernmost point at which the moon rises is a right angle. Divided into 56 seg-

ments, the surrounding circle could, therefore, be used to determine the position of the moon throughout the year. It could also be used to ascertain the dates of midsummer and midwinter and to predict the occurrence of solar eclipses.

Stone circles, therefore, provided prehistoric people with a comparatively reliable calendar—an essential requirement when they settled into organized agricultural and hunting communities after the last Ice Age, in about 10,000 B.C. But although early people gradually learned to use the heavens as a means of regulating life, they also stood in awe of the celestial bodies. They regarded them as dwelling places or even as manifestations of powerful gods who controlled them and all worldly events. Thus began one aspect of the study of the heavens, now known as astrology, which paid particular attention to the relationship between the movements of stars and planets and the supposed influence of these upon human affairs, an interest maintained today.

**The pyramids at Giza** are sited about 6 miles (10 kilometers) west of the Nile River and about 9 miles (15 kilometers) southwest of Cairo. Dating from between about 2600 B.C. and 2500 B.C., they are still among the largest buildings ever erected. Square in transverse cross-section, almost all of the many Egyptian pyramids were carefully positioned with their faces aligned north-south and east-west. Other structural features of the pyramids also have astronomical significance. For example, the entrance passage of the Khufu (Cheops) pyramid pointed directly toward Alpha Draconis, the star closest to the north celestial pole at the time the pyramid was built.

# Astronomy as a science

Approximately contemporary with the megalithic cultures of western Europe, but flourishing independently of, were the much more advanced civilizations of Egypt, Babylon, India, and China. Each had its own system of astronomy, inextricably mixed with astrology, mythology, and religion. Each called upon the support of its own particular gods, kings, wise men, and mythical heroes to present its political, religious, or social aspirations to the people.

In Egypt, for example, astronomers made careful observations of the positions of the stars—especially the positions and times at which various stars rose and set. Of particular importance was the precise date of the summer heliacal rising (the emergence of a star from the light of the sun) of the bright star Sirius. This event portended the annual flooding of the Nile River, which was vital to the agricultural economy and hence, to the lives of the entire population of the Nile valley. The ancient Egyptian astronomers were also highly competent mathematicians—a skill that is apparent from the design (both external and internal) and positioning of the pyramids.

### Middle-Eastern astronomers

In addition to the Nile River, the Tigris, Euphrates, and Indus rivers were also sites of flourishing civilizations in the 2,000 years before the birth of Christ. Their religious beliefs and cultures were incorporated into, and characterized by, their particular types of astrology and their special forms of mythology and folklore relating to the stars. Observations that may originally have had purely spiritual or religious purposes gradually became more scientific and thus encouraged the development of astronomy.

There were four main factors that enabled these ancient but advanced cultures to develop a relatively sophisticated astronomy: they were located in a part of the world that had clear skies throughout most of the year; they had a leisured elite with spare time to study the heavens; they had a written language, which provided them with a means of recording their observations; and they had the mathematical knowledge to make practical use of their astronomical findings. These favorable conditions were common to the civilizations of Babylon, Assyria, the Sumerians of Mesopotamia, the Egyptians at the time of the pyramids, the Greeks, and later, the Phoenicians and the Arabs.

In addition to using their knowledge of the heavens to make calendars and predict various regular events, these ancient civilizations also developed considerable skill in using the stars for finding directions. Consequently, they began navigating ships across the seas and caravans across the featureless deserts.

In Mesopotamia, however, in about the seventh century B.C., astronomy, and particularly the aspect of it known as cosmology (which concerns the universe as a whole) became closely involved with the Zoroastrian religion, which also devoted considerable attention to astrology, so that the two studies became linked. Later, Babylonian priests put astronomy back on a scientific and mathematical footing. But farther east it remained amalgamated with, and was often totally incorporated into, astrology.

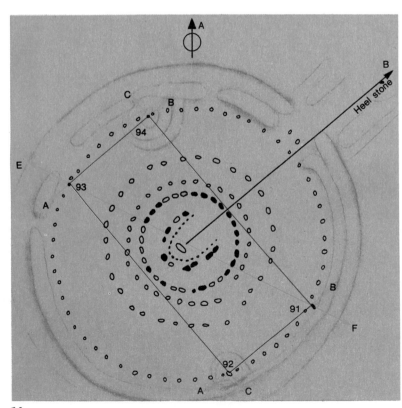

**The megalithic monument** of Stonehenge *(above)* consists basically of several concentric circles of standing stones. The diagram *(left)* shows the positions of existing stones (solid black) and of the holes in which stones originally stood (outlined). There are many astronomically significant alignments among the various positions. The station stones (91 to 94) form an accurate rectangle, with the two short parallel sides indicating midwinter sunset (A) and midsummer sunrise (B) (the latter also indicated by Stonehenge's axis, center to Heel stone) and the two long sides showing the positions of moonrise (C) and moonset at major standstill. The diagonal (91 to 93) indicates moonset (E) and moonrise (F) at minor standstill. In addition, the moon undergoes an 18.61-year cycle in which its northernmost rising point moves between 50° north of east (major standstill) and 30° north of east (minor standstill).

A ziggurat, a large pyramidal stepped temple (a reconstruction of which is illustrated), was built in the center of most major Babylonian cities. Many ziggurats were dedicated to celestial gods—the one at Ur, for example, was dedicated to Su'en, the moon god. As in many other ancient civilizations, Babylonian astronomy was inextricably mixed with religion, mythology, and astrology. Moreover, the priests tended to be the best-educated sector of the population; thus they were largely responsible for the development of Babylonian science, including astronomy. The Babylonian empire lasted from about 2700 B.C. to 500 B.C., during which time the priests did much to demystify astronomy and put it back on a scientific basis.

## Astrology

Despite modern science's lack of regard for astrology, the work of the early astrologers was of great value in the development of astronomy, principally because of their accurate observations and records of star positions. But the conclusions that those astrologers drew from their observations depended far more on supernatural beliefs than on scientific principles. For example, from calculations known only to themselves, they plotted charts called horoscopes, from which they attempted to predict and influence future events.

Such interpretations of celestial phenomena were in accord with the belief. This belief was widely held in Europe before the discoveries of Copernicus and Galileo in the sixteenth and seventeenth centuries. It is still popular in many parts of the world today. As a result, in many parts of the world the astrologers themselves became extremely influential, consulted by the rich and the powerful. Astrology, therefore, became at best a pseudoscience occupied—even obsessed—with attempts to predict (and influence) the rise and fall of kings and governments and the course of national events.

Only the Hebrews, with their belief in one God whom they regarded as creator and arbiter of all things, strongly repudiated the views and claims of astrologers. Despite this, however, the Old Testament contains some 25 references to stars and astronomy.

Astrology also had an influence on the development of sciences other than astronomy. In early medicine, for example, each part of the human body was considered to be under the influence of a specific part of the celestial sphere. And alchemy, the embryo science of chemistry, adopted astrologers' planetary symbols for various elements. For example, the planet Mars, named after the Roman god of war, gave its symbol to the metal iron.

Regarded as a whole, astrology can, therefore, be seen as an attempt to explain the apparently baffling mysteries of the natural world, not merely the celestial phenomena investigated by modern astronomers, and to establish a methodical interpretation of them. Although modern science now disagrees with astrology's method, our understanding of the universe has benefited by its attempt to impose a logical order on natural phenomena.

An Egyptian mummy case showing the goddess Nut surrounded by signs of the zodiac. Despite the antiquity of this relic, which dates from the early A.D. 100's, many of the signs are the same as those used today; easily recognizable, for example, are Leo (the Lion), Libra (the Scales), Pisces (the Fish), Taurus (the Bull), and Gemini (the Twins).

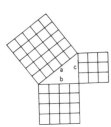

**Pythagoras' theorem**
states that, in a right-angled triangle, the square on the hypotenuse is equal to the sum of the squares on the other two sides; i.e.,
$$a^2 = b^2 + c^2$$

# The ancient Greeks

Of all the ancient civilizations, the Greeks probably made the most significant advances in astronomy, as they did in many other sciences, all of which they regarded as part of natural philosophy. Their civilization began to emerge as a major culture in about 900 B.C. and lasted until about 146 B.C., when the Romans took control. Greek astronomy began to develop as a science between about 600 B.C. and 450 B.C., although, in general, most of the Greeks' important scientific achievements were made between 300 B.C. (after the conquests of Alexander the Great in the Middle East and India) and A.D. 200. During this period, the Greeks not only made numerous contributions of their own, but also collected and preserved knowledge from other cultures with which they came into contact.

The focal point of the Greek civilization was the city of Alexandria (the present-day chief port of Egypt). In its famous library was amassed (and later progressively destroyed) the knowledge of the Greeks, Phoenicians, Babylonians, Indians, as well as, later, that of the Arabs.

It was the mathematicians of India who developed the first really practical number system—although in the third century B.C. Archimedes devised one that enabled large

numbers to be manipulated relatively easily. (He also made one of the first calculations of the size of the universe.) The Greeks also developed algebra, which rapidly became invaluable to astronomers.

## The geocentric universe

One of the earliest Greek scientists was Pythagoras, who lived in the sixth century B.C. He is now best known for his theorem concerning right-angled triangles. This extremely important theorem introduced the concept of numbers into geometry, thereby producing trigonometry, the basis of positional astronomy and of the modern star coordinate system.

Pythagoras also put forward the erroneous idea that the earth is the unmoving center of the universe—a proposal known as the geocentric theory of the universe. This idea received widespread support from Aristotle, Ptolemy, and Eudoxus of Cnidus (who in the fourth century B.C. proposed a complex model of the universe consisting of 27 interconnected concentric spheres with the earth at their common center), among other influential thinkers. This remained the generally accepted theory of the universe until it was finally disproved by Nicolaus Copernicus (1473-1543).

**Aristarchus of Samos** not only proposed a heliocentric model of the solar system (A, *top*), but also tried to determine the relative distances to the moon and sun (A, *bottom*). Assuming the angle the moon at first quarter makes with the earth and sun to be 90°, he measured the moon-earth-sun angle to be 87°. From this he calculated the ratio of the distances to the sun and moon from earth to be 19:1. In fact, the true angle to the sun from earth is 89° 51', and the correct ratio of distances is 390:1. Eratosthenes, the librarian of Alexandria, made the first accurate determination of the earth's circumference (B). Noticing that the midday sun's reflection was visible in the water of a deep well at Syene, he correctly reasoned that the sun's beams must point directly toward the earth's center. He then measured the angle to the sun at Alexandria—480 miles (770 kilometers) away—to be 7.2° ($\frac{1}{50}$ of a circle) and from this he calculated the earth's circumference to be 480 miles × 50 = 24,000 miles (38,620 kilometers). The correct figure is about 24,800 miles (39,900 kilometers). In Ptolemy's version of the erroneous geocentric theory (C, *top*), Earth was orbited by the moon, Mercury, Venus, the sun, Mars, Jupiter, and Saturn. The orbits were epicyclic (C, *bottom*); each planet circled a point that itself revolved around the earth.

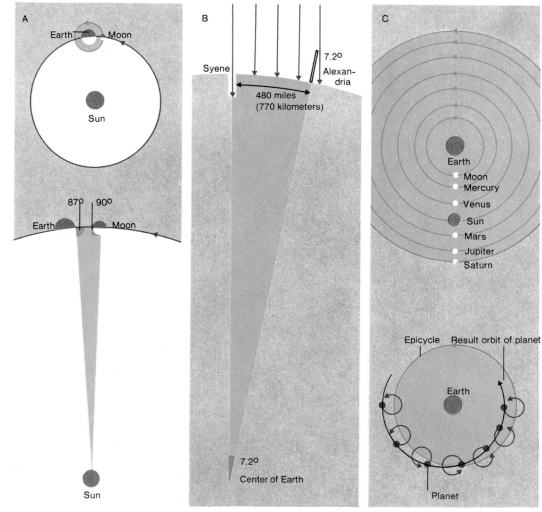

Nevertheless, some Greek scientists did question the geocentric theory, notably Aristarchus of Samos who, in about 280 B.C., proposed what we now know to be the truth—that the earth revolves around the sun. Such dissenting opinions were ridiculed, however, because it could be plainly seen that the earth was stationary.

### Greek observations

The ancient Greeks made more positive progress in practical astronomy. Eratosthenes, the librarian of Alexandria, pioneered the use of geometry in making calculations from astronomical observations. For instance, he calculated the earth's circumference to be about 24,000 miles (38,600 kilometers)—close to the correct figure, 24,901.55 miles (40,075.16 kilometers), at the equator.

Hipparchus made an important contribution when in about 130 B.C. he used stereographic projection to make a map of the stars. This is a good method for translating the positions of stars, assumed to lie on a sphere, onto a plane surface because it results in relatively little distortion. Also, lines of azimuths are arcs of circles and hence easy to draw accurately. The method continued to be used to make star maps until the seventeenth century—for example, on the metal star maps of astrolabes. Hipparchus also compiled a star catalogue (later augmented by Ptolemy). From his many naked-eye observations he discovered that the celestial pole moves by a few minutes of arc over a period of several years, a phenomenon now called *precession* of the equinoxes. He also noted the corresponding slight annual recession of the vernal and autumnal equinoxes (the times of year when day and night are of equal length throughout the world).

Ptolemy was one of the last great ancient Greek astronomers. He made an enormous number of observations and recorded the positions of the stars in his famous *Almagest*, which he compiled in about A.D. 150. In this book, he also elaborated the geocentric theory of the universe and attempted to account for the motions of celestial objects. Like other Greek astronomers before him, he rejected the idea that the earth moves in space. He explained the apparently irregular motions of the planets by ascribing to them epicyclic orbits, in which each planet moves in a small circle around a point that itself moves around a larger circle. (The concept of epicyclic motion was originally developed in about 230 B.C. by Apollonius of Perga.) In this way, Ptolemy maintained the philosophical ideal of perfection, which dominated ancient Greek, and medieval, thought.

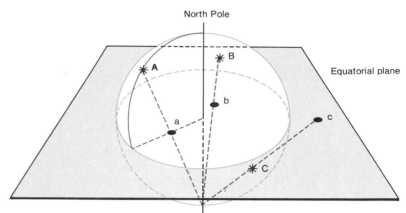

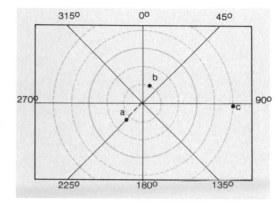

**Hipparchus of Rhodes** developed stereographic projection, a method of mapping the positions of stars in the celestial sphere onto the earth's equatorial plane. Lines drawn from the South Pole to stars A, B, and C *(above)* cut the equatorial plane at a, b, and c, producing the stereographic map *(left)*.

**The astrolabe,** a type of star map, was developed by the ancient Greeks as a combination of three more primitive instruments: the armillary sphere, a skeleton celestial globe; the equinoctial armillary, a metal ring used to determine the arrival of the equinoxes; and the solstitial armillary, a series of scaled rings used to measure the altitude of the sun. Medieval astrolabes (one made in 1548 is shown at left) bore a stereographic projection of the celestial sphere. A typical astrolabe consists of a horizon circle, graduated in degrees (or azimuths) from the north point, and star altitude circles. There is also a sighting bar to measure the altitudes of stars and other celestial bodies.

# Calendars and navigation

Probably the first practical use to which early civilizations put their astronomical knowledge was the devising of calendars, which were essential for organizing the social, economic, and religious life of their society. Prehistoric stone circles, such as those at Stonehenge in Britain and Carnac in France, for example, almost certainly functioned as calendars.

There is, however, a fundamental problem in devising an accurate calendar: the principal units of time (the day, month, and year) are not simple or integral fractions of each other. In simple terms, a day is the time taken by the earth in completing one revolution on its axis. A month was originally regarded as the time taken for the moon to make one orbit of the earth, or the period from one full moon to the next. A year is the time taken for the earth to complete one of its orbits around the sun. But there are several ways of measuring and defining each of these basic units. As a result, numerous different calendars have been developed through the ages, and even today, a number of cultures use calendars that differ from the usual Western kind, such as the Islamic calendar, the Jewish calendar, and several Oriental calendars.

In many calendars, the moon serves to divide the year into months and the phases of the moon are often used to mark religious festivals. The word *month* itself is derived from *moon.* The Chinese of the Shang dynasty (*c.*1766-*c.*1122 B.C.) used a calendar based on a 30-day lunar month, and even in the modern Islamic calendar, the beginning and end of Ramadan (the month of fasting) are fixed by

sightings of the new moon. The way in which the Christian Church calculates the date of Easter also depends on the lunar cycle. Priests of the Mayan civilization, which flourished in Central America from about A.D. 250 to the ninth century, devised several elaborate calendars, one of which was of 360 or 365 days and was based on the periodicity of the orbit of the planet Venus. The first calendar that related days, months, and years was the Metonic calendar. This was based on the lunar cycle of 19 years, after which the moon's phases recur on the same days of the year. Devised by the ancient Greek astronomer Meton in about 432 B.C., this calendar was later adopted by the Persians. It is still used today to define Passover in the Jewish calendar.

The calendar most used today is based principally on the sun. A day consists of 24 hours and a normal year of 365 days, divided into 12 months of between 28 and 31 days each. This leads to certain discrepancies, the most significant resulting from the fact that the solar, or tropical, year is 365.262 days long. Compensation is made by adding an extra day to February every fourth year, creating a "leap year" of 366 days (except certain century years).

## Navigation

As civilization developed, people began to travel for trade and exploration and it became increasingly important to be able to navigate accurately, particularly when a ship was out of sight of land. By the third century B.C., there was great competition among the merchants and traders who plied the Mediterranean Sea in sailing ships. Sailors navigated mainly by using the positions of the stars. As a result, astronomy came to be used for navigational purposes, principally because it is relatively easy to calculate latitude by measuring the declinations of stars.

Today a navigator can calculate his latitude by measuring the altitude (in degrees above the horizon) of the Polestar, Polaris, which is less than 1° away from the north celestial pole. But when people first began to travel extensively 2,000 years ago, Polaris was a considerable distance from the celestial pole. It is only in the last 300 or 400 years that the precession of the earth's axis has brought Polaris usefully near the pole. Instead, the early navigators had to calculate latitude from the position of Kochab, which was then the nearest star to the celestial pole.

## The beginning of cartography

With increased trade and travel by land and by sea, maps also became increasingly important. The early maps of the Mediterranean Sea (around which many of the ancient civilizations developed) are relatively accurate with regard to latitude, but many are grossly in error concerning longitude. This is because differences in longitude are best calculated from the differences in time at which the sun reaches its highest point. The early sailors did not have clocks sufficiently accurate for this purpose.

**The Mayans of Central America** devised several calendars, each for a specific purpose, such as marking religious festivals. The symbols carved into the stone pictured (which dates from about the eighth century A.D.) have a calendrical meaning but do not represent a 365-day calendar. Most of the various Mayan calendars consisted of a series of named days and months; to identify a specific date, an elaborate system of numbers, day names, and month names was used.

They therefore had to use dead reckoning to estimate longitude, which they calculated from estimates of their speed and the number of hours that they had been under sail. In fact, the determination of longitude remained largely a matter of guesswork until the first accurate chronometers were constructed in the eighteenth century.

Fortunately for the early sailors, the Mediterranean Sea is relatively safe. The Atlantic Ocean, however, is much more hazardous, and accurate navigation is much more important. Despite this difficulty, the Phoenicians successfully navigated out of the Mediterranean and sailed as far as Britain, where there is evidence that they went to trade before the Roman occupation.

By about A.D. 140, a navigators' fraternity had developed. In each major port scribes were employed to sketch charts of the ports and to copy out tables of star declinations and other astronomical information, from which latitudes could be calculated. For instance, it was well known that the stars of Ursa Major, the Big Dipper, appeared to just dip into the sea at their lowest point when viewed from the latitude off Alexandria. But early sailors soon learned not to rely on the planets and the moon for navigational purposes. They thought that the "restless stars" (planets) were deceptive because they appeared to move about the night sky, and the moon was regarded as a "wanton woman and a mystery."

**Part of an Egyptian calendar,** dating from about 1230 B.C. On this papyrus calendar, the black hieroglyphs denote lucky days and the red symbols represent unlucky days. The Egyptians used three different calendars: a lunar calendar based on the rising of Sirius (the Dog Star), used for agricultural purposes; a 365-day civil calendar used for administration; and another lunar calendar based on the civil year, used for religious purposes.

**The number system** of the Mayans was remarkably sophisticated: any number could be written using combinations of only three signs: a dot, a bar, and an oval-shaped symbol. Numbers from 1 to 19 were written using dots and bars; adding an oval below any number multiplied it by 20. Adding another oval below the first again multiplied the number by 20 (except in reckoning dates, when the second oval multiplied the numbers above by 18). In the Mayan calendar, two numbers were commonly used, one before the day name and the other before the month name.

**An early 17th-century map** of the Mediterranean Sea shows directions between major ports. (The map was drawn with the Sea's long axis running vertically.) Such early maps were often grossly inaccurate regarding longitude, the determination of which requires a precise means of telling time, which was not developed until the 18th century. (The first timepiece sufficiently accurate for navigational use was made by the English horologist John Harrison. Between 1735 and 1762, he constructed four chronometers, the last of which was found to be accurate to within five seconds after a voyage to Jamaica.)

# The constellations

The positions of the stars in the celestial sphere have remained almost unchanged since prehistoric times. Each of the early civilizations grouped the stars into various constellations. Historically, some constellations were taken to represent gods or mythical beings (or sometimes their dwellings). Other groups were thought to resemble animals or objects on earth—although in most cases, seeing the resemblance demands a vivid imagination. Stories and myths were woven around the gods and animals, however, and this helped people to remember the constellations' names and positions. For example, Orion, the Hunter, is seen to be keeping at bay Taurus, the Bull.

The various civilizations gave different names to their own constellations, but many of the modern names are of Greek or Roman origin. Early Arab astronomers were responsible for naming many of the individual stars. This dates from the time when Arab culture and astrology flourished in the valleys of the rivers Tigris and Euphrates, during the first millennium A.D. Navigators and explorers at that time began to venture farther into the Southern Hemisphere and gradually became aware of new constellations in the southern skies.

### The zodiac

Of special interest to early astronomers and astrologers were the constellations of the zodiac. These form a broad band across the sky along the line of the ecliptic (the path through the heavens followed by the sun, the moon, and the planets of the solar system). The 360 degrees of the ecliptic were divided into 12 sections, each corresponding to a zodiacal sign; this division into 12 was probably made because there are 12 complete lunar cycles (actually about 12.4) in one year. As a result, the sun "occupies" each sign for approximately one calendar month.

The constellations of the zodiac were named in the order in which the sun appeared to occupy them; the first sign being Aries, the Ram, chosen some 20,000 years ago. The start of the zodiac—called the First Point of Aries—was selected to coincide with the position in the sky where the plane of the ecliptic crossed the celestial equator. When the sun is at this point, its declination is at a minimum (0°), and the lengths of day and night are equal throughout the world; this is also called the *vernal equinox* and marks the commencement of spring in the Northern Hemisphere on March 20 or 21. After the vernal equinox, the sun occupies the successive signs of the zodiac until, at the next vernal equinox, it is once again at the beginning of its cycle.

The exact point on the celestial equator at which it is crossed by the ecliptic recedes by about 50 seconds of arc each year. This means it has receded by about 28° of arc since the early astronomers devised the zodiacal system; as a result it now lies in the sign of Pisces (the Fishes), instead of in Aries. Despite this recession, however, the vernal equinox is still sometimes called the first point of Aries, and it has retained the old symbol $\gamma$, which is also the sign of the constellation of Aries.

### Using the stars as signposts

The linking of the stars into groups and geometric patterns, as constellations, was of great help in locating individual stars. The simplified patterns still serve as signposts for identifying stars or neighboring constellations. With the exception of the moon, the most prominent feature in the night sky is the Milky Way, or Lactea Via, the poetic name for the great luminous belt of stars that encircles the whole of the celestial sphere. In its Greek mythological interpretation, Hercules was at the breast of Juno while she slept, and some of her milk fell

**The constellations,** especially those of the zodiac, played an important part in ancient mythology and religion. In this Roman marble relief (which dates from about A.D. 400), for example, Mithras, the Roman sun god, is shown slaying Taurus the Bull, surrounded by the signs of the zodiac.

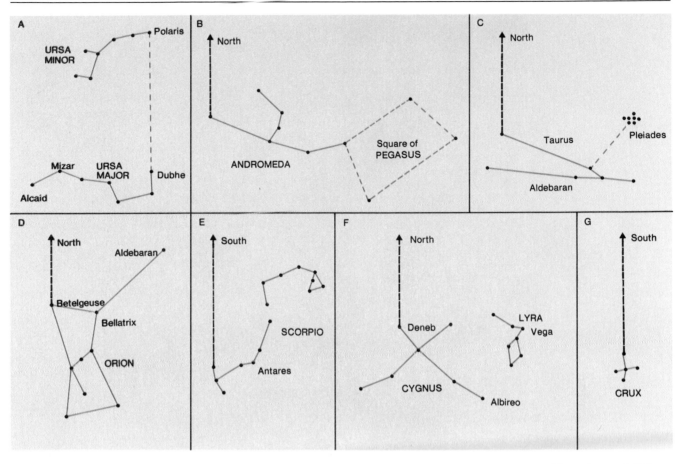

and spread across the vault of the heavens. The Arabs and Persians had their own myth and regarded the Milky Way as a great river alongside which grazed gazelles, camels, and stallions. They described various star clusters as tents, date palms, oases, and even a treasure chest full of glittering jewels.

The constellation of the Big Bear (Ursa Major) is the best known to those who live in the Northern Hemisphere. The hind part of it consists of a group of seven bright stars that roughly form the shape of a plow (or of a saucepan or dipper). Its configuration makes it an excellent signpost for most of the major stars and constellations of the northern sky.

For the stars and constellations near the celestial equator, seen to best advantage in the winter months, Orion is the clearest signpost. It is perhaps the most spectacular constellation of all. Orion's belt points to Aldebaran, the eye of the Bull (Taurus), which is being hunted by Orion, and leads on from there to the Pleiades. In the other direction, the belt points to Sirius (in Canis Major), the dog of Orion, the Hunter.

There are similar sets of constellations in the Southern Hemisphere, the most notable of which is the Southern Cross (Crux). This configuration helps to locate the south celestial pole, although there is no visible star near that point in the sky. It also locates Canopus, Rigel, and the False Cross. Ptolemy drew up a list of 48 constellations, of which 21 appear in the northern half of the celestial sphere and 15 occur south of the celestial equator. The remaining 12 form the zodiac, those special constellations that are arranged at equal intervals along the path of the sun in the plane of the

ecliptic. Today, there are 88 named constellations, many of which are scarcely visible to the naked eye. The total number of stars visible without a telescope (brighter than magnitude 6.0) is about 6,000.

**The major constellations** A-F (above) can all be seen from the Northern Hemisphere; constellation G is visible in the Southern Hemisphere and a few places in the Northern Hemisphere.

**On mid eighteenth century** star charts, the figures tended to correspond only minimally to the constellations they depicted.

# The celestial sphere

Although the ability to measure distances to celestial objects is a relatively recent development in astronomy, the actual positions of the stars in the night sky have been defined and recorded on maps for thousands of years. Irrespective of whether a star is 1 or 1,000 parsecs from earth, its position can be pinpointed on an imaginary sphere surrounding the earth—the celestial sphere.

The concept of a star-studded celestial sphere was designed to enable the positions of the stars to be located in the same way that positions on earth are defined, in terms of latitude and longitude. The imaginary celestial sphere is divided into a grid system that corresponds directly to the terrestrial grid of lines of latitude and longitude. In the astronomical system, however, the two coordinates are right ascension (abbreviated to RA), equivalent to celestial longitude, and declination, equivalent to celestial latitude. These coordinates are measured with respect to an imaginary celestial equator, which is the extension into space of the earth's equator. Similarly, the celestial poles are extensions of the earth's axis and lie, therefore, directly above the earth's true North and South poles. Thus a star on the celestial equator has a declination of 0°. Just as the

earth's North Pole has a latitude of 90° N, Polaris (the polestar), located almost exactly at the north celestial pole, has a declination of about 90° N.

The ecliptic (an imaginary circle on the celestial sphere) represents the plane of the earth's orbit around the sun. Because the earth's axis is inclined at an angle of 23.44° to the plane of the ecliptic, the celestial equator is also inclined by 23.44° to the ecliptic. The celestial equator and the ecliptic meet at two opposite points, which mark the equinoxes. The sun rises at one of these points (the vernal, or spring, equinox, also called the First Point of Aries), on March 20 or 21, and at the other (the autumnal equinox, or the First Point of Libra) on September 22 or 23.

Just as the terrestrial longitude system needs a zero point, so does the celestial sphere, from which all measurements of right ascension can be made. The earth's was arbitrarily chosen, and internationally agreed upon in 1884, to be the Greenwich meridian. The celestial sphere's point was defined—in a similarly arbitrary way—by the ancient Greeks, who chose the vernal equinox as the zero point of right ascension, a system that has remained unchanged to this day.

**On the celestial sphere** the lines of right ascension—the astronomical equivalent of terrestrial longitude—are spaced one hour apart, each interval corresponding to 15° of a circle. This system is used because, to an observer on earth, the imaginary celestial sphere appears to rotate through a complete 360° circle every 24 hours. Thus, it revolves through 15° every hour. The zero point of right ascension is the vernal equinox, one of the two equinoctial points at which the celestial equator crosses the ecliptic. The right ascension coordinate of a celestial body can be measured in degrees but is more usually expressed in hours and minutes. The other celestial coordinate, declination, is measured in degrees north (denoted by +) or south (denoted by −) of the celestial equator. Thus A in the illustration has a right ascension of about 4 hours and a declination of about +25°.

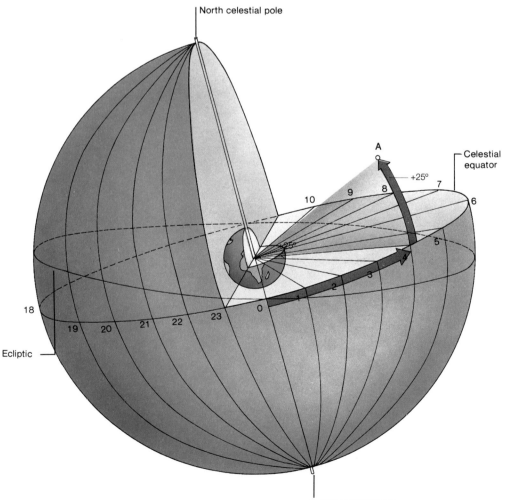

North celestial pole

Celestial equator

Ecliptic

South celestial pole

Instead of measuring right ascension in degrees, it is usually expressed in terms of hours, minutes, and seconds, so that the position of a star is related to its apparent motion across the sky. Thus, the imaginary lines of right ascension on the celestial sphere are spaced at intervals of one hour.

The declination of a heavenly body is measured in degrees north (designated by a plus sign) or south (designated by a minus sign) of the celestial equator—in the same way that latitude on earth is measured relative to the terrestrial equator.

### Star time

As a result of dividing the celestial sphere into hours of right ascension (one hour being the time taken for one hour of right ascension to pass overhead), the time-keeping system used to locate a star is governed by the positions of the stars on the celestial sphere rather than by the position of the sun in the sky.

The movements of the sun and stars are solely apparent motions caused by the rotation of the earth about its axis. Nevertheless, the star day (called the sidereal day) is slightly shorter than the normal solar day. This is a result of the earth's yearly orbit around the sun. By the time a day has passed, the earth has moved through $\frac{1}{365}$ of its orbit, which is equivalent to a time period of 3 minutes, 56 seconds. Thus, a solar day is this length of time longer than a sidereal day. Astronomers use sidereal time because it gives the right ascension of a celestial object, without the need to compensate for the longer solar day.

### The ecliptic and precession

Slight variations in the mutual gravitational attraction between the sun, moon, and earth cause small perturbations in the movement of the earth. This, in turn, affects the celestial coordinate system. The most marked of the perturbations is known as *precession.* Analogous to the circular motion of the spindle of a spinning top, precession is a periodic, slow, continuous rotation of the earth's axis; it takes 25,800 years for the axis to complete one cycle. At present the earth's axis points toward Polaris but, as the axis precedes, it will point to other stars. Eventually, in 25,800 years time, it will again point to Polaris.

Because of precession of the earth's axis, the relationship between the celestial equator and the ecliptic also changes over a period of 25,800 years. During this cycle the positions of the equinoctial points relative to the ecliptic slowly change, moving through successive signs of the zodiac. A few thousand years ago, the vernal equinox (the zero point for measuring right ascension) was in the constellation of Aries, but today it is in Pisces and is slowly approaching the next sign, Aquarius. Thus precession affects the celestial coordinates of heavenly bodies. This means that in addition to giving the right ascension and declination of a star, the date on which the star had these coordinates must also be given to enable the star to be located precisely.

### Observing the stars

Because of the earth's rotation, the celestial sphere also rotates about its axis, with the result that the stars appear to rise and set at different angles from different parts of the earth. On the equator, the stars rise perpendicularly to the horizon. Moreover, all stars, irrespective of their declinations, can be seen during the course of the year; Polaris appears just above the horizon. At the terrestrial North Pole, however, only stars with northern declinations are visible, Polaris being directly overhead. In middle latitudes, the stars appear to rise obliquely from the horizon and some—the circumpolar stars—never rise or set, but follow circular paths around the celestial poles.

**A sundial** makes use of the sun's apparent motion across the celestial sphere (caused by the earth's 24-hourly rotation about its axis). In this portable eighteenth-century example, the inclination of the horseshoe-shaped dial can be altered to match the instrument's latitude.

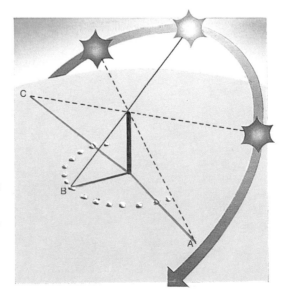

**A shadow clock** consisted simply of a vertical stick in the ground and a surrounding semicircle marked off in hours. When the sun rose in the east, it cast a long shadow (A). As the sun moved across the sky, the shadow passed around the semicircle, becoming first shorter (reaching its minimum length (B) at midday) then longer. By sunset, the shadow had reached the other side of the semicircle (C). Such simple time-keeping devices were very inaccurate, mainly because they did not allow for the changing position of sunrise and sunset during the year.

# The sun-centered universe

There were few noteworthy advances in astronomy between the seventh and fifteenth centuries. The old philosophical ideas of Aristotle became settled into an academic tradition akin to religious belief. Science and religion were so closely linked that astronomers and other scientists became circumscribed by theology, and the earth remained firmly at the center of the universe.

In the sixteenth century, the revolution in astronomy that was to lead to the scientific era of the eighteenth century was instigated by Nicolaus Copernicus, whose interest in astronomy was so keen and perceptive that his name has become immortalized through his work and writings. He postulated—in spite of fierce opposition—that the earth does not occupy the central position in the universe, but that in common with the other planets, it orbits around the sun. This heliocentric model was regarded as heretical and morally wrong by the ecclesiastical authorities. It was because of

this opposition that the few astronomers who had begun to question the old geocentric theory of the universe did so rather secretly, out of fear of being imprisoned for their unorthodox and, therefore, unacceptable views.

## Brahe, Galileo, and Kepler

At that time, astrology continued to be indulged in by most ordinary people. The result was that the accurate forecasting of planetary positions and occultations became a matter of great practical importance and personal prestige. In calculating this astronomical information, however, it was found that the system of epicycles, devised to account for planetary motion, grew to be too complicated and became full of accumulated errors. This confusion acted as a spur to Copernicus and encouraged him to work on his heliocentric ideas, which he persevered with despite threats of persecution.

Following the death of Copernicus in 1543, three notable astronomers entered the public eye: Tycho Brahe, Galileo Galilei, and Johannes Kepler. Between 1560 and 1640, they made a great impact on the progress of astronomy. Brahe was a tireless observer and one of the most methodical astronomers in history. Like Kepler, he was a contemporary of Galileo, but he did not have the advantage of Galileo's telescope and made a vast number of naked-eye observations using only a giant quadrant. He compiled numerous charts of the planets and discovered a supernova in 1572. He could not, however, reconcile his observations with his orthodox religious views, which still required belief in a geocentric universe.

## Galileo and the telescope

Galileo will always be remembered as the person who, in 1609, first made serious use of the telescope to study the heavenly bodies. The first telescope, however, was probably made by Lippershey, in Holland, in 1608, after experiments with spectacle lenses. Galileo astonished the scientific world by his observations of the moon, with the telescope making the lunar mountains and craters clearly visible on the surface.

The telescope also revealed thousands of stars that had not been visible to the naked eye. It showed the planets as definite disks, and made visible the phases of Venus. It revealed for the first time the fact that the sun is spotted with blemishes (sunspots), which move across its surface. Among the most spectacular new sights were the rings of Saturn and the four main moons orbiting around Jupiter.

The most significant result of these epoch-making discoveries was the fact that they exposed the misconceptions of the old geocentric model of the universe. Despite being compelled by the church to denounce his own ideas as false, Galileo, nevertheless, remained an ardent supporter of Copernican theories. Against all opposition, there was a growing acceptance of the new heliocentric model

**Copernicus** championed the theory that the sun lies at the center of the universe (which we now call the solar system). He assigned circular orbits to the planets in the order (out from the sun) Mercury, Venus, Earth, Mars, Jupiter, and Saturn. He acknowledged that they do not, however, move in perfect circles and devised a system of epicycles to account for this. Each planet was assumed to move in a circle superimposed on its large circular orbit round the sun.

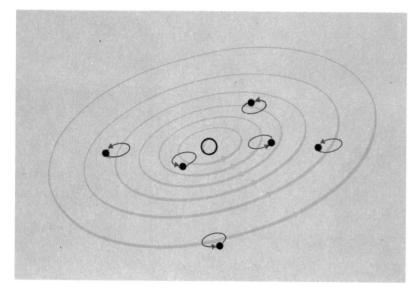

**Newton,** with his law of universal gravitation, provided the physical explanation for the mathematical relationships established by Kepler and others. Newton also made some of the first reflecting telescopes; a replica of one is shown here. The main telescope tube is about 9 inches (23 centimeters) long.

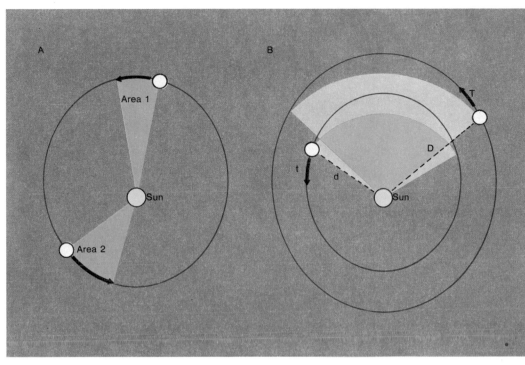

**Kepler's laws,** published between 1609 and 1619, described planetary motion. The first law (A) states that a planet's orbit is an ellipse, with the sun at one focus. According to the second law, a planet sweeps out in equal times segments of equal area; Area 1 equals Area 2. Kepler's third law states that the square of a planet's orbital period is proportional to the cube of its mean distance from the sun. For the planets in diagram B, of periods t and T, $t^2$ is proportional to $d^3$, and $T^2$ is proportional to $D^3$.

**Tycho Brahe** made most of his thousands of astronomical observations using a large quadrant. Similar instruments (but smaller) became adapted for navigational purposes, such as this example equipped with filters for taking sightings of the sun.

of the universe, with the newly termed solar system at its heart.

Kepler, using information recorded by Brahe, demonstrated that the planets (including Earth) did not move in circles, as Ptolemy's followers declared, but in ellipses. He also showed that a planet's speed varies as it orbits around the sun. Summarized in Kepler's laws of planetary motion, his calculations further discredited the old geocentric model and paved the way for a scientific explanation of the planets' orbits. They also established the principles that allowed Isaac Newton to develop his theories of universal gravitation later that century.

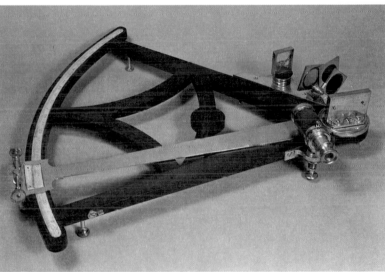

# Star positions

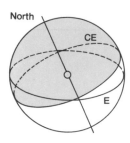

Early astronomers and navigators, from about the seventh century A.D., used the astrolabe to find or define the positions of stars. The original instrument was designed by the Arabs, using ingenious geometry at a time when spherical trigonometry was unknown. Star positions were given in terms of altitude (angle above the horizon) and azimuth (distance around a horizon circle). The astrolabe could also be used to tell the time by the stars or the sun. It gave devout Muslims the prescribed times for prayers and provided a reliable sun or star compass for travellers and navigators.

The medieval astrolabe was, in effect, a sort of calculator for transforming the coordinates of right ascension and declination of any star at a specific time into its corresponding altitude and azimuth. This capability was of great convenience in finding out just where to look in the sky for a particular star. The circular plate representing the ecliptic was divided into 12 segments, often represented by the signs of the zodiac, which served also as calendar dates.

### The planisphere

The modern equivalent of the astrolabe—and much more convenient to use—is the planisphere. The example illustrated below is designed for use in the Northern Hemisphere at latitude 51° N. It consists of a star chart using a polar projection, with all the dates of the year inscribed around the edge (corresponding to the zodiacal signs on an astrolabe). Computer-plotted altitude and azimuth curves, bounded by a horizon circle, are printed on a transparent overlay, which can be rotated over the star chart. All stars that fall within the horizon circle should be visible (on a clear night) at the time and date set on the outer ring. A transparent cursor is calibrated in angles of declination above and below the celestial equator.

### Star charts

Modern star charts are drawn with respect to coordinates of right ascension and declination. Often a computer is used to plot the star positions, using information from one of the major observatories. The charts on these pages show all stars of magnitude to 5.0 and of declination 50° and larger (with positive declinations for the Northern Hemisphere and negative declinations for the Southern Hemisphere). All are visible to the naked eye. An indication of magnitude is given by the size of the spot. The largest spots represent a magnitude of 0.0, and the smallest spots represent magnitude 5.0.

The charts also indicate the official boundaries of the constellations, whose names in conjunction with Greek letters or numbers are the basis of the systematic naming of the stars. Some stars also have their own names, given to them over the centuries by various astronomers since the time of the Greeks and Arabs. For example, the two "pointers" in the constellation Ursa Major (the Big Bear) are called by the names Dubhe and Merak. On a star chart they are labelled $\alpha$ and $\beta$ (and termed Alpha Ursae Majoris and Beta Ursae Majoris). They are located at right ascension 11 hours and declinations of $+62°$ and $+56°$, respectively.

### The northern sky

Polaris (the polestar) lies close to the northern celestial pole and is part of the constellation Ursa Minor (the Little Bear). Its nearest prominent neighbor, Kochab (Beta Ursae Minoris), forms another point in the same constellation. Both are of second magnitude. Ursa Major contains several bright stars, the most prominent being Alcaid and Alioth, both in the "handle," and Dubhe, the bright orange "pointer" to the polestar. Ursa Minor and Ursa Major give the most easily recognized orientation in the northern sky. From them it is easy to locate Arcturus (magnitude $-0.1$) in Boötes by following the curve of the "handle" of the Big Dipper. Arcturus is slightly orange in color.

Just as the two "pointers" in Ursa Major can be used to locate Polaris, so the other two stars in the quadrilateral part of the constellation point away from the polestar toward Regulus (Alpha Leonis), the blue-white first magnitude star that is the brightest star in Leo. Between Regulus and the Milky Way are the two bright stars Castor and Pollux, Alpha and Beta Geminorum respectively. Castor is of second magnitude and is a multiple star; the orange Pollux is of first magnitude. An imaginary line, drawn from Pollux through the third bright star in Gemini, the second magnitude Alhena, and across the Milky Way, will locate the giant, red variable Betelgeuse, in Orion. This is easily identified by the three stars Beta,

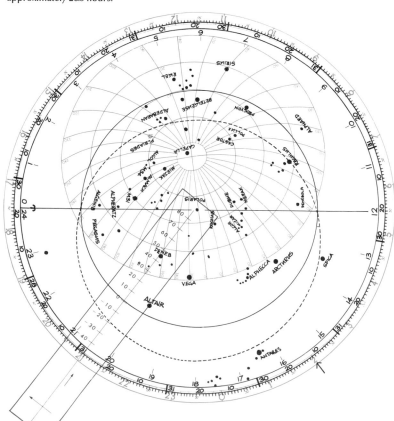

Epsilon, and Zeta Orionis, that form Orion's belt. The brilliant Rigel (Beta Orionis), of magnitude 0.1, is on the opposite side to Betelgeuse (Alpha Orionis).

Cassiopeia, like Ursa Major, is circumpolar in the Northern Hemisphere and so is another useful locator. The small double zig-zag of stars can be found in the Milky Way on the opposite side of Polaris to Ursa Major. If the line from Polaris is continued beyond Cassiopeia, Andromeda can be identified. This is the location of the spiral galaxy M31 (NGC 224), estimated to be more than 2 million light-years away.

Between Cassiopeia and Gemini, along the path of the Milky Way, are Perseus and Auriga. Nearer to Cassiopeia, Perseus contains an eclipsing binary star, Algol (Beta Perseii), the magnitude of which varies from 2 to 3.5. Auriga, between Perseus and Gemini, contains

Capella (Alpha Aurigae), of magnitude 0.1 and one of the brightest stars in the sky. It is a giant star of the same spectral type as our sun, but 46 light-years away.

Adjoining Auriga is Taurus, in which the central star is the orange, first magnitude Aldebaran (Alpha Tauri). Close to Aldebaran is the open cluster of the Hyades and, beyond this, the bright open cluster of the Pleiades.

On the opposite side of Cassiopeia to Perseus and Auriga is Cygnus, a beautiful constellation in the shape of an X. The leading star is Deneb (magnitude 1.3), which, with Altair in Aquila, and Vega in Lyra, makes up the so-called Summer Triangle. Vega (magnitude 0) has a blue color that can be observed with the naked eye. First magnitude Altair can be identified by its brightness and also by the two less bright stars beside it.

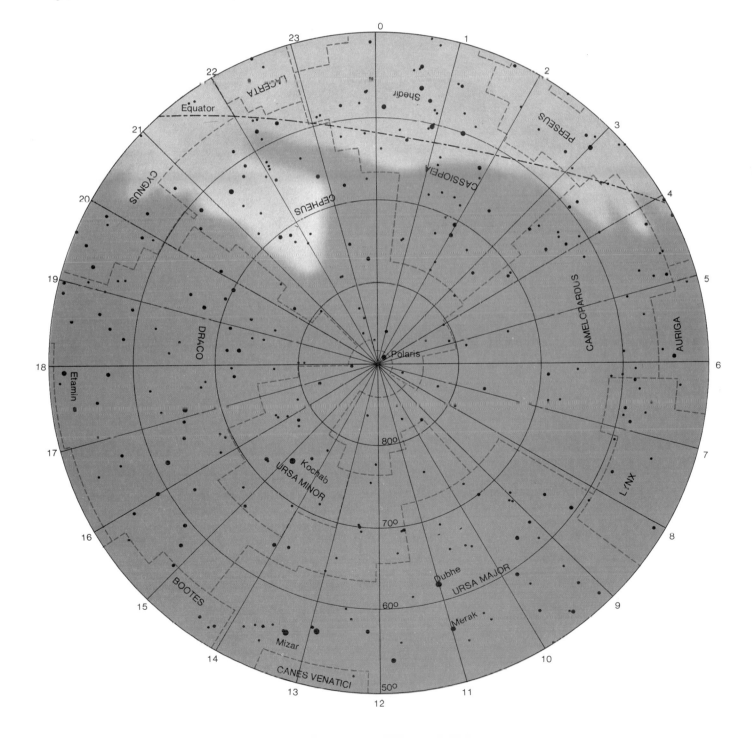

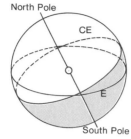

**The southern celestial sphere,** where CE is the celestial equator and E is the ecliptic.

### The southern sky

Crux Australis, the Southern Cross, is the orientation point in the southern sky, although it is not in fact at the southern pole. It is a small constellation, more kite-shaped than cruciform, of four stars all of first or second magnitude. Alpha Crucis is a binary, and Gamma Crucis is a red giant.

Adjacent to Crux are three constellations that were formerly one: Carina (keel), Puppis (poop), and Vela (sail) of the Argo. Carina stretches away from Crux to its largest star, Canopus, a supergiant of magnitude −0.7. Beyond Puppis, and close to the Milky Way, can be seen Sirius, the Dog Star, brilliant leader of Canis Major, with a magnitude of −1.4.

Close to Crux is one of the most brilliant constellations, Centaurus, the leader of which is the binary Alpha Centauri (magnitude −0.3),

the nearest bright star to earth, only 4.3 light-years away. Also associated with Centaurus is the outstanding globular cluster Omega Centauri (NGC 5139). On the other side of Alpha Centauri is the easily identified Southern Triangle, with its bright orange leader. Farther along the Milky Way, moving away from Crux, is Scorpius, with the enormous red giant Antares at its heart. A diameter of 300 million miles (480 million kilometers) has been calculated for this star.

Most remarkable of the "Southern Birds" is Grus, the Crane, with its bluish Alpha and orange Beta, both of second magnitude. The sweep of the body of Grus points toward the spectacular Small and Large Magellanic clouds (Nebecula Minor and Major), some 200,000 light-years from earth. Apart from the spiral nebula in Andromeda, these are the most distant heavenly bodies that can be seen

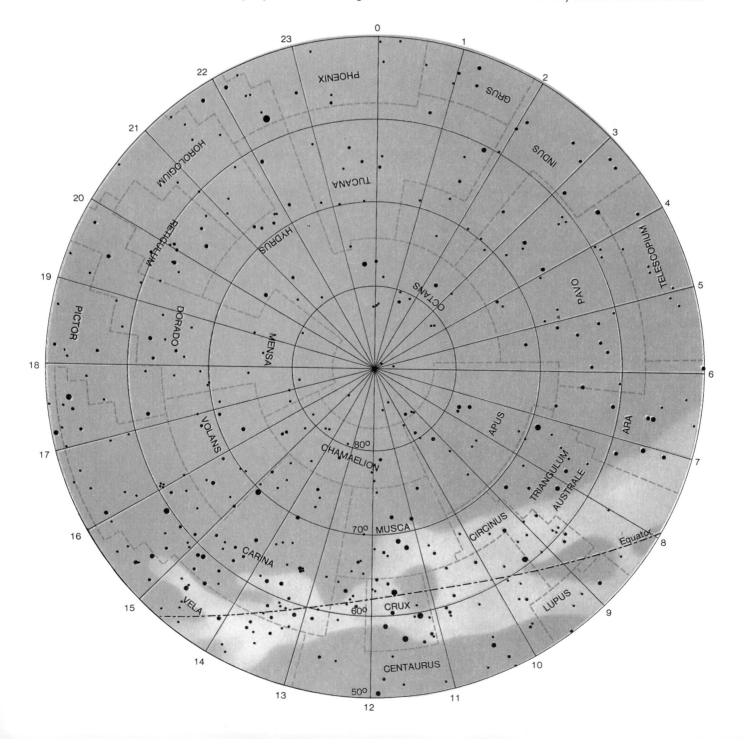

by the unaided eye. Also near the imagined
flight path of Grus is the brilliant star Achernar
(magnitude 0.5), in Eridanus.

### Distances of stars

Early astronomers found it extremely difficult
to estimate the distances to the stars. Some
stars (those nearest the earth) have different
angles with distant stars when they are measured on two occasions, six months apart
(when the earth is on opposite sides of its
orbit around the sun). Thus, the angles are
measured from each end of a baseline approximately 190 million miles (300 million kilometers) long. This phenomenon, in which relatively near stars appear to move in relation to
the background of more distant stars, is called
parallax. For example, a star with a parallax of 1
second of arc is 3.26 light-years away, a distance known in astronomy as 1 parsec. A light-
year is the distance light travels in one year,
equal to 5.88 trillion miles (9.46 trillion kilometers).

Most stars are too far away to exhibit detectable parallax, and at least for the purposes
of amateur astronomy, their positions can be
regarded as fixed. But modern sophisticated
instruments in major observatories are capable of measuring star distances with increasing accuracy. They are sufficient to reveal that,
over the years, some stars do show a very
small proper motion. For this reason, star atlases and catalogues have to be updated every
few years. This real movement of the stars in
our galaxy (their proper motion) is quite separate from the apparent small changes in position that result from the precession ("wobble")
of the earth's axis and the recession of the First
Point in Aries (the vernal equinox).

### The wanderers

Star positions were well and accurately known
before the invention of the telescope. But the
orbits and positions of the planets, or "wan-
derers" as they were once called, could not be
accurately accounted for. Therefore, they
could not be inscribed on an astrolabe or plotted on a star chart. Understanding came with
the revolutionary work of Galileo, Brahe, and
Kepler which, together with Newton's contribution, finally swept away the Greek idea of an
earth-centered universe and established the
present model of the solar system.

Kepler worked out that the orbits of the
planets are elliptical (and from this assumption
derived his laws of planetary motion), but had
no knowledge of gravity and the physical basis
for the orbits. He assumed that some mystical
force or "magnetic threads" held the planets in
their orbits.

Then, in 1687, with remarkable intuition,
Newton postulated the existence of a universal
force of gravity. He explained how gravity not
only attracts all objects toward the earth, but
also exists between the sun and the planets;
between the earth and the moon; and indeed
between any two masses. The Greeks had simplified celestial mechanics according to the
simple doctrine that "matter behaves according to nature." This view was unarguable, but it
stifled scientific inquiry. Newton was able to
formulate, in mathematical terms, the basic

laws of motion. With these, he was able to ver-
ify Kepler's laws mathematically and to apply
them to the orbits of planets and their moons,
all using the single law of gravitational attraction. This fundamental law states that the gravitational attractive force between any two objects is proportional to the product of their
masses, and inversely proportional to the
square of the distance between them. The
same law governs the orbits of artificial satellites and space probes, which are so much a
part of the twentieth century.

**Early forms of star maps**
included globes of the celestial sphere. This eighteenth-century Arab example
is made of brass and has silver studs to represent the
stars. Star angles and bear-
ings can be read off the
scales, which are engraved
in degrees, in groups of six.

**The position of the moon
and planets** could not be
plotted on star maps or
globes, but their motions
could be simulated on a
mechanical model called an
*orrery*. In this example, the
brass sphere at the center
represents the sun and the
two white balls near it are
Mercury and Venus. A min-
iature moon orbits the
globe representing Earth.
All move round their re-
spective orbits when the
white handle is turned.

# Through the telescope

The development of the telescope was the key to the great advances in astronomy that took place during the seventeenth and eighteenth centuries. Galileo introduced refracting telescopes, which use lenses to produce a magnified image. Newton, and most of the astronomers who followed him, employed reflecting telescopes, in which the chief optical components are curved mirrors. The principle of the reflecting telescope is similar to that of the large dish-shaped aerials that today's radio-astronomers use to collect microwave radio signals emitted by stars and other celestial objects.

Galileo did not invent the telescope, although he was one of the first to use the instrument for astronomy. His main contribution stemmed from his improvements to the making and selection of lenses (his later telescopes had a magnification of about 33 times). The most important function of an astronomical telescope, however, is not to magnify. Stars are so far away that they never appear as more than points of light, even when viewed through the most powerful telescopes. For this reason an astronomical telescope's chief function is to increase the amount of light that can enter the eye from a distant object such as a star. That is, to make objects visible that cannot be seen with the unaided eye.

### Power and brightness

The extra light-gathering power of a telescope enables an astronomer to see thousands of stars that are invisible to the naked eye. This light amplification is related to the diameter of the object lens (in a refractor, or the mirror in a reflector) of the telescope. It is equal to the area of the object lens divided by the area of the pupil of the human eye (taken to be about 0.25 inch across when the eye is conditioned for viewing in the dark). For example, a telescope with a lens or mirror 6 inches (15 centimeters) in diameter has a light-gathering power of 625. It can be used to see stars of brightness down to 12 on the magnitude scale. This is about 250 times less bright than a star of magnitude 6, which can just be seen with the unaided eye by someone with good eyesight. The magnitude scale is logarithmic; bright stars have low, or negative, magnitudes (the sun, the brightest object in the heavens, has a magnitude of −27); dim stars have high positive magnitudes.

The "power" of a refracting telescope is apparently limited only by the size of its objective lens. But in practice, this limit is soon reached because of the difficulty of manufacturing large glass lenses. Also, image quality deteriorates because large lenses suffer from chromatic and other aberrations. The result is in out-of-focus images surrounded by colored fringes of light. Aberrations can be corrected to some extent by combinations of lenses made from different types of optical glass, but such achromatic lenses are extremely expensive in large sizes. Reflecting telescopes, as introduced and developed by Isaac Newton, avoid these difficulties. Mirrors can be made larger than lenses, although even mirrors become difficult to make when they exceed about 13 feet (4 meters) in diameter.

### Telescope mountings

There are two principal ways of mounting an astronomical telescope so that it can be aimed at any point in the heavens. The simpler, and less expensive, type is an altitude-azimuth mounting, usually referred to as an *alt-az mount*. The telescope is mounted on a horizontal axis so that it can be pointed up or down at any angle from the horizon to the zenith, that is, at any altitude. The instrument (on its horizontal axis) is then mounted onto a vertical axis so that it is free to turn and point in any direction of the compass. From north (0°) through east (90°), south (180°), west (270°) and back around to north through a whole 360° turn—that is, it can turn to any azimuth. With such a mounting, a star's position is given in terms of its altitude (angle above the horizon) and azimuth (bearing around from north).

The second main type of telescope mounting is called an *equatorial mounting*. It is mechanically similar to the alt-az mount, but with an important difference. The vertical axis is inclined at an angle equal to the latitude of the telescope's site, so that the axis points to the celestial pole; it is termed the *polar axis*. When the telescope is aimed at right angles to the polar axis, it therefore points at the celestial equator and continues to do so as it is turned about the equatorial axis. The altitude axis becomes a declination axis, indicating the angle the telescope's line of sight makes with the celestial equator.

**William Herschel** (1738-1822), the German-born astronomer who lived and worked in Britain, built this large reflecting telescope in 1789. It had a curved polished metal mirror 4 feet (1.2 meters) in diameter and a focal length of 40 feet (12.2 meters). Regarded as one of the great technical feats of the time, it remained in use in its original form for more than 20 years.

**This image of Jupiter** was taken by the Wide Field & Planetary Camera-2 on the Hubble Space Telescope. The Hubble Space Telescope can resolve details in Jupiter's cloud belts and zones as small as 200 miles (320 kilometers) across. This detailed view is surpassed only by images from spacecraft that have traveled to Jupiter.

**Among the first discoveries** made by Galileo, with the newly developed telescope, were the four large satellites of Jupiter (now called the Galilean satellites). These are readily visible through even a low-powered telescope.

On an equatorial mounting, a telescope is free to turn about two axes at right angles to each other. Movement counterclockwise around the polar axis correlates with the right ascension of, say, a star (its angle around the celestial equator). The movement about the equatorial axis corresponds to the star's declination (its angle above or below the celestial equator), expressed as a positive angle (above) or as a negative angle (below).

Many equatorially mounted telescopes have graduated scales called the *right ascension circle* and *the declination circle.* Using these, an astronomer can set the scales to the known right ascension and declination of a star, planet, or comet. The telescope is then correctly aimed at the object and can be kept trained on it simply by turning the telescope slowly about the polar axis in order to compensate for the earth's spin. This compensation must be at a rate of 15° every sidereal

**The portable equatorial telescope** *(right)* was designed in 1775 by the British instrument-maker Jesse Ramsden, who introduced many innovations to optical instruments used in astronomy. There are four main types of telescopic instruments. A Galilean telescope *(far right,* A) is a refracting telescope with a converging object lens and a diverging lens in the eyepiece. Together they produce an upright magnified image (similar optics are still used in opera glasses). Later astronomical telescopes (B), like Ramsden's, used two converging lenses, which give an inverted image. In the Newtonian reflecting telescope (C), a curved mirror focuses the light, which is diverted to the eyepiece by a small plane mirror within the telescope. There are also various other reflecting telescope designs. A radio telescope (D) uses a similar principle; a paraboidal "dish" aerial focuses radio waves onto a receiver.

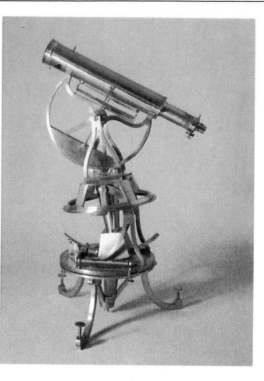

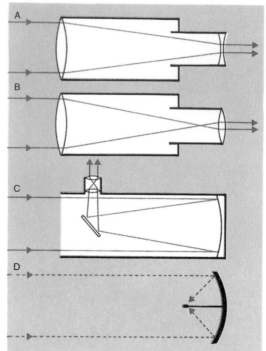

hour, or 1° every 4 minutes. Some telescopes have a motor drive synchronized with a sidereal clock to maintain the aim automatically. The largest modern telescopes are controlled by computer.

**Photographing the stars**

Before the latter part of the nineteenth century, astronomical observations were recorded by positional readings of altitude and azimuth or declination and right ascension; and by means of drawings wherever there was anything of significance to be seen. Photography has revolutionized this often laborious process to such an extent that observatories are now used almost exclusively for obtaining photographs, which are analyzed later, and usually elsewhere.

Early photographs were, almost inevitably, of relatively poor definition, despite long exposure times. Developments in photographic science have, however, benefited astronomy as much as—if not more than—any other field. Special emulsions can be made that are sensitive to infrared or ultraviolet light; extremely fine-grain films can be used for extended time exposures; these factors can achieve remarkable definition in the images that result.

So valuable is photography, in fact, that some very large telescopes have been built that cannot be used visually at all (the Schmidt telescope at Mount Palomar, in the United States, is an important example). This telescope has the additional merit of being able to photograph a relatively large area of sky at one time on a curved photographic plate with an area of slightly more than 10 square feet (1 square meter). This is in marked contrast to most optical telescopes, in which the field of view is narrow.

During long time-exposures, the telescope must track the stars being photographed (which appear to move because of the earth's rotation) with absolute precision to avoid blurring the image. Sometimes an independently moving object, such as a satellite, enters the photographic field. When this happens, a line of light appears on the photograph, marking the object's path.

**Invisible radiation**

Sight is our most acute and sensitive form of long-distance perception. We know about the stars because we can see them, and because of this, optical telescopes are the traditional instruments of astronomy. Nevertheless, it must not be forgotten that light is only one form of electromagnetic radiation, and that it forms only a narrow band in the electromagnetic spectrum.

On either side of the band of visible radiation (wavelengths of which range from approximately 4,000 Å for light at the violet end of the visible spectrum, to 7,000 Å for light at the red end) are electromagnetic radiations which are invisible, but which can nevertheless be perceived. Ultraviolet (of shorter wavelength than light) can be perceived indirectly, by the effect it has on the pigmentation of human skin. Infrared radiation (of longer wavelength than light) can be felt as radiated heat. Film emulsions can be prepared that react to both of these, so that otherwise invisible sources emitting either can be "observed" photographically. Similar photographs can be used to identify the ultraviolet or infrared components of objects that emit light as well.

Of shorter wavelength, and higher frequency than ultraviolet, are X rays and gamma rays. At the other end of the electromagnetic

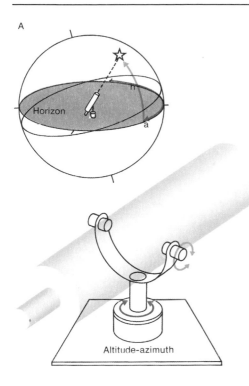

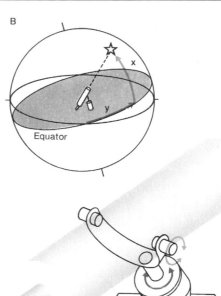

spectrum, with longer wavelength and shorter frequency than infrared, are microwaves and radio waves. Although all these radiations exist in space, only some of them (fortunately) can penetrate the earth's atmosphere. These are visible light, some ultraviolet, some infrared, and a substantial range of radio waves, from wavelengths of approximately $10^7$Å, which is 1 centimeter, to almost 1 kilometer, or $10^{13}$Å.

### Radio telescopes

The fact that radio waves come from beyond the earth was first proposed by Karl Jansky in 1931. But systematic study of the phenomenon did not begin until nearly a decade later. Since then, however, it has developed into what is probably the most important area of astronomical study. This is because the amount of information that can be obtained from radio telescopes (particularly about the more distant reaches of the universe) is so much greater than anything we can learn from the study of radiations in the visible and near-visible range. Furthermore, although such great advances have been made through the study of radio waves, investigations by similar means of extremely short wavelength radiation promises to extend the boundaries of our understanding of distant stars and galaxies. These investigations are made possible by the siting of equipment above the earth's atmosphere, which blocks X rays and gamma rays.

Although the equipment for detecting radio waves can take various forms (for example, a series of aerials extended in line) the main type of radio telescope resembles a radar dish. Like the parabolic reflector in an optical telescope, it collects the electromagnetic waves and focuses them at a point, in this case called the receiver. Radio telescopes of this type can be extremely large, although beyond a certain size they cannot be moved.

Radio waves focused at the telescope's receiver are recorded, then represented for

analysis in one of several ways. They may be plotted graphically, on a revolving drum; converted by a computer into a contour map showing the intensity of emissions; shown as a three-dimensional shape, with "peaks" of increased radio activity; or represented as a multicolored image in which the colors signify wavelengths or intensities of signal received.

**The curved dish aerial** of a radio telescope acts in a similar way to the curved mirror of a reflecting optical telescope. It concentrates radio waves from space onto a receiver supported at the focus of the dish.

# The modern observatory

Most optical observatories are sited remote from human habitation, usually at the tops of mountains. This siting results from the need for dark, clear skies. At high altitudes the chances of cloudless skies are improved because the observer's view is usually above the cloud layer.

Choosing a permanent site for an observatory can be difficult. The Royal Greenwich Observatory, for example, was originally located at Greenwich, in London, but as London pollution worsened and the number of street lights gradually increased, conditions for observing the night sky became intolerable. Between 1948 and 1957, the observatory was moved south and re-established in the grounds of Herstmonceux Castle, near Hailsham in Sussex. Unfortunately, it was not long until atmospheric pollution began to put pressure on this establishment too. An extensive search led to the choice of a volcanic peak on the island of La Palma, in the Canaries, so that the observatory could be based high above the clouds at 7,765 feet (2,367 meters) above sea level.

An observatory is easily recognized by its characteristic cluster of domed buildings, each usually housing a telescope. Most observatories also have laboratory facilities for coating mirrors and for servicing instruments, computer rooms and workshops, as well as residential accommodations. Many observatories are so remote that they have to be totally self-sufficient for weeks at a time, often cut off by adverse weather conditions.

**Telescopes**

Most of the telescopes in observatories use reflecting optics and are of the Cassegrainian design, in which a secondary convex mirror reflects the incoming light back through a hole in the center of the main mirror. Large refractors are less common, because of the problems of lens sag and the long length of tube required.

Many modern telescopes are fully automatic, such as the Anglo-Australian Telescope (AAT), which has a pointing accuracy of one second of arc. Most telescopes are on equatorial mounts (one axis of the mounting lies parallel with the earth's axis of rotation). To track an object as it moves across the sky, it is necessary only to rotate the telescope slowly round the mounting axis. This method of tracking, however, leads to large, heavy, and expensive mountings. Modern mounting designs simply have a vertical and a horizontal axis (the alt-azimuth mount), both of which are driven by motors.

The heart of any reflecting telescope is its main mirror, and until recently this had to be quite thick in order to avoid flexure as the telescope moved. Far more economical designs, using thin mirrors, are now possible, allowing lightweight telescopes to be built. In these designs, deflections in the mirror are detected and corrected automatically by computer-controlled servomechanisms. Such systems, often called "rubber mirrors," are extremely successful, an example being the United Kingdom Infrared Telescope (UKIRT) located in Hawaii.

For improved detail, as well as for studying fainter objects, it is necessary to use larger telescopes. Making single, large mirrors is a difficult and expensive task. The large telescopes of the future will probably have segmented mirrors. Several telescopes incorporating this design have already proved to be successful, namely the *m*ultiple-*m*irror *t*elescope (MMT) at Mount Hopkins, near Tucson, Arizona, and

**Keck Observatory** is located in Mauna Kea, Hawaii. It has one of the world's largest reflecting telescopes, with a reflecting surface 33 feet (10 meters) in diameter made up of 36 mirrors.

**Large reflecting telescopes** present problems of optics, mechanical engineering, and cost. Mirrors of diameters in excess of about 200 inches (5 meters) are difficult and costly to build, and the whole telescope, with its support and drive mechanisms, is a formidable piece of engineering. One method of obtaining effectively larger apertures makes use of six small mirrors arranged in a circle *(left)*. Six 80-inch (2-meter) mirrors, for example, give the same light-gathering power as a much larger telescope *(right)* that has a single mirror with a diameter of 173 inches (4.4 meters). The six smaller mirrors are easier to produce than a single large one, and the whole structure is more compact and simpler to engineer.

the Keck Telescope at Mauna Kea, Hawaii.

Since the Apollo missions to the moon and the spectacular success of the American planetary probes, there has been little point in studying planetary objects with ground-based telescopes. Nevertheless, a precise measurement of the earth-moon distance, with an accuracy of a few inches, can be obtained. This is done by bouncing a pulse of laser light from a special reflector left by Apollo astronauts on the moon. Earth-based telescopes are used to detect the weak, reflected pulse. By timing accurately the journey of the pulse to the moon and back to earth, the exact earth-moon distance is easily evaluated.

### Spectrohelioscopy

The sun is our nearest star and, as such, has been an object of intensive study with a wide range of instruments. The solar astronomer does not suffer from the shortage of light that plagues deep-space astronomers, and therefore usually uses smaller aperture instruments than those used on the night sky. High magnification can be employed to reveal a wealth of detail on the solar surface.

The world's largest solar telescope is the 60-inch (1.5-meter) solar telescope at the Kitt Peak National Observatory, southwest of Tucson, Arizona. Unlike other telescopes, this instrument has its main mirror buried deep in the ground, at the lower end of a tunnel parallel with the earth's axis of rotation. The light of the sun is reflected down the tunnel by a large, driven, flat mirror at the top, open end of the tunnel. This arrangement has

**An Earth-size fireball,** rising thousands of miles above Jupiter's surface, was viewed through the reflecting telescope at Keck Observatory in Hawaii. The fireball was a result of the impact of Fragment G of Comet Shoemaker-Levy 9 in July 1994.

**A Schmidt telescope** has a corrector lens to prevent distortion of the image produced by its large spherical mirror. (A phenomenon called *spherical aberration* occurs when the uncorrected mirror does not focus all light rays at the same point.)

**The Anglo-Australian telescope** (AAT) has a 153.5-inch (3.9-meter) primary mirror and both a prime focus (in the cage at the top) and a Cassegrainian focus (located below the hole in the primary mirror).

two advantages: the only moving part is the flat mirror, rather than the whole massive telescope; and the tunnel can be kept at a uniform temperature (because most of it is underground) and so eliminates any thermal air current that would cause a magnified image to badly "boil."

### The spectrohelioscope

The spectrohelioscope is a type of scanning spectroscope that enables an image of the sun to be formed in one particular wavelength, instead of the usual mixture making up white light. By examining the sun in hydrogen light, the distribution of hydrogen on the sun's surface and in its atmosphere can be viewed. This technique makes visible the arched prominences and solar flares that could otherwise not be seen. A "narrow-band" interference filter is usually used, which passes only an extremely narrow range of wavelengths.

A more difficult observation is the study of the faint solar corona—the extended, intensely hot, outer atmosphere of the sun. The instruments used for this purpose are called coronagraphs; they are essentially telescopes with a special mask to obscure the sun's disc. The design of coronagraphs has to be extremely skillful in order to prevent scattered stray light within the instrument from swamping the weak image of the corona. Improved images of the sun's outer atmosphere were obtained with a type of coronagraph on board Skylab, because on the ground, the earth's atmosphere causes so much scatter.

### Photography

The photographic emulsions used at observatories still consist basically of a silver halide which is decomposed by exposure to light, although today, they are very sophisticated versions of their forerunners. Great improvements have been made in sensitivity, contrast, and grain size; the reduction of the latter allows far more detail to be recorded on a plate. Considerable effort has also gone into "gas hypersensitizing," in which ordinary emulsions are baked in an atmosphere enriched with hydrogen, resulting in a substantial increase in sensitivity and speed.

The age of the photographic emulsion may be drawing to a close, with modern electronic detectors rapidly becoming superior in performance. Even so, a 30-minute exposure from a large telescope can produce a photographic plate that records the images of hundreds of thousands of stars and galaxies. But this information can take many weeks to analyze. The problem is that the quality of the information is considerably lower than that obtained by modern electronic detectors. The true role of photography in astronomy is really in producing sky maps and surveys. For this purpose it will probably remain useful for many years to come.

Optically fast telescopes, called Schmidt cameras, have been developed for producing large-field photographs of the sky. These cameras are made up of a large, spherical primary mirror, with glass correcting plates in front of it to compensate for the aberrations produced by the mirror. The United Kingdom's Schmidt

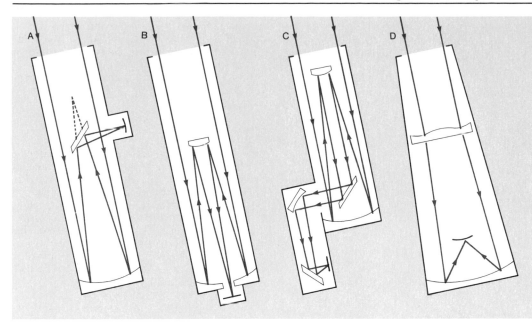

**Four focusing principles** found commonly in astronomical telescopes are (A) the Newtonian telescope, which is often used by amateurs because this type is easy to make; (B) the Cassegrain focus; (C) the Coudé focus which, by producing an image far from the main tube, allows heavy equipment to be attached to the telescope for special observations; and (D) the Schmidt telescope, which provides an image from a very wide field.

telescope, at the Siding Spring Observatory in Australia, has produced a 606-plate survey of the southern skies and careful examination of some of the plates led to the discovery of many new galaxies and nebulae.

### Spectroscopy

It has long been realized that by studying the spectrum of an object, much information can be gained concerning its chemical composition, temperature, movement, and other physical phenomena. Astronomers have, for many decades, applied this technique to the study of stars, galaxies, and nebulae. Originally, a glass or quartz prism was used to break the incoming light into its component colors, and the resulting spectrum was photographed. Modern spectrographs use diffraction gratings rather than prisms. (Gratings are highly reflecting surfaces on which are ruled many very thin parallel lines.) The reflected light forms a spectrum that is dispersed far more than that produced by a prism, enabling more detail to be seen. These gratings have several hundreds of lines per millimeter ruled on their faces, which are commonly a thin film of aluminum deposited on an optically flat glass or quartz block. The modern spectrograph is sensitive enough to show wavelength shifts caused by the line-of-sight velocities of astronomical objects. Thus, a fairly accurate determination can be made of the speed of expansion of nebulae, rotation of galaxies, and expansion of the universe. Photo-

graphic films are still used with spectrographs because they can record the whole spectrum simultaneously. Increasingly, however, electronic detectors of various forms are replacing or supplementing film.

### Photometry

Second only to the spectrometer, the photometer is the astronomer's most useful instrument. Photometric devices accurately measure the intensity of light from the stars and galaxies. They are nearly all based on highly sensitive, light-detecting electron tubes, called *photomultipliers*. In these devices, weak starlight causes electrons to be emitted from the surface of a photocathode, and each electron released can be made to produce many millions of secondary electrons. The output signal is easily measured and recorded and accurately represents the intensity of the light falling on the photocathode.

By measuring with color filters in front of the photomultiplier, it is possible to determine the temperature of the stars, the composition of nebulae, and the chemical processes in supernova explosions. Some modern photomultipliers are capable of detecting the individual photons that make up the incoming light. This enables the powerful technique of photon counting to be used in measuring extremely faint objects.

A particularly useful application of photometry is the plotting of the light-curves of vari-

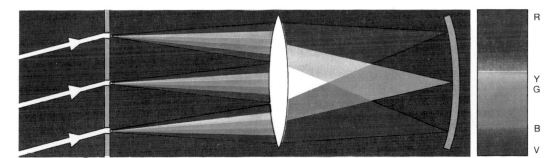

**A diffraction grating** contains many narrow, closely-spaced gaps and is often made by ruling fine lines through a film of aluminum deposited on a glass or quartz block. The grating breaks up white light rays passing through it into their constituent colors, and the lens then focuses each color onto a screen in its appropriate place in the spectrum: red (R), yellow (Y), green (G), blue (B), and violet (V).

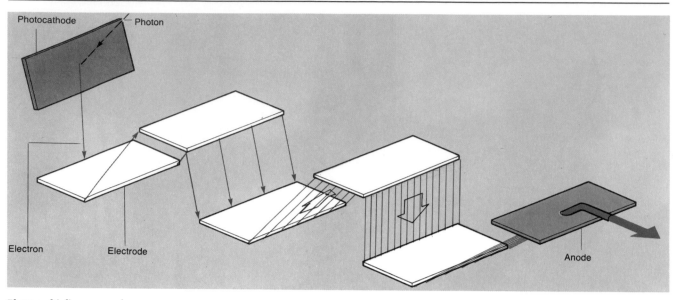

Photocathode — Photon

Electron    Electrode    Anode

**Photomultipliers** are used inside photometers, which allow astronomers to measure the intrinsic intensity of apparently weak starlight. The light rays hit the photocathode, which converts the photons into electrons. These electrons strike electrodes that are coated with a film of electron-emissive material. They then bounce off to bombard successive electrodes, each time multiplying the initial number of electrons. Most photomultipliers have between 9 and 14 electrodes. The anode at the final stage of the photomultiplier collects the electrons as an electric impulse, or current, which is then recorded. The time taken from the emission of the electron to the resulting impulse is only a fraction of a microsecond. Using such an instrument, the brightness of stars can be measured to one hundredth of a magnitude, whereas with the naked eye an observer is able to estimate brightness to only one-tenth of a magnitude.

able stars, particularly where these stars are close binaries. Photometric observations of their varying light output reveal not only their dual nature, but also their masses, separation, relative diameters, and other information.

## Image tubes

One of the most exciting additions to the astronomer's laboratory is the image intensifier. For many years, telescopes were made larger, not in the search for better resolution, but to gather more light. The image intensifier is a form of electron tube in which an image is focused onto an input photocathode. The resulting emitted electrons are accelerated within the evacuated tube by a very high voltage. An electron lens focuses these electrons onto a fluorescent screen (like that in a television tube) which emits a bright flash of light when a high-speed electron strikes it. In this way, a single photon at the input releases a single electron, which is accelerated to hit the screen and causes the emission of many new photons. Such a tube has a "gain" of about 100. That is, the image on the screen is the same as that on the photocathode, but one hundred times brighter.

An image intensifier placed in the image plane of a spectrograph, with the film in contact with the screen, improves the sensitivity of the system dramatically. Often, two or three intensifiers are coupled; the input of one seeing the output of another, and so on. These "cascade" intensifiers are capable of intensifying images by many thousands of times. A three-stage intensifier (used in front of the photographic film on a 12-inch (0.3-meter) telescope) results in shorter exposure times than for plain film (with a 200-inch (5-meter) reflector), such as that at Mt Palomar.

Image intensifiers are used in many instruments: cameras, spectrographs, acquisition and guidance systems. Recently, a completely different and more compact type of tube, called a *microchannel plate* intensifier, has become available. This does the same job as the tubes described previously, but is free from

the pincushion distortion that early tubes produced.

Considerable effort is currently being expended on replacing the output screen of intensifiers with an electronic encoding device. This would permit the electron image to be read out directly into a computer for further processing, rather than converting it back into light. Results are promising, with prototype devices already being tested on telescopes in the United States and the United Kingdom. But these devices are still at too new a stage to have yet contributed significantly to our knowledge of the universe.

### Charge-coupled devices

Since the mid-1970's, a new type of detector has gained popularity in astronomy, called the *charge-coupled device*, or CCD. The CCD is a semiconductor device and is an offshoot of large-scale, silicon-integrated circuit technology. Essentially, it comprises an array of tiny detectors that each store an electric charge in proportion to the amount of light that has fallen on them. The array is then "read out" electronically into a computer memory, where the data is stored for later processing. The CCD was developed as a replacement for television camera tubes, and when used in this way, it had little to offer the astronomer. When cooled to about $-238°$ F. ($-114°$ C), however, it can be used in the so-called "slow scan" mode, permitting exposures of many hours to be made.

Modern CCD's have about 1,500 separate detector elements, or "pixels," each measuring about 25 microns square, making the active area of a CCD array only about 0.47 by 0.32 inches (12 by 8 millimeters). These devices are used as if they were photographic films that can be examined directly by a powerful computer. A further advantage of these detectors is their robustness. Even if a CCD were exposed to direct sunlight, it would be unharmed, whereas image intensifiers and photomultipliers are destroyed if too much light reaches their photocathodes.

### Image photon counting system

Perhaps the one electronic detector system that has contributed more to our knowledge of astronomy than any other is the *image photon counting system* (IPCS). This detector is a four-stage, magnetically-focused image intensifier, coupled via a lens to a plumbicon television camera tube. Magnetically-focused intensifiers are virtually free from the pincushion distortion produced by tubes that employ electrostatic electron lenses. The four stages provide an extremely high amplification of the faint images. A single photon, hitting the input photocathode, produces a bright flash on the output screen, which is "seen" by the television camera. Sophisticated electronics "writes" the position of the original photon in the memory of the computer. This process is repeated for each photon detected, and an image is built up in this way in the computer memory. This then can be processed later and displayed on a video screen or recorded on magnetic tape.

This photon counting system is the most sensitive yet developed for detecting faint images. It has been used almost exclusively for spectroscopy in place of photographic film, although some direct imaging has also been done with the IPCS. Only a few such systems exist due to their great cost, all used on the largest telescopes, such as the Palomar 200-inch (5-meter) and the Anglo-Australian telescope. For imaging applications, the IPCS is largely replaced by the cryogenic (cooled) slowscan CCD, but for applications that require time resolution it remains unrivaled.

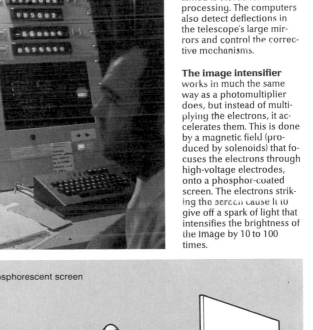

**The control console** for the Anglo-Australian Telescope (AAT) is a vital element in the observatory. The AAT is automatically aimed at a selected object by keying into the console the object's coordinates. The telescope then tracks its target accurately by means of a microprocessor. This determines the movement needed and operates the motors on each axis of the telescope. The data obtained is stored for later processing. The computers also detect deflections in the telescope's large mirrors and control the corrective mechanisms.

**The image intensifier** works in much the same way as a photomultiplier does, but instead of multiplying the electrons, it accelerates them. This is done by a magnetic field (produced by solenoids) that focuses the electrons through high-voltage electrodes, onto a phosphor-coated screen. The electrons striking the screen cause it to give off a spark of light that intensifies the brightness of the image by 10 to 100 times.

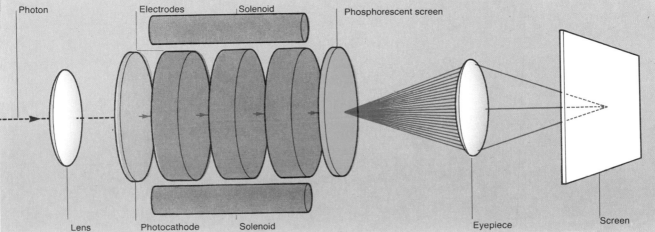

Photon | Electrodes | Solenoid | Phosphorescent screen

Lens | Photocathode | Solenoid | Eyepiece | Screen

# Radioastronomy

In addition to celestial bodies that radiate visible light, the universe contains many objects that emit radiation of various nonvisible wavelengths, such as radio waves. In fact, some astronomical objects emit very little light (or even none at all) and are, therefore, unimpressive when observed visually. They may, however, radiate relatively large amounts of energy at nonvisible wavelengths. The range of such nonvisible radiations is extremely broad, spanning almost all the electromagnetic spectrum (of which visible light constitutes only a small part). Therefore, it is important to study as wide a range of electromagnetic emissions as possible in order to gain the fullest possible understanding of the universe.

Historically, the nonvisible part of the electromagnetic spectrum was first studied in 1931-32, when the American Karl Jansky detected radio emissions (at a frequency of 20MHz—equivalent to a wavelength of 49 feet or 15 meters) emanating from the center of our galaxy. Since then, radioastronomy has developed considerably and has made substantial contributions of our knowledge of the universe.

## The nature of radio waves

Radio waves are low frequency and, therefore, long wavelength electromagnetic radiations. The radio part of the electromagnetic spectrum lies beyond the infrared region and comprises all radiation with a frequency lower than about 300,000 million hertz (300,000MHz) or with a wavelength longer than about 1mm. Because of their low frequency, radio waves are not absorbed by the earth's atmosphere. As a result, radio observations of celestial objects can be made from the earth's surface during the day and at night, both in cloudy and clear weather.

## Types of celestial radio emissions

There are three main types of radio emissions: thermal emissions, synchrotron (or nonthermal) emissions, and radio spectral-line emissions.

Thermal radio-wave emission occurs as a result of the acceleration of electrically-charged particles in a hot gas. When the temperature of a gas is high enough, its neutral atoms break up into negatively-charged electrons and positively-charged ions. Every charged particle moves continuously, interacting with other particles as it does so. (Such interactions are called collisions, although the particles do not normally hit each other.) These collisions cause some of the particles to

**Two of the smaller radio dishes** of the Parkes radio observatory in New South Wales, Australia. The main dish has a diameter of 210 feet (64 meters) making it one of the largest fully-steerable radio telescopes in the Southern Hemisphere. Much of the observatory's famous work on quasars is now done using this large dish.

**The VLA (Very Large Array)** telescope near Socorro, New Mexico recorded this image of galaxy NGC 1316 (blue white) and two accompanying regions (red). The red regions indicate the emission of radio waves, and the blue-white region, visible light.

accelerate, as a result of which they emit radio waves. The higher the temperature of the gas, the greater the number of collisions, and the higher the intensity of radio emissions. Hence, the temperature of a thermal radio source can be calculated from the strength of its radio emission.

Like thermal emission, synchrotron radio-wave emission is produced by the acceleration of charged particles. Unlike thermal emission, however, the acceleration is caused by a magnetic field. The characteristic feature of synchrotron emissions is that the radio waves are polarized (that is, they vibrate in only one plane) unlike those given out by thermal sources. Polarized radio waves have been detected from the Crab Nebula (which also emits unpolarized thermal radio waves). The precise source of these emissions is thought to be the star designated NP 0532, situated in the middle of the nebula. This star produces the magnetic field necessary to accelerate the charged particles. Most other powerful celestial radio sources emit polarized radio waves, which indicates that they are produced by the synchrotron process.

Radio spectral-line emission, the third type of celestial radio emission, is concentrated in a narrow band about one specific frequency— just as an optical spectral line corresponds to a single frequency in the visible electromagnetic spectrum. Radio line emissions usually originate in clouds of hydrogen gas, a relatively common constituent of the universe, which is found in our galaxy's spiral arms, among other places. Therefore, these lines can be used to map the distribution of hydrogen

gas, even in regions where interstellar dust prevents optical observations of the gas clouds.

Line emissions are produced only from the relatively few hydrogen atoms in which the proton and its orbiting electron are initially spinning in the same direction (in the nucleus). In this situation, the hydrogen atom as a whole is in an unstable high-energy state. The result is that the electron changes its direction, spinning in the opposite direction to the proton. When this change occurs, the hydrogen atom falls to a lower, more stable energy state, and the excess energy is radiated as radio waves at the single frequency of approximately 1,420 MHz (commonly known as the 21-centimeter wavelength).

In practice, however, line emissions cover a broader range of frequencies than the 1,420 MHz line. This is because collisions between atoms affect their individual energies. This, in turn, alters the frequency of the radio waves emitted when the atoms fall to a lower, more stable energy state. The extent of this frequency broadening can be used to determine the temperature of celestial hydrogen clouds (typically about $-274°$ F. ($-170°$ C)). Furthermore, the frequency of emissions detected on earth also varies as a result of movements of the clouds (an effect known as the Doppler frequency shift). This phenomenon can be used to calculate the clouds' motions.

Since the discovery of 21-centimeter hydrogen line emission, scientists have found that other molecules also produce line emissions when falling to lower energy states. Each type of molecule can be identified from the char-

The radio interferometer near Manchester, England, has four fixed and four movable dishes on a 3-mile (5-kilometer) track aligned east-west. Every 12 hours, the earth's rotation moves all the dishes through a circle centered on the midpoint of the baseline. Varying the spacing of the dishes and analyzing the signals by computer—earth-rotation synthesis—make the array effectively a 3-mile (5-kilometer) dish.

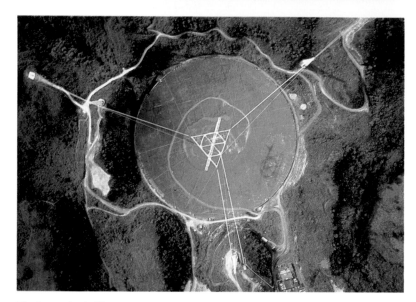

The Ionospheric Observatory at Arecibo in Puerto Rico has the world's largest radio telescope that makes use of a natural hollow in the ground to support the telescope dish.

power of radio telescopes increases with increasing diameter of the radio dish. (The resolving power of both radio and optical telescopes also increases with increasing frequency of the incoming electromagnetic waves. Thus, optical telescopes can, in theory, resolve greater detail than can radio telescopes because visible light has a higher frequency than radio waves. In practice, however, other factors—such as turbulence of the earth's atmosphere—limit the resolving power of optical telescopes, and radio telescopes are generally more effective.)

Nearly all radio telescopes are steerable so that they can track a radio source as it moves across the sky. (This movement is caused by rotation of the earth.) The first fully steerable radio telescope was built in 1957 at Jodrell Bank, England, by the University of Manchester and has a dish that is about 250 feet (76 meters) across. The largest radio telescope of this type is the 330-foot (100-meter) Effelsberg telescope at the Max Planck Institute for Radio Astronomy, Bonn, Germany. There is, however, a practical upper limit to the size of individual radio dishes, due to the difficulty in making very large parabolic dishes that are also accurately shaped—principally, because large dishes tend to deform under their own weight. This limitation creates a problem when astronomers want to study the finest details of distant radio sources, because this requires dishes that are tens of miles across. The problem can be overcome, however, by using radio interferometry.

### Radio interferometry

Radio interferometry is a technique whereby two or more moderate-sized radio telescopes are separated by several miles and (coordinated by means of a cable link) simultaneously study the same radio-emitting object. By combining the signals received by each of the telescopes (which can usually be moved on tracks), it is possible to obtain the same degree of resolving power that would be obtained from a single dish several miles across. In addition, radio interferometry enables the positions of radio sources to be precisely determined. This is very useful for optical astronomers because a radio source may be optically very dim and, therefore, extremely difficult to find without knowing where to look. The angular sizes of radio sources can also be obtained by radio interferometry, as can the distance between two neighboring sources.

Moreover, despite the low frequency of radio waves, radio interferometers can resolve the structure of celestial objects in far greater detail than can optical telescopes. This is partly because of the large effective size of radio interferometers (the effective size being equivalent to the distance between the dishes) and partly because the practical resolving power of optical telescopes is restricted by the turbulence of the earth's atmosphere. But even the best conventional radio interferometers are inadequate for studying extremely small and distant objects, so a technique called Very Long Baseline Interferometry has been developed.

acteristic frequency and wavelength of its emissions. This is the same way that hydrogen can be identified from its 21-centimeter radiation. More than 50 different sorts of molecules have now been detected in space using this method.

### Radio Telescopes

The basic design of most radio telescopes is similar to that of optical reflecting telescopes: both use a parabolic reflector (called a dish in radio telescopes) to collect incoming electromagnetic waves and bring them to a point of focus. But unlike optical reflectors, which collect and focus light, radio telescopes collect and measure the minute amounts of energy in radio waves. (As an indication of how little energy there is in celestial radio waves, it has been calculated that if the energy emitted by a quasar—one of the strongest celestial radio sources—were to be collected by a radio telescope for 10,000 years, it would only be enough to light a small bulb for a fraction of a second.) Because of the infinitesimal amounts of energy involved, the largest possible radio dishes are needed to study radio sources at the edge of the detectable universe. Moreover, the larger the radio dish, the greater the amount of detail it can reveal about the structure of a radio source. That is, the resolving

### Very Long Baseline Interferometry

The principle of Very Long Baseline Interferometry (VLBI) is essentially the same as that of normal radio interferometry, except that VLBI employs several radio dishes hundreds of miles apart, sometimes on different continents. In Europe, one such VLBI array comprises the 250-foot (76-meter) Jodrell Bank telescope in Britain, the 320-foot (100-meter) Effelsberg telescope in Germany, and 14 dishes at Westerbork, Holland. The large separation in VLBI arrays causes difficulties in coordinating the individual dishes and in analyzing their results, so most arrays are controlled by a central computer, which sends instructions to each dish by radio. But even with this arrangement, the signals transmitting the data collected by the dishes back to the computer are often of poor quality. To overcome this problem the individual radio observatories record their data on tapes, which are later collated and analyzed by the computer.

Using Very Long Baseline Interferometry, a small region (less than about 200 astronomical units—0.003 light-years—in diameter) of unusually strong radio emission has been detected in the center of our galaxy. The nature of this object is unknown, although some astronomers believe it to be a black hole that is releasing large amounts of radio energy as it captures dust and stars from the galactic center.

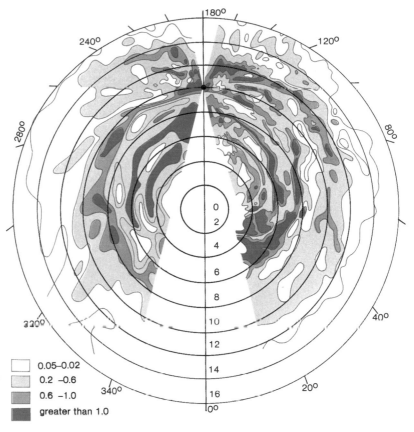

| | |
|---|---|
| ☐ | 0.05–0.02 |
| ▨ | 0.2 –0.6 |
| ▩ | 0.6 –1.0 |
| ■ | greater than 1.0 |

**The radio map** *(above)* shows hydrogen distribution in our galaxy (as atoms per cubic centimeter). The distance scale is in thousands of parsecs from the center. High-density regions correspond to the galaxy's spiral arms. The radar map of Venus *(below)* was made by sending signals from the earth and bouncing them off the planet. Light blue indicates lowland areas; darker colors through to brown represent highlands.

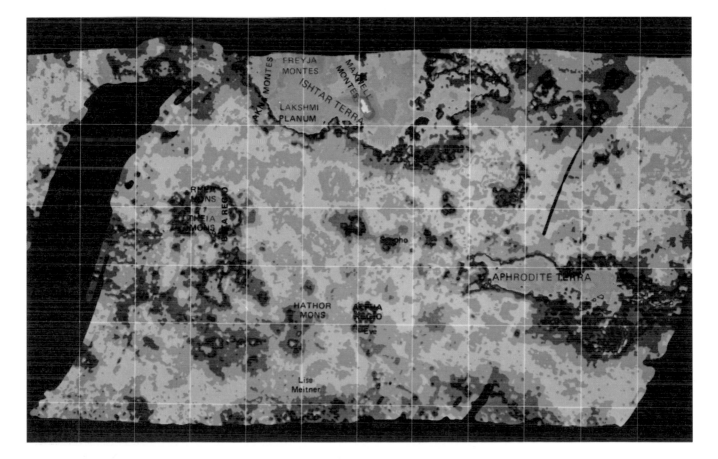

# The amateur astronomer

Many of the world's astronomers are amateurs—in the sense that they do not earn their livings from pursuing the study of the science. This does not imply, however, that all such amateurs pursue their interest with unprofessional skills and equipment. Many indeed have made contributions of outstanding importance to astronomy, and some have equipment that some smaller observatories might envy. The amateur's greatest asset is the opportunity simply to observe the heavens and investigate any object or phenomenon that seems of interest. In contrast, professional astronomers must follow specific programs of scientific research.

Amateur astronomers may be considered to fall into three approximate categories.

The first group includes those who have a general interest in the stars and planets. They can identify the more obvious constellations and follow the special astronomical events that are covered by the press or television. Members of this group are mainly naked-eye observers, although they may also use binoculars or small, tripod-mounted telescopes.

Binoculars (typically 7 by 50 or 10 by 50) with 7- or 10-fold magnification and an objective lens of 2 inches (51 millimeters) in diameter, will reveal many more stars than are visible to the naked eye and will give breathtaking views of the Milky Way. Craters and other surface features of the moon, Jupiter's four main satellites, star clusters, and comets can also be observed.

Small telescopes, with objective lenses of a 2-inch diameter or more, are the next step from binoculars. Such small telescopes, which are capable of magnifications of up to eight times per inch of objective lens aperture, are not intended to be hand-held. They are usually provided with a light tripod, which provides some stability, and with an altazimuth mounting, which is simple to use. This type of stand allows the telescope to be rotated about vertical and horizontal axes and appeals to those who may be mystified by sidereal time and setting circles or who simply want to point their telescopes at some interesting object in the sky.

A large number of books, maps, and star atlases are available to help locate objects in the night sky and can be used with alt-az instruments. Like many of the star charts that are issued monthly, these give altitudes, azimuths, and indicate the times when objects of interest can be observed.

Amateur astronomer observing a nebula in the constellation of Orion. It is important to allow the eyes to adjust to the dark before looking at the night sky. Most people's eyes need from 10 to 30 minutes in darkness in order to adjust.

The moon is a favorite subject of study for amateur astronomers, both for observation and photography. Good photographs of the lunar surface can be obtained with a 35mm camera body attached to almost any equatorially-mounted telescope.

The second group make amateur astronomy their major interest, either buying a relatively powerful telescope or even making a telescope for themselves. Telescopes they are likely to use are of three main types: refractors, reflectors, and catadioptrics, the last combining elements of each of the first two. Amateurs in this group would normally use a refractor with an objective diameter between 3 and 6 inches (75 and 150 millimeters), or a reflector with an objective diameter between 6 and 20 inches (150 and 510 millimeters). Catadioptrics are available with objective diameters of 3 and 14 inches (75 and 355 millimeters), the most popular sizes being 6 inches (150 millimeters) and 8 inches (200 millimeters).

Telescopes used by the second group are almost invariably equatorially mounted, which means that one axis points to the north or south celestial pole in the Northern or Southern Hemisphere, respectively. (This polar axis is parallel to the axis of the earth.) The other axis, at right angles to the polar axis, is the equatorial axis.

Two setting circles are important accessories for the proper use of an equatorial telescope: the right ascension circle is calibrated in hours and minutes of Right Ascension (R.A.); the declination circle is calibrated in degrees. A drive mechanism, which is usually electronic, regulated by a sidereal clock, turns the telescope about its equatorial axis so that, when set for the R.A. and declination of a particular star, the telescope is able to follow that star's movement through the sky.

The sidereal drive actually turns the telescope at the same rate as the earth, but in the opposite direction. This capability is useful enough when observing through the eyepiece, but it is indispensable when photographing the moon, or planets, stars, nebulae, or other celestial phenomena, because long exposures are required.

Astrophotography is itself a rewarding branch of amateur astronomy for which neither exacting skills nor heavy expenditure is required. A single lens reflex camera can be used by attaching the body of the camera (without its lens) to a telescope from which the eyepiece has been removed. This way the primary image of the telescope objective is focused on the camera film. The telescope without its eyepiece simply becomes a powerful telephoto lens. This arrangement, using a telescope with a focal length of about 47 inches (1.2 meters), will give an image of the moon 0.4 inches (10.2 millimeters) in diameter at the focal plane of the camera and will look reasonably clear on 35mm film. Images can be increased in size by using eyepiece projection. Camera adaptors for this purpose can be obtained from most telescope suppliers.

The third group includes the most serious and advanced amateurs of all. They may actually be attached to university departments or observatories and are likely to be well qualified in related branches of physics, mathematics, optics, or electronics.

Particularly interesting subjects for amateur astronomers include:

**The sun**—especially: sun-spots; eclipses; also spectroheliography (for which some amateurs can construct their own equipment). Because it will cause instant, permanent blindness, it is extremely important to remember to never look at the sun either directly, through darkened glasses, or through binoculars or a telescope. Observations can only be made by projecting the sun's image onto a screen.

**The moon**—especially: surface changes; observations of the exact times at which the moon occults stars and planets; and photography, for which the moon is an ideal subject.

**The planets**—especially: the rings of Saturn; the phases of Venus; the ice caps and markings of Mars; the movements of the satellites of Jupiter.

**Comets, meteor showers, and aurora**—amateurs make a particularly important contribution in this area because of the time they can spend simply searching the sky. Most comets have been discovered by amateurs.

**Double stars or binaries**—it has been estimated that roughly half the stars in our galaxy are binaries, showing variable brightness as the two stars orbit and eclipse each other.

**Other deep sky objects**—for example, nebulae; galaxies; star clusters; variable stars.

**A telescope** should always be stable and firmly mounted, especially for high magnifications and photographic work. Light weight telescopes present problems of stability and should only be used at low magnifications.

**A large telescope,** such as this 12-inch (305-millimeter) Newtonian reflector, on a permanent mount, must be shielded when not in use. A geodesic dome is light and serves the purpose.

# The stellar universe

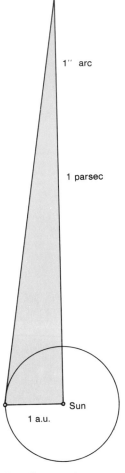

1" arc

1 parsec

Sun

1 a.u.

**Vast distances in space** are expressed in astronomical units, light-years, or parsecs. An astronomical unit (a.u.) is half the diameter of the earth's orbit around the sun. A parsec is the distance to an object (such as a star) that subtends an angle of 1 second of arc at a baseline 1 a.u. long. A light-year is the distance light travels in 1 year (equal to 63,290 a.u., 5.88 trillion miles, or 9.461 trillion kilometers). One parsec equals 3.26 light years or 206,265 a.u.

It is possible to see about 6,000 stars with the naked eye, and using a small telescope as many as 600,000 become visible. More powerful telescopes reveal, in addition to individual stars, many thousands of galaxies. Each of these galaxies contains as many as one trillion stars. The most powerful telescopes can probably detect 1 billion galaxies. Yet despite the immensity of these galaxies, they appear as the tiniest blotches of light surrounded by vast reaches of empty space. The universe, which by definition includes everything in existence, is unimaginably large. To study it, it must be broken down into its constituent parts.

### The basic structure of the universe

An analysis of stars shows that many are part of clusters of as few as 10 stars to as many as 1 million stars. All revolve as a group about the center of the galaxy of which they are a part. This hierarchy continues to build up, with many galaxies being members of galactic clusters, bound together by their mutual gravitational interaction. The local group of about 20 galaxies, including our own, is one example of such a cluster. These clusters are typically tens of millions of parsecs across and contain several hundred galaxies. There is some evidence to suggest that clusters of clusters exist, or "superclusters" of galaxies.

Despite the apparent random distribution of stars, it is generally believed that the universe takes on a uniform appearance when viewed on scales greater than about 1 billion parsecs. It is said to be homogeneous and isotropic on these scales—that is, it looks the same from all points, in all directions. That the universe should have a structure on this large scale is surprising in view of its violent beginnings (according to the big bang theory). Even so, the structure makes it much easier to try to calculate its properties.

### The expansion of the universe

In the 1920's the universe as a whole was discovered to be in a state of expansion. This finding was revealed in the recession of the galaxies: whereby the farther a galaxy is from the earth, the faster it appears to race away. This phenomenon is expressed by Hubble's law, which states that the recession speed of a distant galaxy is proportional to its distance. According to this law, there is a distance from earth at which a galaxy recedes from it at the speed of light. Because it is impossible to see this or any other more distant galaxy, the corresponding distance can be taken as representing the radius of the visible universe. Hubble's constant ($H_0$) relates the distance of a galaxy to its speed of recession. Determining the actual value of Hubble's constant is made difficult by the uncertainties involved in meas-

uring the vast distances to the farthest galaxies. Estimates for the Hubble constant range from 40 to 100 kilometers per second per million parsecs.

The observation that all the galaxies that obey Hubble's expansion law seem to race away from us might lead one to think that the earth is the center of expansion. But the universe expands uniformly at every point, so we see only a small area of its expansion.

The present expansion of the universe suggests that at an earlier stage, the galaxies were closer together. It is thought that there may have been a time when all the matter in the universe, and the space that contains it, was merged into a single globule, which exploded to start the expansion. This is the big bang theory of the origin of the universe. Hubble's constant ($H_0$) is also used to indicate how long ago this initial explosion took place, flinging all matter outward to condense later into the galaxies we now see. But because of disagreement about the value of the Hubble constant, estimates of the age of the universe range from 7 to 22 billion years.

The big bang would have generated vast quantities of radiation from the enormously high temperatures involved. This radiation, now much cooled and diluted by the expansion, would be—and still is—observable in the form of background microwave radiation, corresponding to a temperature of 3 K (−454° F.; −270° C), just above absolute zero.

Stars and galaxies also contribute to the total radiation background, which covers all known frequencies of the electromagnetic spectrum. The universe is, at present, dominated in its evolution by the matter within it. In the first 10,000 years of its existence, however, the universe's development was governed by its radiation content.

### The density of the universe

The density of matter in the universe can be calculated once the number of galaxies per cubic megaparsec and the mass of each one is known. Counts of the numbers of galaxies exceeding a certain luminosity show that there is roughly 1 galaxy per 50 cubic megaparsecs of space. Taking an average galaxy mass as $10^{11}$ solar masses, the density of space averages only 1 atom per 10 cubic yards (7.6 cubic meters). This figure for the density is considered by some astronomers to be an underestimate. They argue that intergalactic space may contain large amounts of dark matter in the form of dust, dead stars, black holes, and cold gas. Such material would be extremely difficult to detect but, if found to exist, could have very important consequences. A high enough density of matter could halt the expansion of the universe and cause it to collapse again, thus resulting in another big bang.

**The trails of stars** photographed using a long exposure trace arcs of light in the sky above the 83-inch (2.8-meter) telescope at the Kitt Peak Observatory in Arizona. The colors of the stars are very distinct, and the brightness of each arc indicates the luminescence and distance of each star. The trails and apparent movement of the stars are due to the earth's rotation on its axis. To ancient astronomers, it seemed that the stars, and not the earth, were moving in the heavens. Many of these stars are larger than our sun, and each exists in a galaxy. Galaxies themselves fill only a hundred-millionth of the known universe, and the space between them is increasing. The scale of the universe is unimaginable; yet, it is expanding. It seems impossible that humans could ever view its total extent.

# Evolution of the universe

How the universe originated and evolved are among the most perplexing questions still facing astronomers—in particular cosmologists, who specialize in studying the universe as a whole. Throughout the ages scientists have tried to solve the riddle of the universe's origin, but it is only in this century that any significant progress has been made.

At the beginning of this century, most astronomers believed that although individual stars and other celestial bodies were moving, these movements "canceled out" each other so that the universe as a whole was static. It was also generally thought that the universe was infinitely large (and, being static, was neither expanding nor contracting) and infinitely old. The universe has always existed in much the same state; there had been no beginning. Then in 1915, serious doubts were cast on the idea of a static universe as a result of Albert Einstein's general theory of relativity—which, even today, is still the best theory of gravitation. (It is not confined only to the force of gravity but deals also with the effects of acceleration.)

When Einstein applied his theory to the universe, he found that his equations allowed for the existence of only nonstatic universes—that is, several different hypothetical models of the universe were possible within the general relativity theory, but none of these possible universes was static. Several years later it was discovered that the spectra of distant galaxies showed red shifts, (Doppler shifts), which indicated that these galaxies were moving away from the earth and, by extension, that the universe was expanding—as predicted by Einstein's general relativity theory. (Red shifts are an apparent change in the frequency of light because of relative motion between the source and the observer. A frequency shift toward the red end of the visible spectrum means that the source and observer are moving apart.)

Since then other findings have also supported the general relativity theory, and it now forms the basis of almost all modern cosmological models and studies of the universe.

## The big bang theory

Using the general relativity theory, astronomers have extrapolated back in time from the universe as it now is to try to discover how it originated. Measurements of its expansion rate indicate that the universe originated in an unimaginably violent explosion that occurred from 10 to 20 billion years ago—the big bang

**A computer simulation of galaxy clustering** is shown in these two illustrations. The first chart *(near right)* represents the distribution of galaxies soon after their formation—spread randomly throughout the universe. The second chart *(far right)* represents the galaxy distribution 14 billion years later; as can be seen, the galaxies have grouped together into clusters.

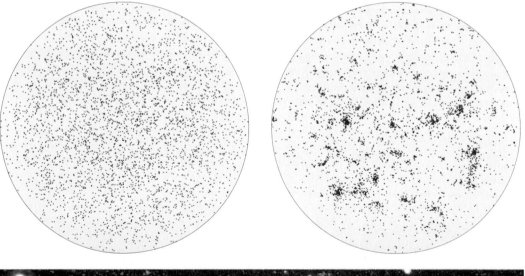

**Galaxies** began to form billions of years ago and were initially distributed randomly. Today, however, most galaxies tend to be in clusters, one of which—Stephan's quartet—is shown in the image-enhanced photograph on the right.

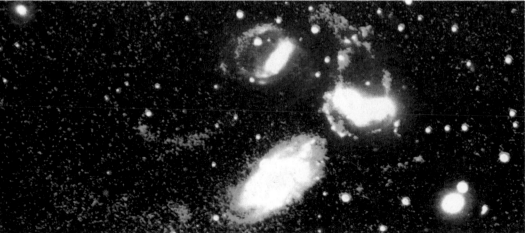

theory of the universe. According to this theory, all the matter that now exists was originally conglomerated in a state of enormous density; this condensed "nucleus" then exploded, throwing out the matter from which the stars, galaxies, planets—and ultimately ourselves—later developed.

But the origin of the matter in the nucleus and the details of the conditions at the precise moment of creation are still unsolved problems. The general relativity theory proposes that at the moment of creation all matter was condensed in a unique state called *singularity,* a state of infinite density and infinitesmal volume. The laws of physics do not apply to this state; without such a frame of reference, it is impossible to describe or explain what happened at the moment of creation. Nevertheless, some scientists believe that the big bang could not have occurred had matter reached a state of singularity. It has, therefore, been postulated that little understood "quantum gravitational processes" intervened to prevent singularity from occurring, thereby enabling the big bang to take place.

Immediately after the big bang, the rapidly-expanding matter was inconceivably hot. At such high temperatures, elementary particles (protons, neutrons, and electrons, for example) can be created, seemingly from nothing. These particles, which are produced in matter-antimatter pairs (electrons and positrons—positive electrons—for example), came into existence about 1 millionth of 1 second after the explosion. By about 100 seconds later, the universe had cooled to a temperature low enough for electrons and positrons to interact with protons and neutrons to form deuterium nuclei.

About three minutes after the big bang, helium nuclei were formed from deuterium. Other nuclei—for example, beryllium nuclei—were also formed, but only in extremely small amounts. (The relative abundance of the heavier elements in the present-day universe is a result of their more recent formation in stars.)

The temperature of the universe continued to decrease, and by about a million years after the big bang, it was cool enough to enable the formation of hydrogen atoms. This point marked the end of the radiation-dominated era, during which the effects of energy (in the form of heat radiation) predominated. At the beginning of the matter-dominated era (which is still continuing), interactions between matter, rather than energy, were (and are) the principal changes.

The big bang was extremely violent and created a great deal of turbulence, as a result of which the rapidly expanding matter was not distributed uniformly throughout the universe. Thus, there were dense regions containing large amounts of matter and less dense areas with relatively little matter. It is generally believed that the high-density regions then began to slowly attract increasing amounts of matter until, about 1 billion years after the big bang, they developed into galaxies. Subsequently, the individual galaxies gradually grouped together to form clusters and superclusters. About 3 billion years later, the first stars began to develop in the galaxies. After a further 6 billion years, our solar system (and

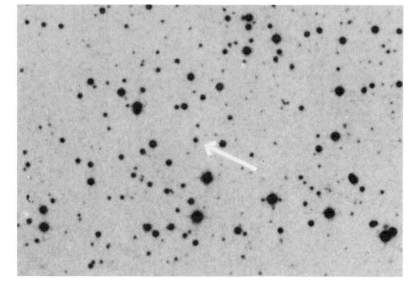

The brightest and most distant objects in the observable universe are quasars similar to the one shown by the arrow in the photograph above. The photograph is reproduced as a negative to make the quasar, which is billions of light years away, more clearly visible.

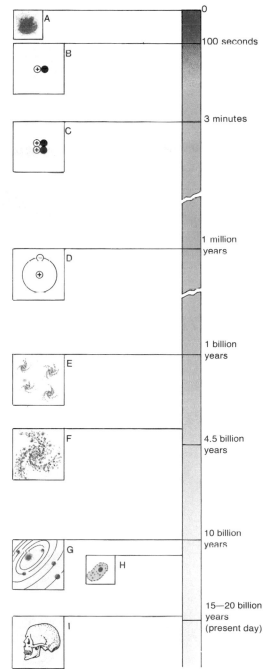

The universe is believed to have originated from 10 to 20 billion years ago, when the dense nucleus containing all matter exploded with inconceivable force in the big bang (A). Expanding rapidly, the universe had cooled sufficiently (to about 10 billion degrees) by 100 seconds later to enable deuterium nuclei to be formed (B). The temperature continued to decrease, making possible the formation of helium nuclei (C), and, 1 million years later, hydrogen atoms (D). Galaxies started to form (E) about 1 billion years after the big bang, and stars developed within the galaxies approximately 3 billion years later (F). Our solar system formed about 4.5 billion years ago (G), and life developed on earth (H) relatively soon afterward—about 3 billion years ago. But modern man (*Homo sapiens*) did not appear until about 300,000 years ago (I).

**A supernova** represents the death of a star. The two photographs show NGC 5253 before (near right) and during (far right) the explosion of one of its stars. If the remnants of a supernova expand and meet an interstellar dust cloud, a shock wave is produced that may cause the cloud to collapse. Some astronomers believe that such a compression may have triggered the formation of our solar system.

therefore the earth) started to form. Life evolved on earth relatively quickly; it is thought that the first life-forms (probably simple single-celled organisms) developed about 3 billion years ago—within about 1 billion years of the earth's formation. Modern man *(Homo sapiens)* is a newcomer, the earliest fossil remains being only some 300,000 years old.

**Testing the big bang theory**

According to the big bang theory, most of the helium that is present today was first formed about three minutes after the big bang itself. From this it has been calculated that the universe should now consist of about 23 per cent helium and 77 per cent other elements (mainly hydrogen)—a prediction that has been sup-

ported by measurements of the abundances of the various elements in our galaxy and in other galaxies; thus these measurements are evidence in favor of the big bang theory.

Another test of the validity of the big bang theory derives from a discovery, made by the American physicists Arno Penzias and Robert Wilson, concerning the intensity of background radiation. If the universe began with an enormous explosion, there should still exist a much-cooled relic of the incredibly high temperature that originally existed. Because the big bang involved the entire universe, this relic should be in the form of a fairly uniform background radiation (called isotropic radiation), with minor local variations in intensity reflecting inhomogeneities in the universe when the radiation-dominated era came to an end.

In 1965, Penzias and Wilson detected isotropic background radiation in the microwave region of the electromagnetic spectrum—the type of radiation expected if the big bang theory is correct. Subsequent measurements of the intensity and frequency of the isotropic radiation and of its average temperature, about 3 K (−454° F.; −270° C), also tended to support the big bang theory.

In 1989, NASA launched the Cosmic Background Explorer (COBE) satellite to study the microwave background radiation. COBE confirmed that there is very uniform background radiation at about 2.7 K (−454.8° F.; −270.5° C). Big bang theory also predicts that the background radiation should have irregularities left over from the explosive turbulence of the big bang itself. In 1992, NASA scientists announced that analysis of COBE data had revealed the first such small irregularities, strengthening the case for the big bang. Most scientists believe that the big bang theory provides the most plausible explanation of the origin of the universe.

**The fate of the universe**

In addition to extrapolating backward in time to try to discover how the universe originated and evolved, cosmologists have also extrapolated forward in an attempt to predict the ulti-

**Our sun** is thought to be about 4.6 billion years old. Like other stars, it generates energy by converting hydrogen to helium. As a star consumes its hydrogen, it gets larger and cooler, becoming first a giant, then a supergiant star. Eventually it develops into a white dwarf, a pulsar, or a black hole. A few stars, however, finish their lives as supernovae.

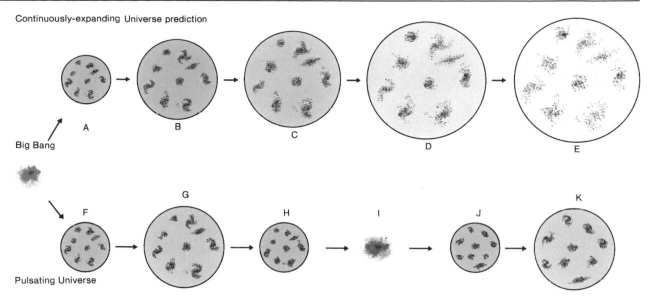

Continuously-expanding Universe prediction

Big Bang

Pulsating Universe

mate fate of the universe. According to the almost universally-accepted general relativity theory, there are only two possible futures for the universe: it will either continue to expand (at an ever-decreasing rate) indefinitely, or it will eventually stop expanding and collapse back on itself. This second possibility could again form a highly condensed nucleus that will explode in another big bang—the pulsating universe theory. Which of these two possibilities is more likely depends on the amount of matter in the universe: the more matter, the more probable is the pulsating universe.

Astronomers have calculated that an average density (throughout the entire universe) of 100 atoms per 10 cubic yards (7.6 cubic meters) is necessary for the universe eventually to stop expanding and collapse. But the most recent measurements indicate that the average density is, at most, one atom per cubic yard. Thus, it is generally thought that the universe will continue to expand indefinitely, gradually becoming less active until, more than a 100 billion years from now, it will be completely "dead," except for the occasional explosion of a black hole.

But some astronomers doubt the validity of this hypothesis. They believe that there is a large amount of material (such as dust, dead stars, and black holes) that has not yet been detected and, therefore, that there might be sufficient matter for the universe to eventually collapse back on itself. If this is the case, the universe will not merely "fade away" to a cold, dead expanse, empty of everything, even gas and dust. Instead, it will eventually stop expanding, become static for a short time, and will then begin to contract.

As this contraction begins, the galaxies will start to converge, slowly at first, then with increasing speed as they are mutually attracted by gravity. About 100 million years before the "big crunch" (the time at which all matter will be conglomerated in an extremely dense nucleus), the galaxies will begin to merge and their constituent stars will collide, exploding as they do so. As the universe continues to contract, it will become hotter. According to the pulsating universe theory, eventually all matter will become condensed into a single, incredibly hot mass, which will then explode—as in the original big bang—thereby causing the universe to expand again. Thus, the universe would undergo a perpetual cycle of big bang, expansion, momentary stasis, contraction, and big bang again. But this theory depends for its plausibility on there being more matter in the universe than has been detected, and the available evidence therefore supports the continuously-expanding universe theory.

**The fate of the universe** is uncertain. Most astronomers believe that it will continue to expand indefinitely (A to E), becoming increasingly less active as more and more stars die and the galaxies disperse into tenuous clouds of dust and gas. But a few scientists—adherents of the pulsating universe theory (F to K)—think that there is sufficient matter in the universe to make it stop expanding and collapse back on itself. It will eventually form a highly-condensed mass which will then explode in a second big bang; thus the universe would be recreated. Moreover, this cycle of events would repeat itself endlessly, and the universe would therefore exist forever.

# Stellar evolution

Stars are believed to be born in groups from the collapse of large, cold clouds of interstellar material composed chiefly of hydrogen gas. Whenever the mass of such a cloud exceeds the Jeans mass (named after the British astrophysicist James Jeans), the gravitational force within it is greater than any outward thermal pressure and causes the cloud to collapse.

### Protostars

Observations suggest that if the Jeans mass of a cloud is equal to many solar masses, the collapse of the cloud leads to the formation of the same number of stars as there are solar masses, each star having approximately one solar mass. These stars are then part of a star cluster. As the whole cloud collapses, regions within it undergo their own localized contractions in a process called *fragmentation*. The temperature of these regions starts to rise, because their density is so high that heat cannot escape. Eventually, the temperature rises far enough for outward thermal pressure to halt the collapse of the localized regions, and the fragmentation ends. These now stable, noncollapsing regions of high density and temperature are called *protostars*.

The next stage in a star's evolution depends on its mass. For a protostar of a mass similar to that of the sun, the collapse of the cloud leads to the formation of a hot, central region. This core contracts to form the nucleus of the future star. The outer regions of the protostar draw closer to the core, and the temperature at the center increases. About 60 million years after the interstellar cloud originally started its collapse, the temperature becomes high enough for nuclear fusion reactions to begin. The reactions keep the star stable for many millions of years, during which time it shines using energy derived from its conversion of hydrogen to helium.

For a star of more than one solar mass, the collapse is such that the initial nucleus expands quickly, and thermonuclear reactions begin much more rapidly. As a result, the nucleus becomes so bright that radiation pressure prevents much of the outer parts of the protostar from moving inward to further increase its mass, and only about one-third of the protostar's initial mass burns by hydrogen conversion. The corresponding stages of a star of 10 solar masses may last only 200,000 years.

### Main-sequence stars and supergiants

When the hydrogen-burning reactions begin in a newly born star, the star is at the Zero-Age Main Sequence (ZAMS) stage. A star of one solar mass burns its hydrogen for about 10 billion years and for this time remains on the main sequence. According to this analysis, the sun, which is about 4.6 billion years old, is a middle-aged star.

As the hydrogen fuel is used up in a star's core, its energy production decreases, and the core slowly starts to collapse. The unburnt hydrogen in the shell outside the helium-filled core is gradually converted to helium, which becomes part of the core, and the resulting radiation halts the overall contraction. The collapse of the core itself continues, however, because it has to reach an even higher temperature to burn its helium and produce more energy-rich elements. This process continues until the helium core makes up about 10 to 15 per cent of the star's entire mass, when it reaches the Schönberg-Chandrasekhar limit—which determines when the core must start contracting. Under its own weight, and the weight of the outer layers, the core contracts rapidly; the surrounding envelope expands and the star becomes a red giant. During this time, the contracting core becomes hot enough for the helium in it to "burn" and produce carbon, which stops the core from collapsing any further. Over a period of a few tens of millions of years, the star grows into an enormous, very luminous, yet relatively cool, red giant. Our sun will reach this stage about 5 billion years from now. It will expand about 30 to 40 million miles (48 to 64 million kilometers) to reach the planet Mercury. The earth's temperature will increase so drastically that life will cease to exist there.

**The birth of a star** is not yet fully understood, but astronomers believe that protostars condense from interstellar clouds of gas and dust in a process of fragmentation. These fragments of cloud contract until the pressure and temperature at their centers rise and slow the rate of collapse. The central regions collapse faster than the outer layers. When the temperature of the contracting core is high enough to start the hydrogen-burning reactions, the contraction halts and the star joins the main-sequence band.

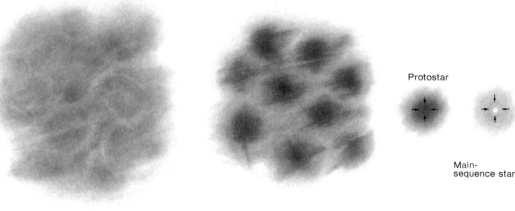

Interstellar gas cloud

Fragmentation

Protostar

Main-sequence star

## White dwarfs

A star may remain a giant or supergiant for several million years before all nuclear reactions cease. Gravitational collapse then occurs with no outward pressure to stop it, and the final result may be a white dwarf. Such a star is small (about the same size as the earth) but has about 1 million times the density of water. The temperature at the surface is a few tens of thousands of degrees, yet the luminosity is quite low—about one thousandth of our sun.

If the core of a star has a final mass at this stage of less than about 1.4 solar masses (the Chandrasekhar limit), then the collapse stops at the white dwarf stage. With the passage of time, the remaining heat and light will be radiated away, so that the star eventually becomes a black dwarf. Even if a star begins its life with a much greater mass, it is possible for its final collapse to be stopped at the white dwarf phase if it can shed the extra mass at some stage. Stars of from 4 to 8 solar masses become red supergiants and eventually explode in a supernova explosion.

## Neutron stars and pulsars

If the mass of a star's core is between about 1.5 and 3 solar masses, the star's collapse is thought to continue until very high densities are reached. At such densities, electrons collide with protons and produce neutrons. Eventually, so many neutrons are created (relative to the number of protons) that the nuclei of atoms begin to break up, and virtually nothing but neutrons remain, forming a neutron star.

Neutron stars have some bizarre properties. Each has the mass of several suns, yet is only about 12 miles (19 kilometers) across. The outer layer of a neutron star is solid, although the star that gave birth to it was gaseous.

In 1967, radio-astronomers discovered a radio source that gave a very brief burst of radio energy once every 1.34 seconds. Other such sources, known as pulsars, were soon tracked down, and one, in the Crab Nebula, was found to have a period of 33 thousandths of a second. To have such a rapid rate of spin,

this object must be very small. The position of this particular pulsar corresponds with the site of a rare and spectacular phenomenon observed by Chinese astronomers in A.D. 1054—the violent end of a star's life in a supernova explosion.

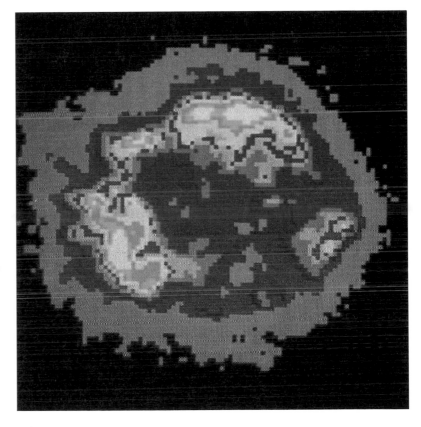

**Cassiopeia A** is a supernova remnant in the constellation of that name and lies 9,000 light-years away. It is a classic young shell of gas and dust and is the remnant of an explosion that occurred c. 1604 A.D. Its outer filaments are moving at a velocity of up to 5,590 miles (9,000 kilometers) per second. As the remnant expands, its gases lose heat, resulting in the decreasing emission of radio waves.

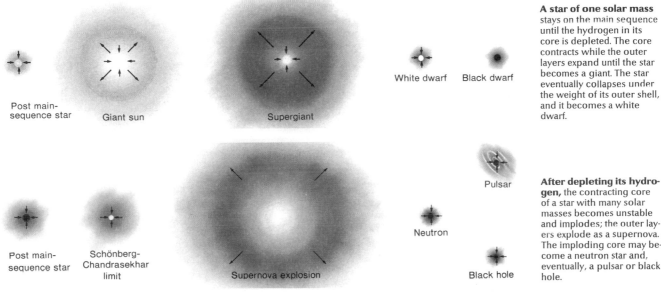

Post main-sequence star    Giant sun    Supergiant    White dwarf    Black dwarf

Post main-sequence star    Schönberg-Chandrasekhar limit    Supernova explosion    Neutron    Pulsar    Black hole

**A star of one solar mass** stays on the main sequence until the hydrogen in its core is depleted. The core contracts while the outer layers expand until the star becomes a giant. The star eventually collapses under the weight of its outer shell, and it becomes a white dwarf.

**After depleting its hydrogen,** the contracting core of a star with many solar masses becomes unstable and implodes; the outer layers explode as a supernova. The imploding core may become a neutron star and, eventually, a pulsar or black hole.

# THE ELUSIVE OBJECTS CALLED
## *black holes*

**A spiral-shaped disk** of hot, whirling gas in the core of galaxy M87 was photographed by the Hubble Space Telescope in 1994. This discovery was the first convincing visual evidence of the existence of black holes.

**B**lack holes have such strange characteristics that scientists doubted their existence for years. Since the late 1960's, however, most of these doubts have been dispelled, and astronomers, armed with the latest technology, have set out to find these elusive objects.

In May 1994, the findings of the Hubble Space Telescope gave scientists the most conclusive observation of black holes yet—a swirling concentration of matter at the center of a galaxy known as M87. According to the reports, this phenomenon could be explained only by the presence of a huge black hole with a mass of up to 3 billion times the mass of the sun.

## How black holes are formed

Today, scientists believe that black holes come in various sizes. Many are formed from the collapsed remnants of very large stars. Others, like the one in M87, are supermassive objects formed at the heart of galaxies. And mini black holes, much smaller than a pinhead, may have been created during the big bang, the explosive birth of the universe some 15 billion years ago.

While a star burns fuel, it produces an outward push that counters the inward pull of gravity. When no more fuel remains, its core cools and shrinks, the internal pressure drops, and the star can no longer support its enormous weight. What happens next varies, depending on the mass of the star and its remaining core.

A star with a mass of about four to eight times the mass of the sun usually ends its life as a supernova, collapsing under its own weight. As it collapses, atomic particles in its core fuse, causing a shattering explosion that rips apart the outer layers of the original star. When a core mass of between 1.4 and 3 times the mass of the sun remains, it becomes a neutron star.

A star with a mass 8 to 25 times the mass of the sun may also collapse and explode but may not stop at the neutron-star stage. If the remnant is more than three times the mass of the sun, it may shrink to a tiny point so small and so dense that its gravitational attraction is strong enough to prevent even light itself from escaping. This point then becomes the center of a black hole.

A star that contains more than 25 times the mass of the sun may collapse without creating an explosion. If its remaining mass is at least three times that of the sun, it will shrink to form a black hole.

Some scientists believe that supermassive black holes may be at the center of many galaxies. In such a galaxy, huge gas clouds and swarms of stars rotate in a swirling mass. At the center of the galaxy, stars and gas clouds may become so closely packed that they are drawn together by gravity, eventually forming a single large mass. Continued gravitational contraction produces a black hole with the mass of millions or billions of suns.

Innumerable mini black holes may have formed during the big bang. The tremendous pressures within the explosion could have squeezed pockets of subatomic particles to incredibly high densities, converting them to mini black holes.

## Searching for black holes

A black hole is invisible, but its incredibly powerful gravitational field wreaks havoc on surrounding matter. And these effects can be detected in the form of X rays.

Scientists have the best chance of finding a black hole in binary star systems. In such systems, a black hole can strip gas from its partner. If this happens, the gas falls violently toward the black hole in a tightening spiral called an *accretion disk.* As the gas gets closer to the black hole, it accelerates to nearly the speed of light. Compression and friction cause the gas to become progressively hotter, raising its temperature up to tens of millions of degrees. The hot gases emit enormous amounts of radiation, which can be detected by scientific instruments.

Scientists believe this process is generating the powerful X rays being emitted from the first black hole to be identified—Cygnus X-1 in the constellation Cygnus. Once its position was known, astronomers discovered that this X-ray source had a companion star—a massive blue supergiant. To find the supergiant's dark companion, scientists used a process of elimination.

First, the orbital motion of the supergiant told scientists that the mass of the unseen object must be 6 to 15 times the mass of our sun. Second, it could not be a normal star, because a star so massive would almost certainly be visible. And third, it could not be a neutron star, because a neutron star cannot have a mass more than three times that of the sun. That left only one other possibility—a black hole.

Today, scientists have identified a few other possible black holes formed from dead stars: V404 Cygni, another suspicious object in Cygnus; LMC X-3, an erratic X-ray source in a nearby galaxy called the Large Magellanic Cloud; and the dark companion of A0620-00, an orange sunlike star that whips around in the Monoceros constellation.

Although just one star in millions is massive enough to end its life as a black hole, most galaxies contain at least 100 billion stars, so black holes resulting from collapsed stars would hardly be rarities. There may be millions of black holes in the Milky Way alone.

**A dark region of dust** about 800 light years across rotates in the bright nucleus of Galaxy NGC 4261. Astronomers believe that only a huge black hole could generate enough gravitational force to cause such a disturbance.

# The stars

When we look at the clear, moonless night sky, we can see thousands of small dots of light, almost all of which are stars. The few bright objects that are not stars are the planets of the solar system. There are, however, easily observable differences between the planets and true stars: all stars twinkle, whereas the planets do not (unless the air in the earth's atmosphere is extremely turbulent). And, by looking at the sky on successive nights, the planets can be seen to have moved by a relatively large amount when compared with the apparently stationary background of stars. In addition, most of the planets are close enough to earth to appear as disks (or sometimes crescents, depending on their phase) when viewed even with low-powered binoculars. A more fundamental difference is that stars, unlike the planets, generate their own energy (emitted in the form of light and other radiation) by nuclear fusion. Planets are visible only because they reflect sunlight.

The sun is our nearest star, situated at an average distance from the earth of about 92,960,000 miles (149,600,000 kilometers) or one astronomical unit. The next nearest star is Proxima Centauri, slightly more than 25 million million miles (40 million million kilometers).

Despite the immense distances to the stars, and the fact that we cannot see the surface of any star except the sun, we can nevertheless determine some of their individual characteristics. These would be temperature, size, chemical composition, brightness (luminosity), and their groupings. Some stars, such as the sun, are solitary, whereas others may be part of multiple star systems, associations, or stellar clusters.

### Distances to the stars

It is very difficult to measure accurately the distances to stars. This is partly because they are so large and partly because of the apparent smallness of the stars when observed from earth. Moreover, the observed brightness of a star is not in itself a reliable indicator of distance. Stars that appear to be equally bright seem also to be equally distant. Thus, an extremely remote, but intrinsically very bright, star may seem to be the same distance from earth as a much closer, but fainter star.

Despite these difficulties, stellar distances can be measured. There are two main ways of doing this. One is by using the stellar parallax effect, the other by comparing the unknown star with a nearer one whose distance is known. The stellar parallax method relies on the effect whereby a relatively near object appears to move in relation to a distant background as the observer moves. In astronomy, the relatively close object is a "nearby" star (whose distance is to be found), which is observed in relation to the background of more distant stars. The observer uses the movement of the earth in its orbit as a known, sufficiently large change in position. When the earth is at one side of its orbit, the angle to the nearby star is measured. This measurement is repeated six months later, when the earth is on the other side of its orbit. The distance to the nearby star can then be calculated by simple trigonometry.

But the angular changes for even nearby stars are minute. Proxima Centauri, for example, has a parallax angle of only 0.75 of a second of arc, equivalent to the angle subtended by a small coin at a distance of about 2,000 yards (1,800 meters). This parallax method

**Stellar parallax** can be used to determine the distances to relatively close stars. The angle to the nearby star is measured when the earth is at one extreme of its orbit, and again when the earth is at its other orbital extreme. Since the distance between these orbital extremes is known, the distance to the star can be calculated by trigonometry.

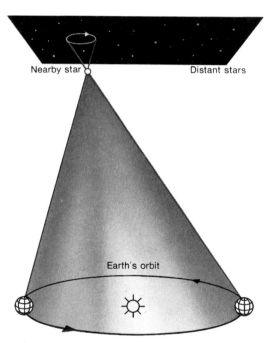

Nearby star

Distant stars

Earth's orbit

**The Big Dipper** is a familiar star pattern in the Northern Hemisphere, being visible throughout the year. To the naked eye its individual stars appear to be equally—and infinitely—distant. In fact, the farthest star Alcaid (η Ursa Major) is 210 light-years away from the earth, more than 3 times the distance to the nearest star Megrez (δ Ursa Major), which is 70 to 80 light-years away.

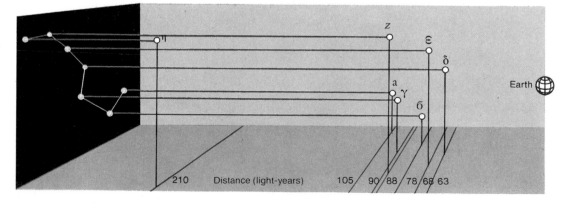

210    Distance (light-years)    105 / 90 / 88 / 78 / 68 / 63

is practicable only for those stars that are less than about 300 parsecs (978 light-years) away. For this reason, distances to more remote stars—by far the majority—are determined using the comparative method.

Analysis of the light from stars enables them to be classified into several different types. The unknown star is first classified and is then compared with a nearby star of the same type. This second star's intrinsic brightness and distance has previously been determined by means of stellar parallax. Working from the assumption that stars of the same type have the same intrinsic brightness, the distance to the unknown star can be determined from the difference between its intrinsic brightness and its apparent brightness.

Another method of assessing stellar distances is to study the periodic variations in brightness of variable stars (such as Cepheid variables) or, more rarely, the brightness of exploding stars (supernovae).

## Magnitude

The absolute, or intrinsic, brightness of a star can be determined only when its apparent brightness and distance are known. Once this is done for a "nearby" star of one particular type, the distances to other stars of the same type (and brightness) can be calculated.

There are enormous differences in the intrinsic brightnesses of different stars—the brightest star known is about 10 billion times more luminous than the faintest. So it is more convenient to refer to the brightness of stars in terms of their apparent magnitudes—that is, their relative apparent brightness.

The ancient astronomers arranged the stars visible to the naked eye on a six-point scale of magnitude: first magnitude for the brightest stars down to sixth magnitude for those that were only just visible. In the nineteenth century, it was discovered that the brightest stars are about 100 times brighter than the faintest stars visible to the naked eye—a difference of only 5 magnitudes on the original scale—so a new scale of magnitude was devised. On this new scale, which is the one used today, a difference of 1 magnitude between stars means that one star is 2.512 (the fifth root of 100) times brighter (or fainter) than a star of the next magnitude. The scale ranges from +28.0 for the faintest star observable with the space telescope, to −27.0 for the brightest star (which is the sun).

The absolute magnitude of a star is a meas-

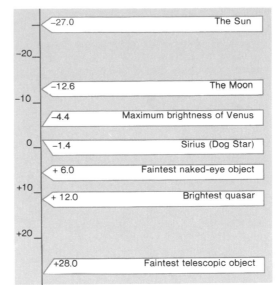

| | |
|---|---|
| −27.0 | The Sun |
| −12.6 | The Moon |
| −4.4 | Maximum brightness of Venus |
| −1.4 | Sirius (Dog Star) |
| + 6.0 | Faintest naked-eye object |
| + 12.0 | Brightest quasar |
| +28.0 | Faintest telescopic object |

**The apparent magnitude** of an astronomical object is a measure of how bright that object appears to be, irrespective of its intrinsic (or absolute) magnitude. On the magnitude scale, a difference of one magnitude equals a difference in brightness of 2.512 times. The brighter an object, the lower its magnitude number. For example, the sun—the brightest celestial object—has an apparent magnitude of −27.0.

ure of its intrinsic brightness and is defined as the apparent magnitude a given star would have if viewed from a distance of 10 parsecs.

### Star color

Even with the naked eye it is possible to see that stars vary in color: for example, Aldebaran (Alpha Tauri) is orange; Betelgeuse (Alpha Orionis) is red; Rigel (Beta Orionis) is blue; Sirius (Alpha Canis Majoris) is white; and our sun and Capella (Alpha Aurigae) are yellow. From our experience of hot objects on earth, we know that color differences reflect differences in temperature. Because the physical laws of radiation are thought to apply to all objects, we can assume that the different colors of the stars also signify temperature differences. Thus, blue stars are hotter than white stars which, in turn, are hotter than red stars.

The subtle variations in stellar colors and, therefore, temperatures can be assessed by observing the stars through colored filters. When viewed through a red filter, for example, a red star appears bright red, whereas a blue star is barely visible. Such precise color analyses are not made visually but by using photographic plates or standard filters attached to photomultipliers.

### Spectral classes

The surface temperatures of stars (ascertained

**Thousands of stars** can be seen on a clear night. Most of those visible to the naked eye lie in the Milky Way, which appears as a broad, relatively faint band that divides the sky in two. Viewed through a telescope, the night sky looks even more impressive. This photograph, for instance, shows the North American Nebula as it appears through a telescope; to the naked eye, however, the nebula is only just visible.

from their colors) can be used to classify them into a number of spectral classes. These classes are denoted by letters of the alphabet and—from hottest to coolest—are O, B, A, F, G, K, and M. For example, O-type stars are blue and very hot, with temperatures above 37,000° F. (20,500° C); A-type stars are white and have temperatures of about 17,000° F. (9,430° C); and M-type stars are red and relatively cool, with temperatures of only about 5,500° F. (3,000° C).

Each of the spectral classes is numerically divided into ten subcategories, with zero denoting the hottest stars within the class through to nine for the coolest. Thus the hottest stars are 00, followed by 01, 02 through to 09 for the coolest stars, within class 0; the next coolest category is B0, followed by B1, B2, and so on down through each of the lettered classes to M9, which is the coolest category of all. In this system, the sun is a G2 star; it has an effective surface temperature of about 10,000° F. (5,500° C).

### Stellar sizes

The sizes of stars vary considerably, from supergiant stars several hundred times larger than the sun, to dwarf stars that are much smaller than the earth. The sun itself is a medium-sized star, with a diameter of about 865,000 miles (1,392,000 kilometers), nearly 109 times the diameter of the earth. In contrast, Antares—one of the largest stars known—has a diameter about 330 times that of the sun,

whereas van Maanen's Star—one of the smallest stars—is only about 6,100 miles (9,800 kilometers) across, considerably less than one-hundredth of the sun's diameter.

With the exception of the sun, the diameters of stars are difficult to measure. Some can be measured by lunar occultation, which involves analyzing the light from a star in the time it takes for the star to be hidden by the moon as the moon moves across the sky. But this method can be used only for those relatively few stars that lie in the zodiac and can be obscured by the moon.

Another technique, called *speckle interferometry,* is more widely applicable. It involves photographing the unknown star and then subjecting the photograph to computer analysis.

### The Hertzsprung-Russell diagram

The most informative way of showing differences in the brightness and surface temperatures of stars is with a special type of graphical diagram called a Hertzsprung-Russell (H-R) diagram. This method was developed independently by the Danish astronomer Ejnar Hertzsprung in 1911 and the American astronomer Henry Russell in 1913. In the H-R diagram, the absolute magnitudes of stars are plotted against their temperatures (or spectral class or color, all of which are equivalent). When this is done, it is found that most stars lie within a wide band—called the main sequence—that runs from the upper left to the lower right of the diagram. The sun is a typical main-se-

**The diameters of stars** vary greatly, from a few thousand miles in dwarf stars to hundreds of millions of miles in supergiants. So vast are the supergiants that Antares, for example, would extend as far as Jupiter if it were where our sun is. But the diameter of a star is not a reliable indication of its mass. Some extremely large stars consist mainly of gas and, therefore, have relatively low masses; some dwarf stars are very dense and are more massive than much larger stars.

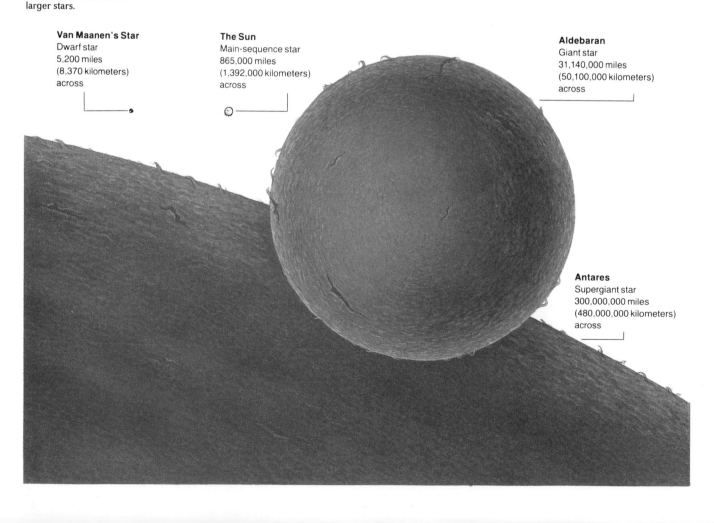

**Van Maanen's Star**
Dwarf star
5,200 miles
(8,370 kilometers)
across

**The Sun**
Main-sequence star
865,000 miles
(1,392,000 kilometers)
across

**Aldebaran**
Giant star
31,140,000 miles
(50,100,000 kilometers)
across

**Antares**
Supergiant star
300,000,000 miles
(480,000,000 kilometers)
across

quence star and lies about midway along the main sequence.

Stars can be classified into characteristic types according to their positions on the H-R diagram. For example, the stars outside the main sequence, nearest the top of the diagram, are very large; these types of stars are called supergiants. In contrast, stars toward the bottom of the diagram are very small; these are called white dwarfs. Within the main sequence itself, there is a general increase in stellar mass from the lower right corner up to the top left.

## Chemical composition

There is a surprisingly high degree of uniformity in the chemical composition of stars, and it is necessary to examine a great many to find any striking variations from the norm. A typical star, such as the sun, consists almost entirely of hydrogen and helium. Spectral analysis of the sun's atmosphere shows that it comprises 75 per cent hydrogen, 25 per cent helium, and 1 to 2 per cent other elements. But spectral analysis can measure only the abundance of elements in the surface layers of stars, and more indirect methods must be used to determine the composition of their interiors.

Evidence about the composition of stellar interiors has come mainly from studies of the occurrence of the extremely rare element technetium in stellar atmospheres. This element is radioactive and decays rapidly, yet has been detected in the atmosphere of certain giant stars. From this it has been concluded that technetium is being continually created within these stars. Because technetium can be formed only by the nuclear transformation of other elements, there must, therefore, be a decrease in these other elements, which indicates that the stars continuously change their internal compositions.

The **Hertzsprung-Russell (H-R) diagram** illustrates the relationship between stars' absolute magnitudes (a measure of their intrinsic brightness and defined as the apparent magnitude a given star would have if viewed from a distance of 10 parsecs) and their spectral classes (or temperatures). On the H-R diagram, stars can be classified into four main types: supergiants, which are extremely large and highly luminous (and therefore have low absolute magnitudes); giants, which are slightly smaller and less luminous than supergiants; main-sequence stars (by far the largest group), which are medium-sized stars of a wide range of temperatures and luminosities; and white dwarfs, which are small and dim and also tend to be relatively hot.

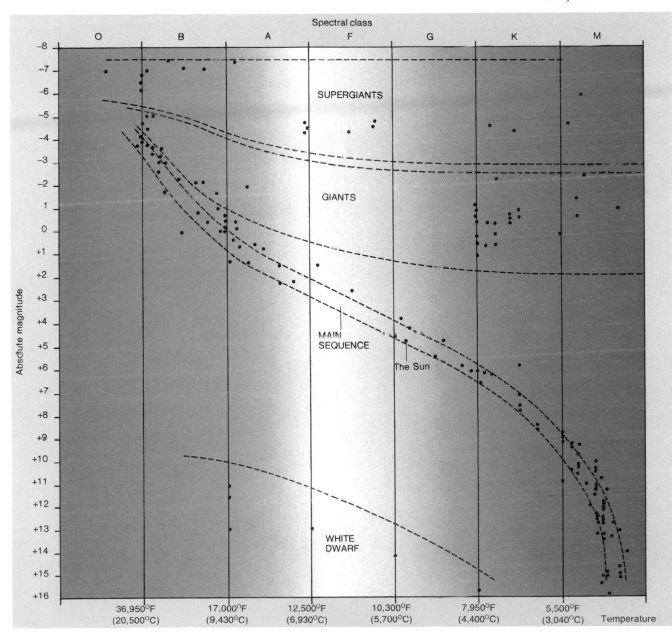

# Variable stars

Among the various types of stars, there are some that differ in that they have a cyclic variation in brightness. This variation parallels a corresponding variation in size, rather like a balloon that is periodically inflated and deflated. The time it takes for such a pulsating star to go through one cycle of variation and return to its original brightness is called its *period*. A period ranges from seconds for some stars to years for others. A few pulsating stars can be seen with the naked eye, although the modern detection technique is to photograph a star field and then compare the result electronically with a photograph of the same field taken at a different time. By this method, any stars that have changed in brightness can be recognized, and hundreds of pulsating stars have now been catalogued. Their strange structural properties provide clues to the history of stellar evolution, and their behavior provides information about the scale of the universe.

### Cepheid variables

The most studied group of pulsating stars are the Cepheids, named after the prototype star Delta Cephei. All have regular periods, which last from 1 to 50 days. They are a relatively rare local sight because there are only about 700 known Cepheids in our own galaxy. Delta Cephei is a good example of its type, varying between an apparent magnitude of 3.6 and 4.3, with a period of 5.4 days. Another Cepheid in our galaxy is the North Star, Polaris, whose period is about four days. Although Polaris continues to pulse, its variation in brightness has declined steadily during the 1900's. The absorption lines in the spectrum of a Cepheid star show Doppler shifts. This indicates that its size may change by 5 or 10 per cent through the course of one pulsation. Surface temperature varies, and the star is brightest during its hottest phase.

It is the observable pulsations in Cepheids that give astronomers a means of measuring distances to stars in other galaxies. These pulsations also provide information about the structures and distances within our own galaxy. The period of a Cepheid star, which is measurable in days, is directly related to the average intrinsic brightness of the star. Using this correlation, the value of the intrinsic brightness can be deduced. By comparing this value with the average brightness of the star, as seen from earth, the actual distance of the star from earth can be calculated. The technique is analogous to judging the distance

**Eta Carinae,** one of the brightest and most massive stars in the Milky Way, lies at the center of the Eta Carinae Nebula in the southern part of the galaxy. In the early 1600's, the star was easily visible—its magnitude varied irregularly between 2 and 4. At the beginning of the nineteenth century it began to brighten increasingly. By 1843, it reached a magnitude of −1 and was the second brightest star in the sky (Sirius being the brightest). It then faded and now varies irregularly around the 7th magnitude. Eta Carinae is estimated to be about 100 solar masses and is, therefore, not very stable. Periodically, it casts off a shell of gas, which is seen as an attempt to restore its stability. This puts it into the class of explosive, or catastrophic, variables in which the variation in brightness is caused by an explosive ejection of outer layers.

**Light curves** of Delta Cephei and RR Lyrae stars show the relationship between period and luminosity in variable stars. The principle, worked out by Henrietta Leavitt in 1912, states that the longer a star's period is, the brighter it becomes. The average period of Delta Cephei is 5.4 days, and it reaches an apparent magnitude of 3.6. (Luminosity increases as magnitude becomes smaller.) RR Lyrae stars have periods that last only hours, and they reach an average apparent magnitude of 7.1; they are, thus, less bright than Cepheids.

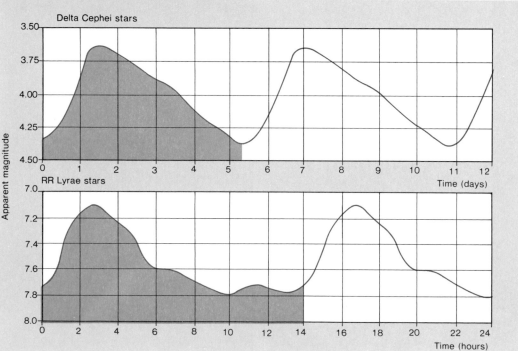

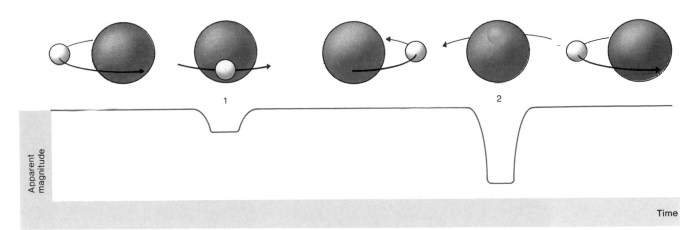

Apparent magnitude

1

2

Time

of a car at night from the brightness of its headlights.

Cepheid stars fall into two distinct groups: classical Cepheids, called Type I Cepheids, which are massive young stars that generally appear in open clusters; and W Virginis stars, or Type II Cepheids. This second group comprises older, low-mass stars, most of which occur in globular clusters. But the most important difference between the two groups is that they do not follow the same period-luminosity relationship. Type II Cepheids are 1.5 magnitudes fainter than Type I. The calculated distance measurement depends, therefore, on the type of Cepheid observed. This distinction between the two classes of Cepheid stars was made during the mid-twentieth century, after which all distance measurements had to be revised. This is because Type I Cepheids are intrinsically brighter than had originally been thought. The new findings also meant that the galaxies containing Type I Cepheids are farther away than was originally assumed. The difference in magnitude of 1.5 corresponded to a doubling of the distance to these galaxies. Popular writers of the time, however, reported that the universe had doubled in size!

### RR Lyrae variables

RR Lyrae variable stars pulsate in the same way as Cepheids, but they have shorter periods, lasting from one day to only a few hours. These stars are also referred to as *cluster variables* because they are found in globular clusters. All RR Lyrae stars are in the same stage of evolution, having a similar mass, age, and chemical composition. In addition, they all have a similar intrinsic brightness (of approximately 0 on the magnitude scale), making dis-

tance measurements even easier to calculate for RR Lyrae variables than for Cepheids. Once the exact intrinsic brightness of a star has been determined, a comparison with the apparent brightness gives its distance. The distance of the cluster in which it appears can then be deduced, as well as the luminosity and sizes of all the cluster stars.

### Long-period variables

Giant red and supergiant stars are the most numerous types of variable stars. Their periods are not as consistently regular as those of Cepheids and RR Lyrae stars. Most of their periods are from three months to two years. The brightest example of this type is Mira, a giant red star in the constellation of Cetus. At its faintest, it is invisible to the naked eye, having an apparent brightness of 9, but it becomes brighter over a period of 11 months and at maximum brightness, is a quite prominent object in the night sky.

### Eclipsing binaries

Many stars are part of a double-star system, each member travelling in its own orbit around their common center of mass. Occasionally, the orbits of the double stars are so aligned that, seen from the earth, each star masks the other as the two move around each other. The light from the pair (called an *eclipsing binary*) varies, not because of a variation in the intrinsic luminosity of the stars, but simply because one star periodically blocks out the light from the other. The most prominent eclipsing binary star in the local system is Algol, in the constellation of Perseus.

**Eclipsing binary stars** orbit around their common center of mass and alternately block each other's light. The yellow star in this example emits more light than its bigger red companion. When the small star passes in front of the larger one (1), the total amount of light emitted decreases slightly. But when the smaller, brighter star moves behind the larger one (2), the total apparent magnitude is greatly reduced. Eclipsing binaries of the same size may completely occlude each other.

# Novae and supernovae

Novae and supernovae are apparently similar, but unrelated, stellar phenomena. A nova is a faint star that brightens suddenly by blowing off its surface layers before returning to its original form. A supernova is a star that explodes and scatters nearly all of its constituent material into space.

## Novae

Stars are generally regarded as being unchanging on a human time scale, so the appearance of a newly visible star, or nova, is unusual. A nova may quickly brighten by hundreds or millions of times and often changes from being invisible to the naked eye to a clearly defined star in the night sky. Generally novae brighten suddenly (within weeks or days), fade drastically during the following few weeks, then continue to fade more gradually for several years. Some novae are recurrent; they brighten and decline regularly with periods that vary from a few years to decades.

Spectroscopic studies of novae show that the absorption lines undergo a Doppler shift to the blue, indicating that the sudden increase of brightness corresponds to an explosive expansion that ejects the surface of the star into space. After several years, the ejected gas can be seen through a telescope as an expanding cloud around the star. The distance of the nova can be determined by correlating the Doppler shift of this gas cloud with the rate at which its angular size is increasing.

Most novae belong to double-star systems in which one of the pairs is a red giant and the other is a white dwarf, or condensed star. The internal gravitational forces of a red giant are relatively weak. Some of the red giant's surface material may be pulled toward the nearby more massive white dwarf (which exerts a stronger gravitational pull). Matter falling toward the white dwarf may trigger off huge explosions, which may recur every few years, throwing off the accumulated matter from the white dwarf's surface.

Each year there are two or three dozen nova outbursts in our galaxy. The brightest of recent years appeared in the constellation Cygnus in August 1975. Within two days, the nova had become brighter than the nearby star Deneb (one of the brightest stars in the sky), then, within a week, it had faded to below naked-eye visibility.

Sometimes, the brightening of a nova can be detected only in the X-ray part of the spectrum. One such X-ray nova was noticed in the constellation of Monoceros (the Unicorn) in 1975. When old photographs of the same area of the sky were examined, it was found that the star had been an optical nova in 1917, thus confirming the recurrent nature of nova flare-ups.

## Planetary nebulae

The very hot stars that lie in the center of an expanding shell of gas are believed to be related to novae. The central star is the contracting core of what would have been a red giant, and the tenuous halo of gas is the remnant of a previous explosion. They were originally misnamed planetary nebulae because of their resemblance to the greenish planetary disks of Uranus and Neptune when viewed through early telescopes.

## Supernovae

One of the most spectacular and rare sights in the sky is a supernova explosion, which marks the death of a massive old star. On average, such an explosion occurs only once every 15 years in galaxies like the Milky Way. The conditions within a supergiant star suddenly become so unstable that the star violently explodes, ejecting into space a fast-moving cloud of material. In the following weeks, the supernova emits a huge amount of radiation, sometimes as much as that emitted by the rest of the entire galaxy in which the supernova lies.

A supernova explosion is thought to begin with the accumulation of an iron core (the remains of previous stages of nuclear burning). The core heats up until the iron undergoes a nuclear transformation. But unlike the previous elements that have been used in the star's nuclear reactions, iron takes up energy while changing into other elements, leaving no extra energy for further heating of the core. As a result, the core shrinks and eventually becomes so unstable that it collapses, causing matter to fall into it from the surrounding layers of the star. Shock waves are produced that travel outward from the core, creating heavy elements such as uranium. Within seconds there is a cataclysmic explosion that destroys the star, blowing off its outer layers, leaving only remnants of the core to remain. The heavy elements (which are produced either near the center of the star or during the explosion itself) are blown off into space and enrich the interstellar gas.

When a new star forms out of such en-

**The Ring Nebula** (M57; NGC 6720), in the constellation of Lyra, is one of the best known planetary nebulae. It lies more than about 2,000 light-years from earth, but is relatively bright and therefore easy to observe. The brightly-colored ring is a shell of ionized gas ejected from the central blue star during a previous explosion (thought to have occurred about 10,000 years ago). The gradation of colors across the ring is caused by different degrees of ionization. The temperature near the central star is high, and gaseous oxygen is doubly ionized (to $O^{2+}$), giving the green color. At the outer edge of the gas shell, the temperature is lower, and the red color of ionized hydrogen predominates.

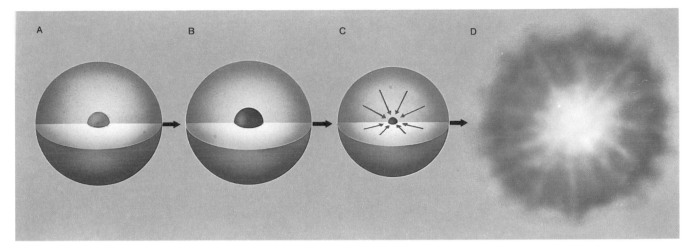

riched gas, the heavy elements form part of a planet (or planets) that may become part of a new star system. Thus, all the heavy elements that are vital to life and make up our familiar world, were first formed by nuclear reactions that took place within supergiant stars.

## Supernova remnants

The gas cloud ejected by the explosion of a supernova spreads out into space, perhaps for millions of years. During this time, the stellar remnants radiate huge amounts of energy, not only as visible radiation (light), but also as X rays and radio waves. Scientists believe that subatomic particles—*neutrinos*—are also ejected. Neutrinos are believed to have so little mass that they can pass through matter un-

disturbed. The two most recent supernovas in our galaxy were seen by Tycho Brahe in 1572 and by Johannes Kepler in 1604. Although visually unspectacular, Kepler's supernova appears as a striking astronomical feature when observed at radio wavelengths. Because of their rarity, our knowledge of supernovae is mainly gathered from galaxies other than our own. An international search program has been initiated to ensure that they are detected and recorded. In February, 1987, a Canadian astronomer, Ian Shelton, using a telescope in Chile, discovered Supernova 1987A, the brightest supernova and nearest to earth since Kepler's observations in 1604. Studies of the neutrinos given off by Supernova 1987A seem to prove the theory of how a massive star becomes a supernova.

**A supernova explosion** starts when a star accumulates a metallic core (A), which heats up (B), and collapses (C). The outer layers fall into the core and then explode (D), totally destroying the star.

**The Veil Nebula** (NGC 6992) is a supernova remnant formed as a result of a supernova explosion about 30,000 years ago. Still expanding, the nebula will eventually become indistinguishable from interstellar gas.

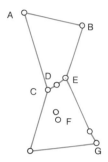

**The constellation Orion** is a multiple star system comprising, among others, A, Betelgeuse (Alpha Orionis); B, Bellatrix (Gamma Orionis); C, Delta Orionis; D, Epsilon Orionis; E, Zeta Orionis; F, Theta Orionis, and G, Rigel (Beta Orionis).

# Multiple stars

Most stars in our galaxy are not single, like the sun, but are under the gravitational influence of neighboring stars, whose close proximity probably indicates that they share a common origin. Two prominent "double" stars, which can be seen with the naked eye, are the pair Alcor and Mizar, in the constellation Ursa Major (the Big Dipper). A telescope reveals that Mizar (which was the first component of a double star to be discovered) is itself part of a double system of stars called Mizar A and Mizar B. Spectroscopic observation further shows that Mizar's two visual components are also themselves binary stars, making Mizar a quadruple star. There is evidence that Alcor varies in its velocity in space, which suggests that it too is a binary star. There are many multiple stars, but they seem stable only when part of a hierarchical network of double stars, in which each pair acts as a component in an even larger set of binary systems.

**Identifying double stars**

Nearby binary stars in our galaxy are close enough to observe visually, but often the individual stars are not far enough apart to be seen as separate units. They can, however, be detected spectroscopically, even in other galaxies. When a double-star system consists of two different kinds of stars—for example, one hot star and one cool one—it produces an overlapping composite spectrum that quite clearly shows the existence of two stellar objects. Even if the pair are similar in nature, they can still be identified as two separate stars because each spectrum exhibits a Doppler shift as the stars orbit around each other. The shift indicates whether the star is receding from us in its orbit, or approaching.

If two closely associated stars orbit in the same plane as the earth's orbit, the doublet changes in brightness because one star periodically cuts off the light from the other one as they rotate around each other. Such a combination is called an *eclipsing binary star*.

**The Orion configuration**
*(right)* symbolizes the Hunter, with Betelgeuse and Bellatrix forming the two shoulders, the band of three stars representing the Belt, the three stars below them forming Orion's Sword, and Rigel marking the left upraised foot. Orion is, however, one of the few constellations in which the stars are connected by more than visual associations. The giant stars in the Belt are assumed to have a common origin, as are those in the Sword. The Belt stars are thought to be more than 5 million years old and those in the Sword region are younger, estimated to be about 1 or 2 million years old. Betelgeuse is the exception in the constellation, being relatively far from the other stars and the only red supergiant in the group.

**The orbits of binary stars** vary depending on the mass of each star and the position of their common center of mass. If two stars similar in mass (A) have a common center of mass that lies halfway between them, the stars have a circular orbit. When one star is much greater in mass than the other (B), with the common center of mass near the center of the more massive star, the smaller star orbits its larger companion. If the two stars differ in mass (C) and have a common center of mass that is some distance from the more massive star, they may follow elliptical orbits. The orbit of the more massive star (M) will be smaller than that of its lighter companion (m). Spectroscopic binaries (D) cannot be seen visually; their movement is revealed by the Doppler shift of their spectral lines. When a star moves toward the earth in its orbit (1), its spectral lines shift toward the blue end of the spectrum. As the star reaches a point where it is neither approaching nor receding (2), the spectral lines remain in their current normal position. Continuing its orbit, the star moves away from the earth (3) and the spectral lines shift toward the red end of the spectrum.

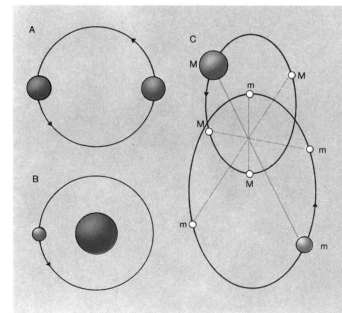

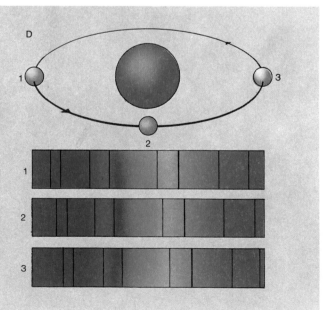

The presence of a very faint star in a double star system can be inferred from subtle disturbances in the motion of the brighter one. The star Sirius A (the Dog Star) is such a binary. Its companion star, Sirius B (often called the Pup), is a white dwarf and its existence was inferred astrometrically long before sophisticated telescopic techniques allowed it to be detected visually. Similarly, an analysis of Barnard's Star indicates that it has two companions whose masses are not much more than that of the planet Jupiter; the objects may therefore be planets, not stars.

## Stellar masses and sizes

It is difficult to determine accurately the mass of a solitary star, but if two stars are physically associated (as they are in a binary system), their individual masses can be deduced by studying their orbital motions. Most visual binaries, however, take many years to complete their orbits—many have not yet completed one orbit since their original discovery. For this reason, eclipsing binaries, with periods of only a few days, are much more useful for astronomers in estimating the masses of stars. Also, the Doppler shift in their spectra shows the speed at which the stars are traveling. From a knowledge of the period and velocity of a binary star, the size of the orbit can be calculated. Their individual masses are then determined by taking into account the gravitational effects that are necessary to produce such an orbit. And by observing how long the light of one star is eclipsed by the other (and knowing the speed of each), the sizes of the two stars can also be calculated. But if the two eclipsing binary stars are very close together, their mutual gravitational attraction is extremely strong, with the result that many stars of this type interact by pulling material from each other. This makes calculations of individual masses imprecise.

## Variable binary stars

Not only does the light from eclipsing binaries vary when they eclipse, but their brightness often also varies when they are close together and interact. This characteristic makes it difficult for astronomers to differentiate variable binaries from intrinsically variable stars—whose brightness varies because of internal factors. Some binary stars (such as the prototype W Ursae Majoris) may be so close to each other that they are in contact, and the binary system consists of two stellar cores orbiting round each other and surrounded by a common envelope. The orbits of some stars (typified by Beta Lyrae) are so close that one becomes distorted by its companion, making it a semi-detached binary star. Wolf-Rayet stars are often part of a close binary system that consists of a massive luminous main-sequence star and a less massive, but even more luminous companion. The intense luminosity of the small star expels the outer part of its atmosphere in the form of a dense stellar wind. This wind produces a complex but characteristic spectrum, which may be the result of the interchange of mass between the two stars.

Telescopes launched above the earth's atmosphere have detected many X-ray sources associated with binary systems. If one member of a pair is a supergiant star and the other is a compact object—either a neutron star or a black hole—X rays may be emitted.

## Mass-luminosity relationship

In spite of the difficulties, accurate values for stellar masses have been obtained for stars on the main sequence (the main band of stars on the Hertzsprung-Russell diagram). If these values are plotted on a graph against their magnitudes, they lie on a straight line that demonstrates the direct relationship between stellar mass and luminosity. Other graphs indicate that mass, luminosity, and surface temperature of main-sequence stars are all related: the more massive a star, the brighter it is.

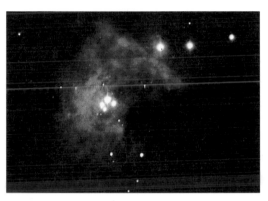

**The Trapezium,** seen with the naked eye, is a star that lies in the center of Orion's Sword surrounded by the Great Nebula—the brightest nebula visible. The star, Theta Orionis, was discovered in 1611 to be a multiple system of four stars. They are approximately equidistant from each other at a distance of about 10 to 20 arc seconds and are thought to have a common origin. Computer simulation of the gravitational attraction between the stars indicates that the Trapezium is a disintegrating system and that in a few million years, it will no longer consist of four stars, but probably of the two most massive stars, which will orbit each other.

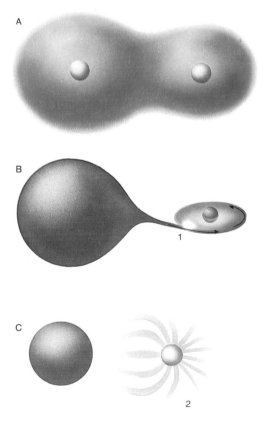

**Variable binary stars** often vary in brightness due to the gravitational effects arising from their proximity to each other. Close binary systems (A) occur when two stars expand as they consume their nuclear fuel, so that they virtually engulf each other. The stellar cores remain separate but they are surrounded by a common envelope of material. Semidetached binaries (B) are close binaries where one star is distorted by the gravitational pull of the other. Gas is drawn from the less massive star to the more massive one—often a white dwarf—and as it strikes the disk of gas around the heavier star, a hot spot (1), brighter than the two stars, is created by the impact. Wolf-Rayet stars (C) occur in close binary systems where one star is much larger than its smaller, yet more luminous, companion. The smaller star is so bright that it expels the outer layers of its atmosphere as a stellar wind (2), which reaches speeds of up to 1,860 miles (3,000 kilometers) per second.

# Star clusters

A brief glance at the night sky reveals that it is not uniformly bespangled with thousands of stars. Some areas are sparse, whereas others contain a profusion of stars that tend to be grouped into clusters. There are two distinct types of clusters—open (or galactic) and globular—and each is fundamentally different in nature and appearance.

## Open clusters

There are more than 1,000 open clusters in our galaxy. Most of the conspicuous ones are known only by their catalog numbers; although some of the more familiar examples have been given names—such as the Pleiades, a group of hot, young, bluish-white stars in the constellation of Taurus. The six brightest member stars can be seen with the naked eye, and modern telescopes reveal hundreds of others within the group. Another open cluster in the same region of the sky is the Hyades cluster, whose most prominent stars form the V-shape that outlines the face of Taurus, the Bull. An open cluster usually contains from ten to several hundred distinguishable stars, which are interspersed with prominent patches of gas and dust. A cluster is seldom larger than 10 parsecs across.

## Globular clusters

A few globular clusters are bright enough to be seen with the naked eye, and they appear

**The open cluster NGC 3324** is remarkable because its brightest star is red, whereas most of the rest of the cluster is blue. These young blue stars have converted almost all of their hydrogen to helium. As a result, their centers have contracted to maintain the former level of energy production (although the outer layers expand), making the stars (now blue giants) shine even brighter. The red star has passed this stage and has expanded to become a supergiant. It has cooled down more than the blue stars but seems brighter because much of their energy is emitted as invisible ultraviolet light.

**The globular cluster M3** (NGC 5272) in the constellation Canes Venatici (the Hunting Dogs) is one of the four great globular clusters in the Northern Hemisphere. It is not a very dense cluster, although it contains more than 44,000 stars. It is difficult to distinguish between individual stars without using a telescope, and so M3 is seen with the naked eye as a single star, even though it is 48,500 light-years away.

as fuzzy, luminous balls of light. But telescopic observation reveals that most are spherical stellar systems that contain several thousand stars. They are densely packed toward the central regions and become more dispersed at the edges. The stars are so tightly packed at the center of a globular cluster that if the earth were situated there, the nearest stars would be light-months away, and the brightness of the night sky would always be comparable to full moonlight. A cluster has an average size of 100 parsecs across—a small space for so many stars—and contains no interstellar gas. There are about 100 globular clusters in our galaxy.

Astronomers have recently observed that a few globular clusters are associated with intense bursts of X rays. Each burst is equivalent to about 1 million times as much energy radiated by the sun in a similar time. One current interpretation is that a massive black hole may exist in the center of many globular clusters.

**Composition and location of cluster stars**

Spectral analysis of the two groups shows that open and globular cluster stars have basically different chemical compositions. The open cluster stars are similar in composition to the sun—75 per cent is hydrogen, most of the rest is helium and less than 1 per cent is composed of heavier elements. In globular clusters, the abundance of heavier elements is 10 times less even than that in open cluster stars.

As well as differing in composition, the two stellar groups occupy distinctive regions within our galaxy. Open clusters occur in the spiral arms, and globular clusters tend to congregate around the central halo. Also, their motions within the galaxy –which is itself rotating—follow different patterns. The open, or galactic, cluster stars move round the nucleus of the galaxy in much the same way as the planets move around the sun, in fairly circular orbits in the same plane. In contrast, the globular clusters follow a galactic path analogous to that of comets within our solar system that have elongated orbits approaching the sun from all directions. The stars in globular clusters move in highly eccentric orbits with a high inclination to the galactic plane.

During the 1940's, when Walter Baade was studying the stars in the Andromeda galaxy, he first noticed that there was a fundamental difference between stars in the central regions of galaxies and those in the spiral arms. He described the two kinds in terms of two different "populations." The stars in the spiral arms, whose brightest members include young, hot, blue stars (typical of open cluster stars in our galaxy), he called Population I stars. He called the cool, red stars that he found to be typical of the central areas of Andromeda (with similar properties to the globular cluster stars in our galaxy), Population II stars.

**Stellar evolution**

Once the concept of two stellar populations was established, astronomers could determine the age and evolution of stars. This was done by comparing the Hertzsprung-Russell diagrams for both types of cluster stars with those for field stars, such as the sun, which move singly rather than in clusters. The

The movement and situation of open and globular clusters in our galaxy differs greatly. Whereas open clusters (A) are found in the spiral arms of the galaxy and orbit the galactic center (B) in the plane of the spiral arms, globular clusters (C) occur around the central halo and orbit it in elongated, elliptical paths. These orbits often take them great distances away from the center, but all known globular clusters (with one exception) return from the outer regions of the galaxy.

Hertzsprung-Russell diagram for a typical open cluster is similar to that of stars such as the sun. The diagram for stars in globular clusters indicates that most of them fall in the red giant zone. In terms of stellar evolution, because the globular clusters consist mainly of mature red giant stars, and the open clusters are composed of young, bright, blue stars, astronomers assume that the latter must have formed at a later stage than the former. This assumption explains the lower abundance of elements heavier than helium in the Population II globular cluster stars, which must have formed when there were few heavy elements in the area.

A Hertzsprung-Russell diagram reveals the evolution of open and globular clusters. Open clusters lie on the main-sequence band—the brightest, youngest stars in the upper part and the fainter, older stars near the bottom. As they mature, the stars move toward the red giant region, as has M67, the oldest open cluster. The Hertzsprung gap contains few stars because they evolve quickly through this region, as has the Double Cluster h and chi Persei. All globular clusters, older than open clusters, occur in the red giant region—M3, for example, has reached the red supergiant zone.

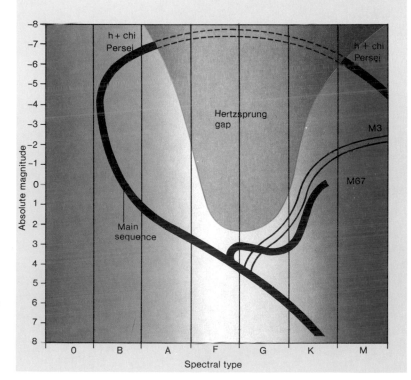

# Nebulae

Even with the unaided eye, faint hazy patches of light can be seen dotted about the night sky. Through a telescope these patches are resolved into various kinds of diffuse nebulae, which are clouds of dust and gas that can be seen in the visible part of the spectrum. In one type, the gas glows. This is an emission nebula. In a dark, or absorption, nebula, the dust appears silhouetted against other glowing material; and when the dust reflects light emitted by other objects, it comprises a reflection nebula.

In the early days of optical astronomy, there was also a category of spiral nebulae, so-called because they appeared to have gaseous "arms" spiraling out from their centers. These "nebulae" are now known to be other galaxies outside our own. A lot of work in classifying nebular objects was carried out by the French astronomer Charles Messier. He was more in-terested in studying comets but drew up a catalog and assigned numbers (called Messier or M numbers) to nebular objects so that he would not confuse them with new comets. A century after this catalog was published (in 1784), a more extensive list (the New General Catalog) was compiled, based on the observations of William Herschel.

### Classification of nebulae

All nebulae are termed gaseous, or galactic (to distinguish them from extragalactic nebulae, the old misleading name for galaxies). There are two types: bright nebulae can be fairly compact in form or can be composed of extremely delicate filaments, or wisps, that are relatively extensive; dark nebulae can be determined against a lighter background of stars, and some have edges that are illuminated like a halo. Whatever its form, the nature of a nebula is determined by the density of the gas and dust from which it is composed, the chemical composition of these materials, and the absence or presence of nearby stars.

An emission nebula is associated with the presence of a hot star or stars (of spectral type B or O, for example). Ultraviolet radiation from the star ionizes hydrogen atoms in the cloud so that it emits light. One of the most famous emission nebulae is the Great Nebula of Orion, in the Sword of Orion; it is so bright that it can be seen with the naked eye. Its luminosity results from the presence of the O-type multiple star Theta Orionis. Another example of an emission nebula is the Rosette Nebula in the Milky Way constellation of Monoceros (the Unicorn).

A dark nebula may be dark when there is no star near it. Also, interstellar material often absorbs light, so that stars behind the nebula appear less bright. But if the nebula itself absorbs sufficient light then the stars are completely obscured. A striking example of a dark nebula is the Horsehead Nebula in Orion, in which a dark dustcloud protrudes into a bright emission nebula. This phenomenon proves that dark nebulae do not simply represent an absence of stars.

Reflection nebulae occur when the stars adjacent to a cloud of dust and gas are not hot enough to cause the cloud itself to emit light, but are bright enough to make the dust particles reflect their light. The Pleiades cluster in Taurus is a good example of bright stars among reflection nebulosity.

### Planetary nebulae

The name of this group of nebulae is misleading because they have nothing to do with planets or a star system at all. Many are associated with a central star surrounded by a disklike shell of nebulosity. These central stars are usually very hot and often their emission is greater in the ultraviolet part of the spectrum. Optically, therefore, the nebula is seen only as a faint ring. Measurements of the Doppler shift in the spectra of planetary nebulae indicate turbulence and motion within the cloud.

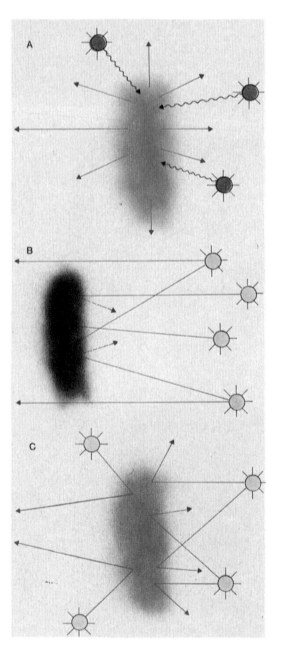

**Nebulae** are classified in three basic types: emission nebulae, dark nebulae, and reflection nebulae. Ultraviolet radiation from nearby bright blue stars excites hydrogen atoms in the gas of an emission nebula (A), and these atoms give off a fluorescent light. An absorption, or dark, nebula (B) is seen as a dark patch, sometimes surrounded by a halo of light; the light from stars behind the nebula is either absorbed or scattered by the nebular material. In a reflection nebula (C), the dust particles in the cloud reflect and scatter the light from stars that are not hot enough to make the nebula itself emit light.

These nebulae are also expanding with a velocity of a few miles per second.

### Supernovae remnants

The nature of certain nebulae suggests that they are the remnants of huge stellar explosions. The Crab Nebula in Taurus is perhaps the most famous example and is believed to consist of material ejected by a star. The supernova that created it was witnessed by Chinese astronomers in A.D. 1054. Its nebulosity is luminous and spreading.

A supernova represents a late evolutionary stage of a massive star. Many nebulae are, however, stellar birthplaces. The formation of a new star is a very slow process because the clouds of gas and dust are extremely rarefied. All stars begin in this way, and the eventual mass of the star depends upon its initial mass when it forms from nebular matter.

### Interstellar matter

Space is pervaded by clouds of cold hydrogen gas that are permeated by cosmic dust. Such clouds do not emit radiation in the visible part of the spectrum, but they do emit radio waves at a wavelength of 21 centimeters. Positive proof of interstellar matter was not obtained until 1904, when stationary lines in the spectrum of a star in Orion (studied by the astronomer Hartmann) indicated that there was material between the star and the observer. Interstellar molecules were not identified until recently; cold hydrogen was detected in 1951, and more molecules are being identified each year.

Interstellar gas has a very low density. There are about 500,000 hydrogen atoms per cubic yard—a lower density than that of the gas in a laboratory vacuum. Grains of cosmic dust, formed by the accretion of matter around molecules, are about $10^{-7}$ millimeters (0.1 micron) in diameter and are about 1,000 million times less common than are hydrogen atoms.

The study of nebulae and interstellar matter brings together optical, radio, and infrared astronomy.

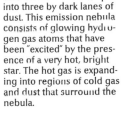

**The Trifid Nebula** is split into three by dark lanes of dust. This emission nebula consists of glowing hydrogen gas atoms that have been "excited" by the presence of a very hot, bright star. The hot gas is expanding into regions of cold gas and dust that surround the nebula.

**Both bright and dark nebulae** occur in the Horsehead Nebula, in the constellation of Orion. The dark dustcloud in the shape of a horse's head and neck extends into a bright emission nebula. The boundary where the two nebulae merge can be seen as a bright rim, where dense, dark droplets of the dustcloud are penetrating the less dense, lighter nebula. Astronomers believe that these droplets may become detached from the main dark nebula, forming dark "globules" that they think are the first stage in stellar evolution.

# Galaxies

Seen through a telescope, the night sky reveals tiny points of light and slightly larger, hazy splotches. The former are stars in our own galaxy—the Milky Way—and the latter are nebulae, stellar clusters or other galaxies, which are complete stellar systems far beyond our own.

There are two broad classes of galaxies: elliptical (probably the most common) and spiral. Spiral galaxies are further divided into normal, which constitute the majority of spirals, and barred spirals. About 3 per cent of galaxies do not, however, fit into any of these categories and are termed irregular galaxies.

Seyfert galaxies comprise about 2 per cent of the spiral groups. Their central regions, or nuclei, are extremely bright and include regions of very high temperatures in which gas moves around violently at speeds of thousands of miles per second. The frequent outward movement of this gas suggests the occurrence of explosions in the galaxy center.

### The shapes of galaxies

The various classes of galaxies are classified by the Hubble system, according to their degree of flatness. The elliptical galaxies range from E0 to E7—from an almost spherical shape to a flattened disk. The normal spirals are classified as S0 (with a large nucleus and little or no arm structure), Sa and Sb (with progressively less tightly-coiled arms and progressively smaller nuclei), and Sc (which have virtually no nucleus and wide open arms). A similar progression occurs with barred spirals: they again range from those with a large nucleus to those with a small nucleus and open arms trailing from the bar, designated as SBa, SBb, and SBc, respectively. The shape of a galaxy,

from spherical to flat with only a small central bulge, results from its mass and the amount of angular momentum. The shape is partly a measure of the intensity of rotational motion of the system. It is thought that elliptical galaxies were formed out of masses of dust that had only a small, overall angular momentum and therefore have no arms.

In spiral galaxies, stars in the nucleus revolve about the center in the same direction as the arms, which trail behind. The origin of the spiral arms is not known, although the spiral pattern is explained by some astronomers in terms of a "density wave." They suggest that a wave of increased density in a spiral shape results in compression of gas and sweeps around the galaxy, initiating the formation of stars in a spiral distribution. Spiral galaxies are thought to be younger than elliptical ones, which contain red, "older" stars and much less nebular material—from which stars are born.

Galaxies vary in size from dwarfs to giants. Andromeda Nebula, in the local group, is one of the largest spiral galaxies known and has a diameter of 60,000 parsecs. Most spiral galaxies have diameters of from 10,000 to 30,000 parsecs. Elliptical galaxies are usually much smaller, and a dwarf elliptical galaxy may only be 2,000 parsecs in diameter.

A galaxy's mass is calculated in terms of solar masses—for example, Andromeda Nebula is thought to have $3 \times 10^{11}$ solar masses. Spiral galaxies are estimated to have masses between about $10^9$ to more than $10^{11}$ solar masses.

### Spectra of galaxies

Despite the distances involved, the electromagnetic spectrum of a galaxy can be quite ex-

A galaxy is usually classified according to its "Hubble" type. The progression from elliptical (E) to spiral (S) was first thought to be evolutionary, but this view is no longer supported. The transition point from elliptical to spiral is represented by class S0. This type of galaxy consists of a spiral disk without arms. Normal spirals (Sa, Sb, Sc) are classified according to the progressive opening of the spiraling arms, as are barred spirals (Sb).

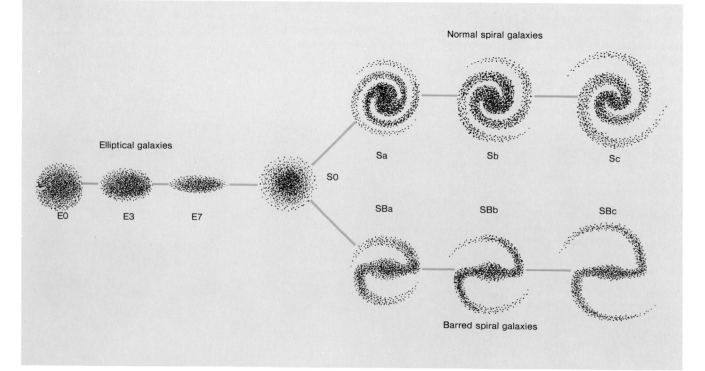

Normal spiral galaxies

Elliptical galaxies

E0    E3    E7    S0    Sa    Sb    Sc

SBa    SBb    SBc

Barred spiral galaxies

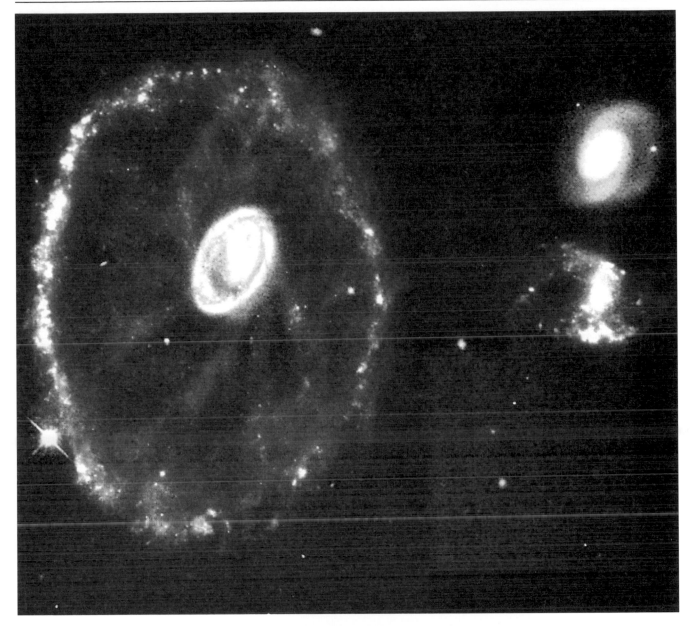

tensively interpreted. The movements of a galaxy—whether it is rotating and whether it is approaching the earth or receding—are revealed by its spectrum. The spectral lines of many distant galaxies show a "red shift": they are displaced towards the red, long-wavelength, end of the spectrum. The farther a galaxy is from the earth, the faster it appears to recede (a phenomenon described by Hubble's law). Also, because of the Doppler effect, the faster a galaxy moves away from us, the longer the wavelength becomes—and the redder the light. This spectral shift can therefore give an indication of how far away a galaxy is. The ratio of the distance of a galaxy to the speed with which it is moving away is known as Hubble's constant, $H_0$.

Galaxies can be counted, like stars, in every direction of the sky—except in the Milky Way, where clouds of dust conceal those beyond. This area is known as the "zone of avoidance." There are about 150 galaxies near enough to enable us to see stars within them. Beyond them are millions and perhaps billions of galaxies and supergalaxies (clusters of galaxies).

**Many irregular galaxies** cannot be adequately explained, and opinions surrounding their origin differ. M82, a galaxy in Ursa Major, was once thought to have undergone a massive explosion some time in the past. It is a powerful radio source, but astronomers now believe that this radiation is the result of much less violent processes inside the galaxy.

**A head-on collision between two galaxies** is captured in this image taken by the Hubble Space Telescope. The ring-like feature is the result of a smaller intruder galaxy—possibly one of the two large objects to the right of the ring—that careened through the core of the host galaxy.

# The Milky Way

Our galaxy is a spiral galaxy about 30,000 parsecs (about 560,000 million million miles or 900,000 million million kilometers) across, which consists of hundreds of billions of stars. Its disk appears as a faint white band that divides the night sky in two; this is the Milky Way. To each side of the band, the number of stars decreases rapidly.

The region in space occupied by the Milky Way is called the galactic plane. The center of nucleus of the galaxy, where the density of stars is at a maximum, lies in the direction of the constellation of Sagittarius. Minimum star density occurs in the opposite direction, toward Taurus.

The sun is off-center, about 10,000 parsecs from the nucleus, which is itself approximately 5,000 parsecs thick and 10,000 parsecs across. The galaxy has three spiral arms (each between 1,000 and 1,500 parsecs wide)—called the Orion, Perseus, and Sagittarius Arms—and the whole system is rotating in space. The group of stars containing the sun, in the Orion Arm, rotates once every 250 million years.

## Stellar populations

Distances within the galaxy are calculated with reference to certain objects, such as globular clusters. These clusters are symmetrical groups of stars that occur as a kind of halo around the region of the galactic center. From the earth, most can be seen on each side of the Milky Way in the part of the sky that lies toward the galactic center. The other principal type of stellar clusters—open clusters—are concentrated in the galactic plane and so, the most are seen from the earth within the Milky Way.

The galaxy may be classified in two regions according to the types of stars they contain. Population I areas have a great amount of interstellar material and "young," bright, hot stars. Open clusters contain Population I stars. In Population II regions, on the other hand, most of the interstellar material has been used up in the formation of stars, which are therefore relatively "old" and are colder than Population I stars. Globular clusters contain Population II stars.

## Evolution of the galaxy

Theories about how the galaxy evolved are based on two main observations: there are more heavy elements in Population I stars than in the Population II type; and Population II stars are moving faster through space than are Population I stars. It is thought that about $10^{10}$ (10 billion) years ago a great mass of light matter, mostly hydrogen, condensed out from the rest of intergalactic material. It then followed a similar evolutionary pattern to that of a star, which forms from interstellar material, and the young "protogalaxy" shrank.

About $6 \times 10^9$ years ago, Population II stars began to form, giving rise to the first globular clusters. At this stage of evolution, heavy elements were still not abundant. The galactic nucleus then formed in this contracting system. But the young galaxy still possessed much kinetic energy (energy of movement), which is why Population II stars tend to have higher velocities. Then star formation ceased as interstellar gas and dust was used up in the nucleus.

The rest of the disk-shaped part of the galaxy evolved from the further condensation of material outside the center of the protogalaxy. Population I stars began to form (and continued to form until relatively recently) from the abundant gas and dust. Previous generations of stars, at the ends of their life-cycles, created heavy elements in their dying stages, thus enriching the disk with the characteristic constituents of Population II stars.

The galaxy's spiral arms are more difficult to account for. Magnetic fields may have dragged them out of the center and maintained their trailing arms. But speculation is hampered by the fact that, in any galaxy, the nucleus sometimes inexplicably releases vast amounts of energy. A complete understanding of this process could dramatically alter the various theories about the origin and evolution of our galaxy and others.

## Observing the Milky Way

Ancient astronomers saw the Milky Way as a girdle across the heavens. Ptolemy, the famous

**Our galaxy** is a fairly typical, spiral-shaped galaxy, and is about 30,000 parsecs across and 5,000 parsecs thick (at its thickest point through the central nucleus). The top diagram shows an edge-on view of a galaxy similar to our own, showing the prominent nucleus and the flatter, more tenuous arms. The spiral shape of the arms is clearly visible in the middle diagram. (Although our galaxy has three spiral arms, their shape is very similar to that illustrated.) The bottom diagram is a schematic representation of our galaxy, showing the relative position of the sun (and, therefore, of the solar system). It lies about 10,000 parsecs away from the nucleus in one of the spiral arms (the Orion Arm). From the earth, most stars can be seen in the direction SB in the diagram, the least in the direction SA.

ancient Greek astronomer, did not think it was a circle, but he did observe how, in places, it divided into two branches. Nobody explained its nature until the beginning of the seventeenth century when Galileo observed the Milky Way through a telescope and saw that it is made up of millions of individual stars. A century and a half later, Sir William Herschel measured the distribution of stars across the sky by means of star counts. He found that the numbers of stars decrease with increasing angular distance from the Milky Way.

The size and structure of the galaxy finally became apparent in the 1920's, with the work of Edwin Hubble. Other spiral galaxies were observed as systems external to our own galaxy but recognized as of the same basic type. Then in the 1940's, the new science of radioastronomy confirmed the spiral nature of the galaxy. The radiation from the cold clouds of hydrogen within the galactic plane revealed the nature of its spiral arms.

Despite these and more recent contributions to our knowledge of the galaxy, much of what we know about its macrostructure still comes from observations of other similar spiral galaxies. Because our own galaxy, although not especially large in cosmic terms, is too large for us conceivably to travel beyond and observe it from outside. Thus, although we know that the galaxy has three spiral arms, for example, we do not know exactly how these arms are positioned in space, nor their relationship to the galactic nucleus.

**The shape of the galaxy** is best seen by looking at external galaxies, such as the one shown here (which is M63), because it is impossible to travel beyond our galaxy to view it from outside. From such observations, it seems that our galaxy is a loose spiral with relatively clearly defined arms.

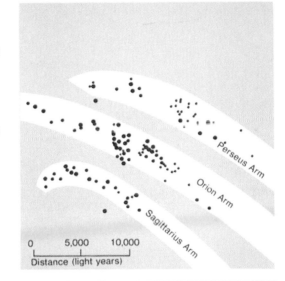

0    5,000    10,000

Distance (light years)

**The spiral arms** are three in number. The middle one is called the Orion Arm because it contains the constellation of that name. The solar system is on the inner edge of this arm. The Sagittarius Arm lies between the earth and the center of the galaxy, which is in the direction of the Sagittarius constellation. The Perseus Arm is so named because it contains many of the stars in the Perseus constellation; this arm lies away from the direction of the galactic center.

**The Orion Nebula** (M42) is a prominent feature of the Milky Way, being the brightest nebula visible from the earth. It lies about 500 parsecs away in the Sword region of the Orion constellation and can just be seen with the naked eye. Viewed through a telescope, the nebula is an impressive sight, with a bright center surrounded by glowing red hydrogen gas.

# Galactic groups

Groups of galaxies (termed clusters—not to be confused with the globular and open clusters of stars that occur within galaxies) are major features of the universe. Their sizes vary enormously, with some galactic clusters containing only a few galaxies and others with several thousands. Moreover, the galactic clusters themselves are part of still larger clusters of clusters—superclusters. Most astronomers believe superclusters to be the universe's largest units. But some astronomers believe that even clusters of superclusters are possible, forming a hierarchical organization of increasingly larger units.

Much of our knowledge about galactic

clusters comes from a pioneering 12-year study by C. Donald Shane and Carl Wirtanen at the Lick Observatory near San Francisco, California. They divided the sky into a number of areas (cells) and counted the galaxies above a certain magnitude in each. At the end of the survey (which involved counting more than 1 million galaxies) they found that some cells contained 10 or more whereas others had none; the average was one galaxy per cell. They also compiled a galaxy distribution map, which showed that, at least to an average distance of about 400 million parsecs, galaxies are grouped into clusters of various shapes.

## The Local Group

Our own galaxy—the Milky Way—is part of a galactic cluster generally known as the Local Group. It contains about 32 galaxies and extends across a spherical volume of space 1 million parsecs in diameter. The Local Group is a fairly typical galactic cluster in terms of the types of galaxies it contains: there are three large spiral galaxies—the Milky Way, the Andromeda Spiral (M31), and the Triangulum Spiral (M33), which are between 15,000 and 50,000 parsecs across; four medium-sized, irregular galaxies with diameters between 3,000 and 12,000 parsecs, including the Large and Small Magellanic clouds (also called Nebecula Major and Minor); and about 25 elliptical galaxies, most of which are relatively small (four are regular ellipticals with diameters between 2,000 and 5,000 parsecs, whereas the remainder are dwarf ellipticals, mostly less than 2,000 parsecs across). Two of the regular elliptical galaxies are companions of Andromeda.

The largest member of the Local Group is the Andromeda Spiral, followed by the Milky Way, the Triangulum Spiral, and the Clouds of Magellan. Of these, only Andromeda and the Clouds of Magellan can be completely seen from the earth with the naked eye—and the Clouds are visible only from the Southern Hemisphere.

Two other galaxies are sometimes also included in the Local Group—Maffei I, an elliptical galaxy, and Maffei II, a spiral. Extremely difficult to observe by optical means because they are obscured by dust, they were not discovered until 1968 (by the Italian astronomer Paolo Maffei). More recent studies indicate, however, that they are not actually in the Local Group, but are part of a neighboring galactic cluster.

## Other galactic clusters

Millions of galaxies have been detected in our part of the universe, and many are parts of clusters. Some clusters are extremely rich in galaxies—the larger ones may have as many as 10,000 members. In the immediate vicinity of the Local Group are several smaller clusters, each containing about 12 galaxies. The nearest one that is rich in galaxies is the Virgo cluster (in the constellation Virgo), about 15,000,000 to 20,000,000 parsecs distant from the earth. It is

**The Local Group** is actually small and is dominated by the Andromeda Spiral (M31). It was originally thought to lie at a distance of 230,000 parsecs, which posed several problems. Certain objects that should have been within the galaxy could not be seen, and globular clusters of stars appeared to be smaller than those in the Milky Way. These problems were solved, however, when Andromeda's true distance was found to be 675,000 parsecs.

**The Triangulum Spiral** (M33) lies about 828,000 parsecs away from our own galaxy and is the third largest member of the Local Group. It is, however, not visible to the naked eye. It has a regular, loose spiral shape with a small, central nucleus. The arms contain a large amount of gas, some of which is massed together to form compact clouds.

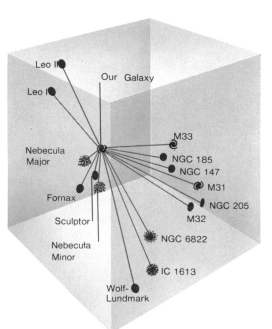

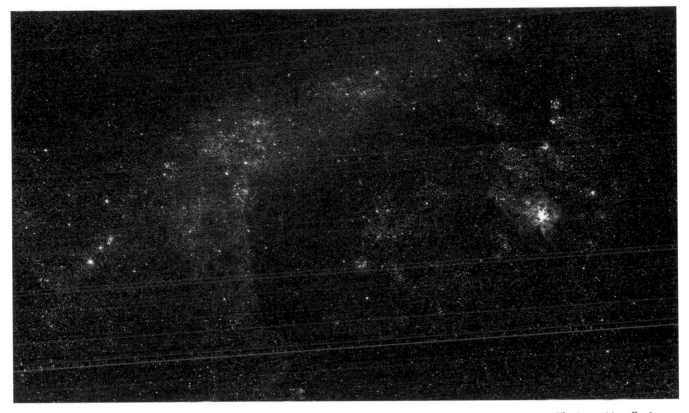

large (about 2 million parsecs across) and contains thousands of galaxies of all types. Other notable rich clusters include the Coma Cluster (in the constellation Coma Berenices) and the Perseus Cluster (in Perseus). All three emit X rays, a phenomenon that some astronomers believe to be characteristic of rich clusters. In addition, the galaxies in the Coma Cluster are concentrated in its center—another feature common to many clusters.

It is now thought that the Local Group, the small neighboring clusters, and the Virgo Cluster form part of a much larger cluster of clusters—called the Local Supercluster. It is believed to contain about a hundred individual galactic clusters and to be about 100 million parsecs in diameter.

### Explaining galactic groups

Since the birth of the universe in the big bang and the subsequent evolution of galactic systems, the galaxies have been—and still are—receding from each other. Despite this general movement, galaxies remain in clusters, each of which seems to be reasonably stable. This relative stability results from the mutual gravitational attraction that binds the galaxies within each cluster, although each galaxy is still sufficiently free to move within its cluster. In the Local Group, the Andromeda Spiral is moving toward the Milky Way.

Starting from the assumption that clusters are stable, it is possible to calculate the gravitational force necessary to maintain that stability, which can, in turn, be used to calculate the total mass of the cluster. But the results of such calculations reveal an interesting anomaly: the galactic clusters appear to contain less mass in the galaxies seen within them than is necessary to maintain their stability. The Virgo Cluster, for example, is observed to have 50 times less mass than it should have. This phenomenon—known as the missing mass problem—has not yet been satisfactorily explained, although one possible reason is that the galaxies within each cluster are still settling down after their formation, and so the clusters are not really stable. Alternatively, there may not be any missing mass because there may exist between the galaxies large amounts of dark, invisible matter (such as dust or gas) that has not yet been detected.

**The Large Magellanic Cloud** (Nebecula Major), about 200,000 light years away, is the galaxy closest to our own. Irregular in shape, the Large Magellanic Cloud is about 40,000 light years across. It is a bright object, easily visible with the naked eye, in the night sky of the Southern Hemisphere. The Small Magellanic Cloud (Nebecula Minor) is an irregular galaxy about 20,000 light years across and about 196,000 light years from Earth. Although it is 75,000 light years away from the Large Magellanic Cloud, both galaxies share a common envelope consisting of a cloud of hydrogen.

**The Virgo Cluster** is the nearest galaxy-rich cluster, situated about 15,000,000 to 20,000,000 parsecs away from the earth. It contains thousands of galaxies of all types—regular and irregular, spiral and elliptical—some of which can be seen in this photograph.

# Peculiar galaxies and quasars

Some galaxies are irregular—neither basically spiral nor elliptical in shape—and so do not fit conveniently into the Hubble classification of galaxies. Of these irregular galaxies, those that can be resolved into nebulae, stars, and clusters are classified as Irr 1; those that cannot be resolved in this way and appear to be amorphous are classified as Irr 2. Yet other galaxies are visually unremarkable, but are significant because they emit forms of radiation other than light, often radio waves. Included in this diverse group are quasars, the most enigmatic of cosmic objects.

### Irregular galaxies

Many irregular galaxies have undergone peculiar changes or exhibit unusual features that cannot yet be adequately explained. For exam-ple, M82—an irregular galaxy with a companion spiral galaxy, M81—underwent a huge explosion in its center a few million years ago, and even today astronomers do not know why this happened. As a result of this explosion, clouds of gas were thrown off, producing the galaxy's irregular shape. Shock waves from the explosion compressed most of the remaining gas into numerous, very hot stars, which clustered together and heated the remnants of the gas and dust clouds to extremely high temperatures.

Some aspects of the behavior of irregular galaxies are reasonably well understood, however, such as what happens when two galaxies interact. The Antennae pair of galaxies (NGC 4038 and 4039) have been interacting for several hundred million years, during which time they have thrown off two curved tails, each of

**Centaurus A** (NGC 5128) is the nearest giant radio galaxy, situated about 5 million parsecs from the earth. Astronomers originally thought it represented a collision between an elliptical and a spiral galaxy (the almost horizontal dark band was thought to be the remnant of spiral galactic arms). Today, however, Centaurus A is believed to be a single system and the dark band is thought to be a girdle of dust encircling the galaxy. Furthermore, two pairs of radio sources have been detected, one pair above the girdle and one below it. Astronomers believe these radio sources were ejected from the main body of the galaxy by two explosions that occurred about 30 million years ago.

**Fornax A** (NGC 1316) is a triple radio source; radio astronomers have detected a relatively weak radio source in the nucleus of the galaxy itself and two stronger sources, one on each side. Around each of the strong sources is a large radio lobe (outlined in green in the diagram), which represents the area of radio emissions. Long-exposure photographs reveal that the visible part—called the optical envelope (colored yellow)—of Fornax A seems to encompass the galaxy NGC 1317. In fact, the two galaxies are not thought to be associated with each other. The loops and ripples indicate that Fornax A consumed at least one other galaxy during the past thousand million years.

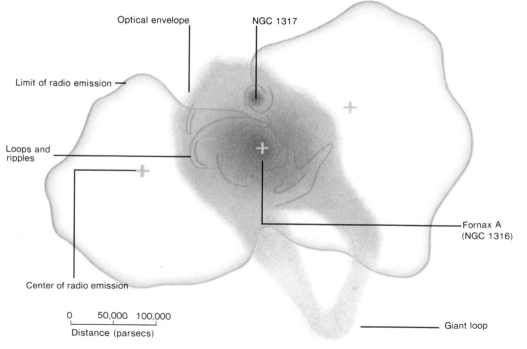

Optical envelope

NGC 1317

Limit of radio emission

Loops and ripples

Center of radio emission

Fornax A (NGC 1316)

0    50,000  100,000
Distance (parsecs)

Giant loop

which is about 30,000 parsecs long. The tails contain stars and gas and were formed as the outlying stars of the two galaxies (originally normal spiral galaxies) were torn away during the interaction.

### Radio galaxies

Most galaxies—regular and irregular—emit forms of radiation other than visible light, and many are sources of radio-wave emissions. Astronomers have detected weak radio signals from many spiral galaxies, including the center of our own, and stronger signals from several ellipticals. Some galaxies, however, are very strong emitters of radio waves, and these are classified as radio galaxies.

The first radio galaxy to be detected was Cygnus A, which emits about 1 million times more radio wavelength radiation than does the Milky Way. When these long-wavelength radiations are plotted on a map, and the resultant radio contours superimposed on a visual image of a radio galaxy, two very different pictures emerge: Cygnus A—a typical radio galaxy—appears visually as a roughly circular bright spot; the radio contours, however, reveal that the strongest radio emissions emanate from two regions (called lobes) situated one on each side of the visible galaxy.

At first, it was assumed that radio emissions were indicative of two galaxies colliding, but too many similar sources have since been discovered for this to be a realistic conclusion. In the case of Cygnus A, some astronomers have theorized that the radio emissions might indicate that a galaxy is undergoing the reverse process—splitting into two parts.

Since the discovery of Cygnus A, many other radio galaxies have been detected and their visible counterparts identified—Seyfert galaxies, for example, which have small but highly luminous nuclei, and are unusual sources of radiation, being a hundred times brighter in the infrared region than is our own galaxy. More recently, X-ray galaxies have been detected. These are optically irregular and contain a huge amount of dust and gas. Collisions in the hot gas are believed to be responsible for the X-ray emissions.

### Quasars

Quasars were discovered while radio astronomers were searching for the visible counterparts of radio sources. It was found that certain radio objects were accompanied by what looked like stars with unusual spectral lines; these starlike objects were called quasi-stellar radio sources, or quasars. Analysis of the spectral lines and their Doppler shifts indicates that quasars are fast-moving, extremely distant objects. They are also very compact and must be highly luminous. (They would not otherwise be visible at the vast distances at which they lie.) Quasars radiate up to a thousand times more energy than a normal galaxy. Most of the 1,300 or so quasars so far discovered are strong X-ray sources as well.

The most interesting question about quasars concerns the nature of the processes by which they generate huge amounts of energy in such compact regions of space. The most popular explanation for this phenomenon is the central black hole hypothesis. According to this, a quasar is like a normal galaxy, but has a central black hole from which it ultimately derives its energy. Gas from the stars in a quasar galaxy is gravitationally attracted to the center and accumulates in a ring (called an accretion ring) that circles the black hole, becoming increasingly hot as it does so and emitting X rays, ultraviolet radiation, and radio waves. Strong magnetic and electrical forces cause streams of electrons to be ejected along the axis of rotation. Ultimately, therefore, a quasar is powered by the energy generated by matter that is gravitationally attracted to the central black hole.

The origin and nature of the central black holes themselves, however, remains a mystery.

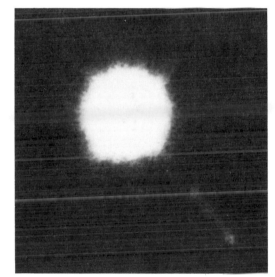

Quasar 3C-273 was one of the first radio sources to be identified optically. Photographs of this object reveal a faint jet joining the stellarlike body to what is the strongest radio source. The development of such quasar jets led to the conclusion that there was motion within them that was more than three times the speed of light. But it is more likely that these "superluminal velocities" are an optical illusion rather than the refutation of Einstein's precept that nothing moves faster than the speed of light.

On this radio map of the inner structure and jet of quasar 3C-273 each contour represents a line of equal radio intensity. Part of the map has been artificially colored to show more clearly how the radio intensity diminishes (indicated by the change from orange through to dark blue) with increasing distance from the three radio centers (shown by the contours enclosing the smallest areas), which are approximately colinear with the jet.

0    300
Distance (parsecs)

# The solar system

The sun, a star, emits enough heat and light to maintain the present climates of all the planetary bodies in the solar system. The corona, photographed here in false colors during a total solar eclipse in 1983, is the outer atmosphere of the sun. It stretches out beyond a distance of half a solar radius where temperatures reach 3,000,000° F. (1,670,000° C). Only since space astronomy have photographs like this of the corona been possible, because on earth, the background light in the atmosphere obscures it.

Comparatively little is known about the formation and early history of the solar system, even though our knowledge of the sun and its planetary system is steadily growing. Various theories exist that explain how the planet earth and its companions were formed about 4.5 billion years ago, but the answer may lie not in the observation of our immediate neighborhood, but of other stars in our galaxy.

### The Titius-Bode law

It has long been known that the distances of the planets from the sun can be fitted to certain mathematical sequences, the most famous of which is the Titius-Bode law. This predictive sequence was first determined by the German mathematician Johann Titius in 1766, and publicized by Johann Bode in 1772. Titius discovered that if the numbers 0, 3, 6, 12, 24, and so on in that sequence, with every number after 3 being double its predecessor, have the value 4 added to each one, and if the distance of the earth from the sun is taken as 10, the end values correspond with the known planetary distances from the sun.

The Titius-Bode sequence was regarded with skepticism by those who thought that any able mathematician could invent a sequence and suit it to the problem. When Uranus was discovered in 1781, however, and was found to conform to the law (with the predicted distance being 191.8 and the actual distance being 196), some astronomers banded together to search for the "missing" planet that would fill the gap at the value of 28. The discovery of Ceres, on January 1, 1801, by Giuseppe Piazzi from his home in Palermo, Sicily, was thought to solve the problem of the gap. But Ceres, at a distance from the sun of 27.7, turned out to be just one in a belt of many thousands of asteroids orbiting the sun between Mars and Jupiter.

Neither Neptune nor Pluto corresponds to its predicted positions within the Titius-Bode sequence, but the search for, and the calcu-

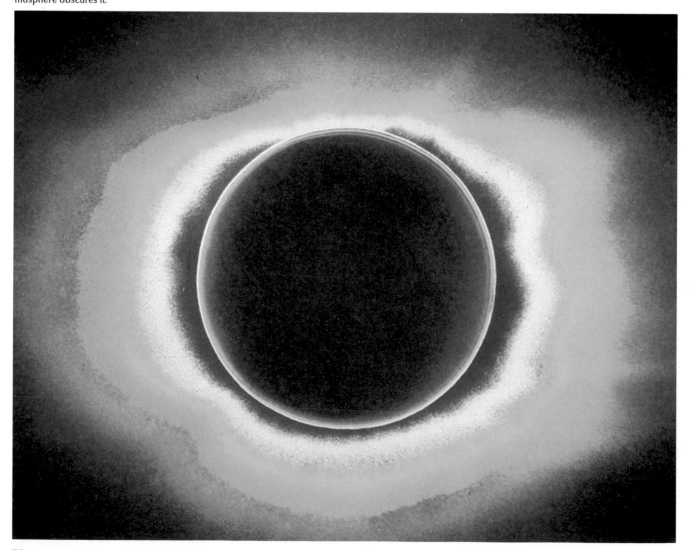

lated positions of, Neptune narrowed the range of possibilities and ultimately aided in its discovery. In fact, Pluto occupies the position that Neptune should hold if it were to follow from Uranus, at an actual distance of 393.0. In spite of this discrepancy, it is evident that the planets are spread out in a fairly distinct arrangement, which could be a clue to the formation of the solar system.

### The rotation of planets

It is accepted that most of the planets in the solar system have, or have had, rotation periods of about 10 hours. Both Jupiter and Saturn maintain this average, whereas it is evident that other bodies have had their periods altered by gravitational interference, such as Earth. The effects of the moon's gravity have contributed greatly toward the lengthening of our day from the 10 hours that it was originally, to the present 24.

The sun's axial rotation period also differs from what it should be. The sun contains almost all the mass present in the solar system, and to match this it should have a proportionate amount of the angular momentum of the system. Consequently, it should rotate in only a few hours; but in fact, the sun's rotational period is nearly a month.

### The origin of the solar system

Virtually all the different theories on the formation of the solar system agree on two facts. One is the age of the system—around 4.5 billion years. This figure has been arrived at from the examination of certain types of meteorites. Particular elements (such as uranium and thorium) decay into lead over time, and scientists can deduce the age of rock particles from meteorites by comparing the respective amounts of these elements and the lead present within the samples.

The other point of agreement is that the

**Comet West** was first discovered in 1976. Comets come from outside the solar system and have extremely elliptical orbits that bring them near the sun, around it, and then take them out of the solar system again. As a comet nears the sun, its frozen nucleus melts and material flows behind it in tails. This comet developed two tails as it approached the sun in 1976. The tails differ in composition: the white tails contain dust particles and the blue tail, on the right, consists of glowing gas. When the nucleus of Comet West retreated from the sun, it was seen to break into four pieces.

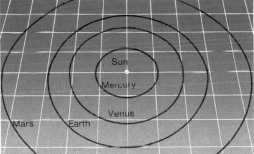

**The orbits of the terrestrial planets** (left) are almost circular, but the outer planets' orbits are highly elliptical. All the planets (except Mercury and Pluto) orbit the sun in more or less the plane of the ecliptic (below)

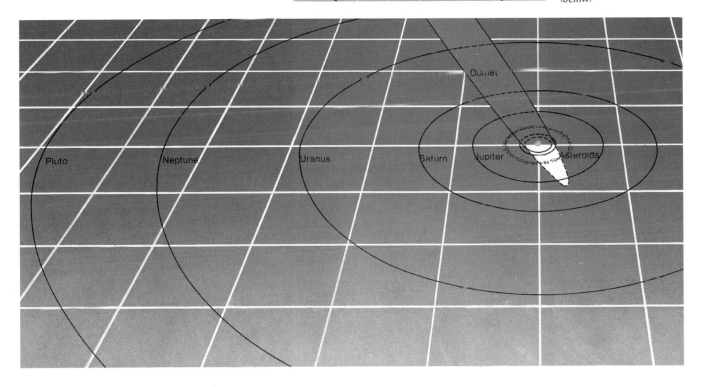

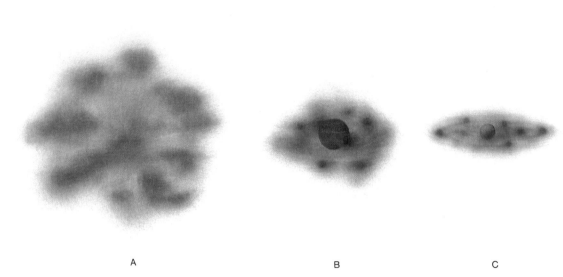

**The evolution of the solar system** is believed to have started with an interstellar cloud of gas and dust that fragmented and condensed (A). Nuclear fusion then began and the sun was born (B). Astronomers also agree that the planets condensed from the gas and dust around the sun (C). Some suggest that as they accreted, the planets were pulled into solar orbit (D). The sun is a young star. As it ages, it will expand (E) to become a red giant (F) and engulf part of its planetary system.

A                   B                 C

planets were formed from gas and dust in the vicinity of the sun. Opinions vary on the origin of this material, ranging from gaseous rings thrown off by the sun to matter pulled from a passing star by the sun's gravity. The gas and dust seem to have condensed into tiny bodies, or planetesimals, which eventually built up the planetary system we know today. This formative sequence would explain the presence of asteroids, which are planetesimals that never accreted into a planet, possibly because of the gravitational influence of the giant planet Jupiter.

Toward the end of the eighteenth century, the French mathematician Pierre Simon de Laplace proposed that the planets were formed from rings of gas thrown off by the young sun, but this theory would not explain the sun's disproportionately low momentum. If the solar system were formed in the way he suggested, then the sun would have almost the correct amount of momentum, which is not the case. According to the Australian astronomer A. J. R. Prentice, however, Laplace's idea would work if the solar core was assumed to have collapsed at a sufficiently rapid rate to push most of the angular momentum outward into the surrounding gas. Prentice's modification of Laplace's original idea has gained some popularity.

### Other planetary systems

Looking to other regions of the galaxy for answers to their questions, astronomers have studied groups of stars, and in particular T Tauri variable stars. T Tauri is the prototype of a particular kind of star that varies irregularly in light intensity. This star, and others of its kind, are young stars in the early stages of evolution. They are throwing off mass, which takes the form of nebulosity surrounding the central star. The density of this matter is not uniform, and the star is seen to vary in brightness as veils of gas and dust pass between the star and ourselves. The ejection of matter from the star in this way would tend to decrease its angular momentum. If our sun had gone through a similar phase, this would explain the

distribution of momentum and rotation that exists in our solar system. The planets themselves could have condensed from the gas and dust around the young sun, building up from local condensations, through the planetesimal stage, and finally into the planets that we observe today.

If T Tauri variables are an indication of possible early processes within our own solar system, then they could also indicate other similar embryonic planetary systems. The idea of a planetary group forming from a nebula surrounding a young star is more credible than that of an accidental creation with, for example, matter being dragged from a passing star. The former notion indicates that the process of planetary formation happens on a fairly regular basis, that other systems may be commonplace, and that they are the standard byproduct of a young star.

On the other hand, the chances of any particular star passing close enough to another to effect a matter transfer on such a scale are very remote. This would mean that our solar system is almost unique. But stellar collisions, or near-collisions, are not the only way that a planetary system could form accidentally—a star could pass through a nebula and draw off matter from the nebula while doing so. This matter could accumulate and condense into planets, although this, too, would be unlikely.

Theories may be proposed unendingly, but without actual observational proof, the idea of extra-solar planetary systems remains just an idea. Even the world's largest telescopes are unable to detect planets orbiting other suns because the light from any nonluminous companions would be obscured in the glare from the parent star. Such objects may, however, be detected from the observation of gravitational effects within other systems.

### Wobbling stars

Two gravitationally bound bodies orbit each other around their mass center—their common center of gravity—the position of which is determined by the relative masses of two objects. For example, because the earth has 81

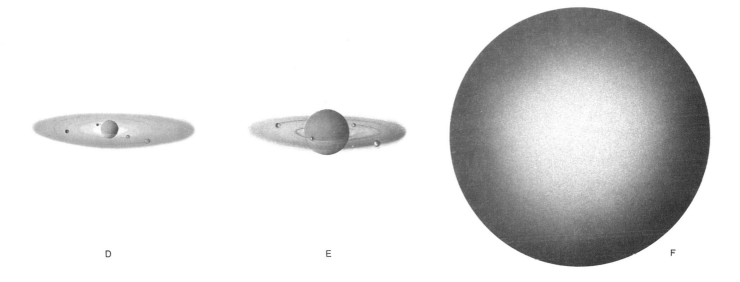

D                    E                    F

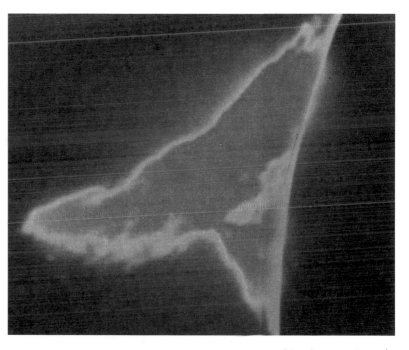

This solar prominence is called a quiescent prominence because it can stay unchanged for several months, supported by magnetic field lines. It may represent cool matter from the corona that is falling down toward the sun's surface.

times the mass of the moon, the center of gravity of the earth-moon system lies 81 times closer to the earth's center than the moon's. This point, the barycenter, lies beneath the earth's surface. As a result of the moon's gravitational effect on the earth, our planet spins around the barycenter, each spin lasting 27.32 days—the length of time it takes the moon to make one complete orbit. This gravitational effect causes waves in the earth's path as it travels around the sun, each wave lasting 27.32 days.

Under favorable conditions, it should be possible to detect similar deflections in the motions of stars—particularly nearby and small stars—with planets in orbit around them. Some astronomers claim to have detected such wobbles in the paths of a few close stars. Peter van de Kamp, a Dutch-born American astronomer, announced in 1975 that he had evidence of wobbles in four stars. In particular, he had observed a tiny deflection of only a few hundredths of an arc second in the path of Barnard's Star, an object only six light-years away and the third nearest star (including the sun). The deviations apparently indicated that there are two large planets in orbit around Barnard's Star, one of which has a mass slightly larger than that of Jupiter, and the other with a mass half that of Jupiter. Van de Kamp also claimed that the star Epsilon Eridani has a planetary companion with a mass six times that of Jupiter.

Other investigators, however, have been unable to duplicate van de Kamp's findings satisfactorily, even when using techniques that were more sensitive than those he used. Most astronomers are coming to believe that van de Kamp's "star wobbles" were caused by miniscule changes in his telescope—for example, when the main lens was cleaned and replaced. The verdict on the existence of other planetary systems remains open for the moment.

Meteorites provide astronomers with important information about the composition and age of the solar system. This stony, iron meteorite contains olivine, which fused to form a bead when the meteorite fell to earth.

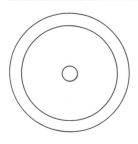

# The sun

As far as life on earth is concerned, the sun is the most important star in the sky. For centuries, astronomers have studied its appearance and behavior in an attempt to discover how it functions. But it is not only the sun's physical properties that have been the subject of study: the determination of the earth-sun distance has also long been a focus of attention. The currently accepted value of 92,960,000 miles (149,600,000 kilometers) for this distance is known as an *astronomical unit*. Such accuracy is essential for astronomers to determine the scale of the solar system and for space scientists to guide spacecraft to other planets.

**Sun's statistics**
Equatorial diameter:
　865,000 miles (1,392,000
　kilometers)
Mass: 333,400 (Earth = 1)
Mean relative density: 1.41
Escape velocity: 384 miles
　(618 kilometers)
　per second
Distance from Earth
　farthest: 94,500,000 miles
　(152,100,000 kilometers)
　nearest: 91,400,000 miles
　(147,100,000 kilometers)
　mean: 92,960,000 miles
　(149,600,000 kilometers)
Mean rotational period:
　About 1 month
Mean surface temperature
　10,000° F. (5,500° C)
Apparent magnitude: −27
Absolute magnitude: 4.8

**The sun** is the nearest star to earth and the brightest object in the sky. It emits electromagnetic radiation of various wavelengths—some of them harmful to life. But the earth's atmosphere absorbs most of these injurious radiations and, in fact, life on earth would be impossible without heat and light from the sun.

### The astronomical unit

The Greek astronomer Aristarchus of Samos was the first to calculate the distance from the earth to the sun. His value of 2,983,000 miles (4,800,000 kilometers), although far short of the true value, was reached through direct measurement. The theory behind his geometric method was sound, but instruments available at the time did not enable angles to be measured accurately.

The first fairly accurate calculation was made by the Italian astronomer Giovanni Cassini in 1672. His value of 86,103,000 miles (138,570,000 kilometers) for the earth-sun distance was only a little short of the currently accepted figure. Since then, calculations of the astronomical unit have steadily improved.

### Sunspots and flares

Observation of the sun reveals many features both on and above its surface. (Such observations are made using special techniques and instruments; looking at the sun directly, with or without a telescope, is extremely hazardous and can instantly produce blindness.) Sunspots mar the bright outer photosphere, and flares and prominences can also be seen. These violent releases of energy within the solar atmosphere result from nuclear processes that take place at the center of the sun.

Sunspots were first studied telescopically in 1610. In that year, the German astronomer Johannes Fabricius published his observations of sunspots, although at about the same time Galileo used their apparent motion across the solar disk to measure the rotational period of the sun. He arrived at a value of just less than one month. In 1863, Richard Carrington, a British astronomer, discovered the sun's differential rotation—that the period at the equator is shorter than that at the poles. Modern estimates of the rotational periods are 26 days at the equator and 37 days at the poles.

A typical sunspot has two regions: a dark umbra and a surrounding penumbra. The umbral temperature is about 4,000K, whereas the penumbra is even hotter at between 5,000 and 6,000K. Sunspots appear dark because even at such high temperatures they are cooler than the surrounding photosphere. (If they were viewed independently of their background, they would shine brighter than an electric arc lamp.)

Sunspots are depressions on the solar surface. In 1769, Alexander Wilson observed a spot on the limb of the sun, which revealed that the penumbra on the far side of the spot was broader than on the foreshortened near side. This effect (the Wilson effect) was explained by assuming that the spots are hollows.

Sunspot activity recurs in a regular cycle, the idea of which was first put forward by the Danish astronomer Horrebow in 1775-1776. During a cycle, spots appear between 30° and 40° north or south of the sun's equator. The region of formation gradually progresses toward the equator until spots form at latitudes of 7° or 8°; maximum sunspot activity occurs at about 15°. This regular change in the latitude of spot formation is known as Spörer's law, after the German astronomer Gustav Spörer, who investigated the phenomenon in 1861. The average length of the sunspot cycle is slightly more than 11 years, although it can vary considerably—from as little as 7.5 years to as long as 17 years.

Associated with sunspots are faculae, discovered by Christoph Scheiner in 1611. These features are luminous clouds, composed mainly of hydrogen, which lie above the solar surface. They usually appear in the region where a sunspot group is about to form, and have an average duration of about 15 days.

Flares are outbursts of energy that also have their origins in sunspot regions. Discovered by Carrington in 1859, these too are fairly short-lived features. Radio disturbances and auroral displays on earth are the direct result of flare activity on the sun.

Prominences are yet another type of eruptive feature in the solar atmosphere. Visible with the naked eye only during a total solar eclipse, they can be studied by spectroscopic observation of hydrogen emissions. There are two basic kinds of prominences: *quiescent* prominences, which are relatively stable and long-lived, and *eruptive* prominences, which can display rapid motion and typically attain heights of more than 20,000 miles (32,000 kilometers) above the surface.

### The neutrino puzzle

Nuclear reactions at the center of the sun produce nearly all the sun's energy. During these processes, neutrinos are released. They are tiny particles with no mass or electrical charge. Neutrinos are emitted from the sun at the speed of light and pass straight through the earth or any other solid body they encounter. As a result, they are difficult to detect and measure. They do, however, react with chlorine to produce argon. To prove the existence of neutrinos, an experiment has been set up involving a tank that contained nearly 130,000 gallons (492,000 liters) of chlorine compound, placed at the bottom of a disused mine in South Dakota. But the experiment has not collected the number of neutrinos that had been anticipated. This may mean that the particles disintegrate on their journey to earth or that the physics of the solar interior is not yet fully understood.

### The production of sunshine

The sun may be the central and most important body in the solar system, but grouped with the rest of the stars, it is classed merely as a yellow dwarf. Virtually all our light and much of our heat comes from the sun, and without its energy, life on earth would cease to exist. The sun is associated with various astronomical phenomena, including the beautiful corona that surrounds the totally eclipsed solar disk, and the ghostly auroras that are produced in the earth's atmosphere as a result of the interaction of energized solar particles with the outer atmospheric layers.

The sun has been observed in many ways for centuries. Records of solar eclipses go

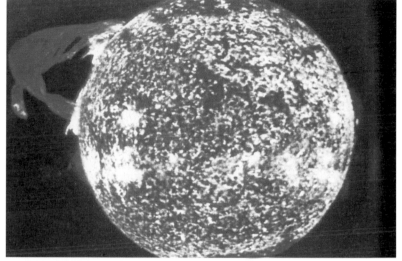

A huge hooped prominence (*above*), one of the largest observed, was photographed (in ultraviolet light) by Skylab. Such arched prominences connect regions of high magnetism and tend to follow the lines of the magnetic field. The gas that forms a prominence is much cooler (between about 20,000 and 70,000 K) than the corona, which has a temperature of 4,000,000° F. (2,220,000° C).

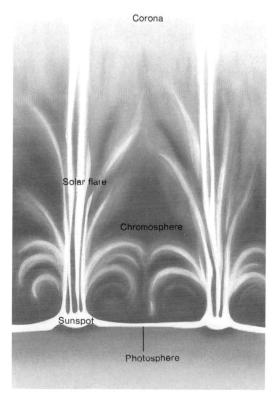

The photosphere, the sun's turbulent surface layer, is only about 340 miles (547 kilometers) deep, but is so bright that it is the only part normally visible. It has several features associated with it, notably sunspots and solar flares (which erupt from sunspots). By studying the sun with special instruments and during eclipses, astronomers have detected other layers. Immediately outside the photosphere is the chromosphere, a broad region several thousand miles thick, and beyond the chromosphere (which is bounded by a narrow transition zone) is the corona, the sun's outer atmosphere.

Corona

Solar flare

Chromosphere

Sunspot

Photosphere

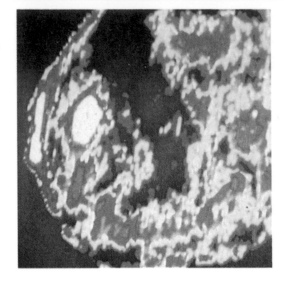

A coronal "hole" is clearly visible (the large dark area) in this computer-enhanced photograph of the sun. Such holes are relatively stable areas in the sun's corona, through which the solar wind emerges.

absorbs electromagnetic radiation at these (and some other) wavelengths.

### The source of solar energy

As with any other star, the sun produces its energy by nuclear reactions in its central core. The temperature and pressure in the core is so intense that hydrogen, initially the most abundant gas in the sun, is converted by thermonuclear fusion reactions into helium. This conversion takes place when four hydrogen nuclei are fused together to make one helium nucleus. The reaction initiates a release of energy that travels by convection through the main body of the sun to emerge as visible radiation at the surface. It is this continuous nuclear process that keeps the sun, and all other stars, shining as they do.

back to early times, and sunspots have been studied since the advent of the telescope in the early part of the seventeenth century. Even ancient civilizations recognized the importance of the sun and worshiped it as a god. In more modern times, the examination of complex features of the sun, such as the corona and prominences, has taken place only during the last 200 years or so. Solar flares have been scrutinized only since the mid-nineteenth century. Space exploration has made possible more detailed observations of the sun. X-ray and ultraviolet emissions could be recorded once measuring instruments were lifted by rocket above the earth's atmosphere, which

### The structure of the sun

When we observe the sun in visible light, the surface, known as the photosphere, can be seen. It is a turbulent region 340 miles (547 kilometers) deep. Closer examination of the photosphere reveals a curious granular structure, each granule measuring 620 miles (1,000 kilometers) across. The granules are fairly short-lived and are produced by turbulent upcurrents of energy from within the sun.

Energy released from the photosphere passes through the almost transparent chromosphere, which is several thousand miles thick. The temperature of matter within this region rises from about 4,500 K at the bottom to about 1,000,000 K in the outer reaches. The

**Sunspots** are relatively cool areas on the photosphere. Near the "edge" of the sun, the penumbra on the far side of a sunspot is wider than on the near side (the Wilson effect), which indicates that sunspots are depressions. During the relatively regular cycle of sunspot activity, the area of sunspot formation gradually moves toward the equator, starting at between 30° and 40° north or south and slowly progressing to latitudes of 7° or 8°.

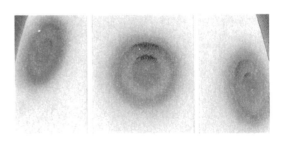

**The number of sunspots** varies cyclically, reaching a maximum approximately every 11 years—the so-called sunspot cycle. The most intensive period of sunspot activity in recent times occurred in 1960, when there were about 200 sunspots in one year.

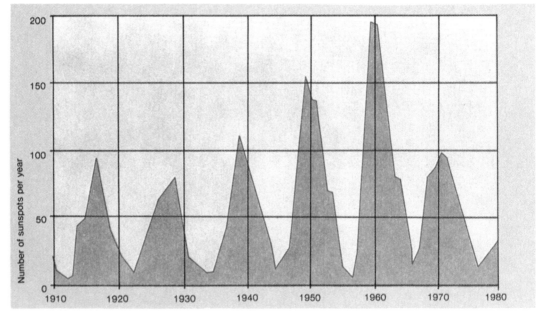

gases of the chromosphere are extremely tenuous. Ultraviolet observations show, however, that it is a very active, dynamic region of extremely high temperatures, through which energy released from the sun passes to the corona and then on to interplanetary space beyond.

## The sun's outer atmosphere

The corona is the outermost layer of the sun's atmosphere. The boundary between the chromosphere and the corona is a thin transition zone within which temperatures rise dramatically to 2,000,000 K. This boundary region is only a few miles thick. Since satellites have been able to carry X-ray telescopes above the dense layers of the earth's atmosphere, studies at these wavelengths have revealed a number of surprises.

The corona is made up of an inner and an outer region. The lower, or inner, corona consists of streams of atomic particles that tend to follow the lines of magnetic regions on the solar surface, forming arches or loops. In places, there are no coronal loops, especially at times of solar minima, when there are fewer active regions on the solar disk, such as sunspots and their associated magnetic fields.

Further examination of the corona reveals large "holes" through which energized particles escape directly into space. Coronal holes are regions with weak magnetic fields where the field lines are open and not looped. The release of particles sometimes dramatically alters the density of solar particle fields in the neighboring interplanetary environment.

The outer corona is more tenuous in nature than its inner counterpart. The temperature is still high, at about 1,000,000 K, although the component particles are much more widely spaced than in the lower corona. The whole corona has no effective outer boundary and

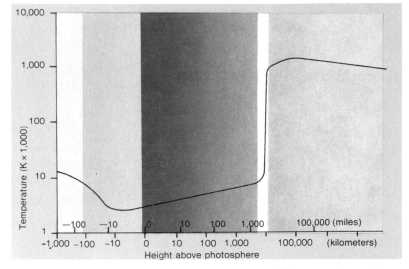

eventually it thins out to become the solar wind. The outer region of the corona can be observed during a total solar eclipse, its misty form reaching out far beyond the solar limb. It marks the last region of the solar atmosphere through which streams of energized particles must pass before they flow out through the solar system as the solar wind.

Light and heat are not the only forms of energy from the sun that affect the earth. The solar wind also produces its own effects. Aurorae, too, are among the many results of interactions between atomic particles from the sun and the outer layers of the earth's atmosphere. Another is airglow, the faint radiance that ensures that the night sky is never totally dark.

**The temperature of the sun** varies greatly from region to region. Although the sun generates energy (and therefore heat) deep below its surface, the temperature is greatest at a height of more than 6,000 miles (9,600 kilometers) above the photosphere.

**The aurora borealis** is caused by particles from the sun that ionize the earth's upper atmosphere. Spectacularly beautiful, aurora borealis is best seen in northernmost latitudes. A similar phenomenon, aurora australis, occurs in southern latitudes.

# The planets

For thousands of years, stargazers have known that the planets of the solar system are different from stars because each of the six visible planets was seen to have its unique motion through the sky, whereas the stars seemed to be motionless. The word "planet," meaning wanderer, derives from the appearance of the individual motions of the planets through the background of seemingly fixed stars. The reason for this appearance is simply that the planets are relatively close to us and they orbit the sun; they are therefore seen to change position in the sky. But the stars do not orbit the sun and are so far away that their movement, although rapid, can be detected only through many years of observation. The same phenomenon could be seen if one were to observe a bird flying past and then to look at an airplane in the sky. The plane would undoubtedly be the faster of the two, although it would actually take much longer to cross one's field of vision because of its distance.

The other visible difference between planets and stars, known to man for centuries, is that stars twinkle, whereas planets do not. This is because planets differ greatly from stars in composition. Stars are vast globes of incandescent gas, creating their own light through nuclear energy production, whereas planets are smaller, darker bodies that reflect the light from their parent stars. If the sun were suddenly extinguished, the planets in our solar system would cease to shine.

The planets within the solar system also differ from each other: tiny, barren Mercury, with its heavily cratered surface, for example, contrasts sharply with our own water-covered planet Earth. In turn, neither of these planets bears any resemblance to the giant gaseous worlds of Jupiter and Saturn. Each member of the sun's family has its own peculiar character-istics that distinguish it from all the other planetary bodies in our cosmic neighborhood.

## The orbits of the planets

The ideas of Ptolemy in the second century involving a geocentric planetary system, with the planets moving around the earth in circular orbits, were gradually superseded by the Copernican heliocentric theory in the sixteenth century. This theory stated that the planets moved in a circular orbit around the sun. It was later improved by Johannes Kepler in the early seventeenth century, who determined that the planetary orbits are elliptical and not circular. It is now known that these orbits all lie in roughly the same plane. The inclinations of planetary orbits are measured with respect to the plane of the earth's orbit around the sun, known as the ecliptic. The orbit of Uranus almost matches that of Earth, with an inclination of less than one degree. The inclination of Mercury's orbit, however, is 7°, and Pluto has the most oblique planetary orbit in the solar system, tilted at 17°2'.

## The rocky planets

The four innermost members of our solar system—Mercury, Venus, Earth, and Mars—are all solid, rocky bodies, a common feature that has defined them as the terrestrial planets. Each bears evidence of surface erosion processes, such as vulcanism or meteoritic bombardment, which have played a significant part in shaping the surfaces we see today.

In 1974 and 1975, Mercury was scrutinized by the *Mariner 10* space probe. A densely cratered surface was revealed, with mountainous regions, valleys, and mare-type areas. The surface of this tiny world is very similar to that of

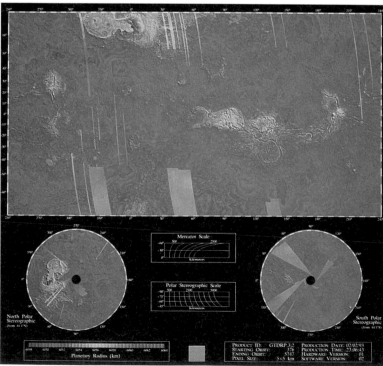

**This map of the topography of Venus** was obtained by the Magellan radar altimeter during its 24 months of systematic mapping. Color is used to code elevation (see color bar), and simulated shading to emphasize relief. Red corresponds to the highest elevation, blue to the lowest. The upper image shows the portion of Venus between 69 degrees north latitude and 69 degrees south latitude in Mercator projection. Beneath it are the two polar regions covering latitudes above 44 degrees in stereographic projection.

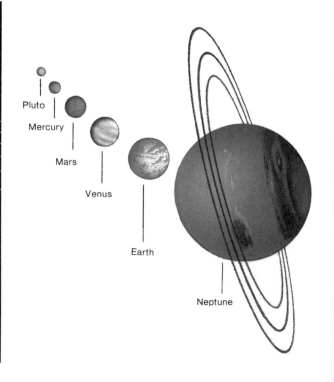

our moon. Venus, however, is completely different from Mercury. It was not until recently that astronomers were able to pierce the dense, yellow-white clouds that cover Venus to photograph the surface below. Radar mapping, carried out in 1978 by the American Pioneer Venus mission, demonstrated a surface that consists mainly of upland regions with two dominant highland areas—Ishtar Terra and Aphrodite Terra. The U.S. spacecraft *Magellan,* which began orbiting Venus in 1990, has also sent back highly detailed images of the planet's surface.

In contrast to Mercury and Venus, most of Earth's surface is covered by water, although the visible terrain displays many features similar to those on the other rocky planets. Volcanoes, meteorite craters, mountain ranges, and valley systems are all in evidence on Earth as they are on its rocky companions. But the prevailing weather conditions are so destructive on our planet that most of these features are relatively short-lived on the geological timescale. On planetary bodies that are almost totally devoid of atmosphere, such as Mercury, virtually the only process to change the surface appearance is bombardment by meteorites, although vulcanism may play a part.

The outermost of the terrestrial planets is Mars, which, apart from Earth, is probably the most geologically active of the four. The effects of wind and water erosion are very much in evidence on the planet's surface. Mars is also considered by some astronomers to be still volcanically active.

The atmospheres of the four rocky planets vary greatly. Mercury and Mars both retain little atmosphere because of their low surface gravity. The atmosphere of Mercury contains traces of hydrogen and helium, and that of Mars is composed mainly of gaseous carbon dioxide with traces of oxygen and water vapor. Earth and Venus, however, with much higher gravity, can retain denser atmospheres and both have cloud layers. Earth's atmosphere includes argon, oxygen, carbon dioxide, nitrogen, other gases, and water vapor. Venus's atmosphere has mostly carbon dioxide, but there are also clouds of sulfuric acid. Argon and nitrogen are also present.

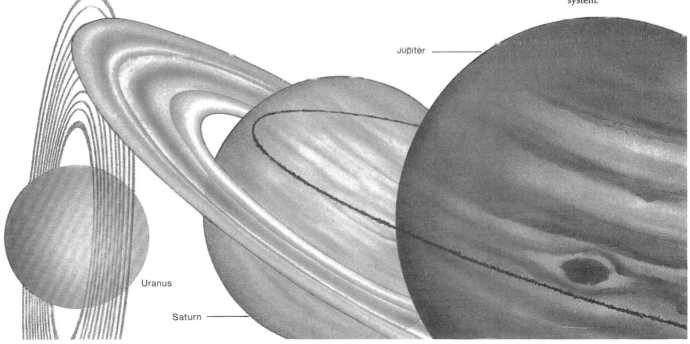

Jupiter

Uranus

Saturn

**Earth** *(right)* **and Mars** *(far right)* are grouped as terrestrial planets, but their physical characteristics differ greatly. Earth, with a surface gravity of 1.00, can retain a dense atmosphere and cloud layers. Mars, however, has a surface gravity of only 0.38, and therefore has a very thin atmosphere; apart from a few plumes of cloud and a periodic haze of carbon dioxide ice crystals, the planet is uncovered. Mars's red appearance denotes a desert terrain, whereas the blue of Earth indicates an abundant water cover.

**Two of Neptune's satellites** Triton and Nereid have very different orbits: Nereid's orbit (A) is tilted to the plane of Neptune's equator (B) by 29° whereas that of Triton (C) is inclined by 157°. Nereid's orbit is highly elliptical; Nereid is about 3.4 million miles (5.5 million kilometers) from Neptune. Triton's orbit is circular, retrograde, and decaying, so that in 10 to 100 million years the satellite will be pulled apart by Neptune's gravity.

### The gaseous giants

Beyond Mars lie the four gaseous planets—Jupiter, Saturn, Uranus, and Neptune. Each of these four worlds dwarfs the inner terrestrial members of the sun's family.

Through a telescope, Jupiter appears as a flattened globe, striated with parallel bands of clouds that mark the outermost layers of the planet's deep atmosphere. Saturn's appearance is essentially the same with its cloud layers less well pronounced than those of Jupiter, but what Saturn lacks in the way of surface detail it makes up for with its magnificent ring system. Saturn's atmosphere consists mainly of hydrogen and helium with small amounts of methane, ammonia, and phosphine. Like Jupiter, its main body is composed of liquid hydrogen and helium. Jupiter, Uranus, and Neptune also have ring systems, but that of Saturn is by far the brightest and most beautiful of the four. Earth-based telescopes reveal three major, distinct rings—Ring A, Ring B, and the fainter Ring C, with a gap between the A and B

rings known as the Cassini Division. The information gathered on the *Voyager 1* mission showed that these rings comprise many narrower ringlets, giving the impression of a gigantic record.

Both Uranus and Neptune are considerably smaller than Jupiter and Saturn—their masses are only six per cent that of Jupiter. The two smaller planets have similar atmospheres with hydrogen, helium, and methane being the most predominant gases. Acetylene has also been found on Neptune. Jupiter and Saturn are known to have solid rocky cores and magnetic fields; the *Voyager 2* probe found evidence, in January 1986, of a magnetic field around Uranus. And in August 1989, *Voyager 2*'s sensing instruments detected a magnetic field on Neptune that is about as strong as Earth's.

Both Jupiter and Saturn have large families of satellites with well over 15 smaller bodies orbiting each planet. Uranus has 15 moons and Neptune has eight.

### The outermost planet

Since its discovery by Clyde Tombaugh in 1930, the planet Pluto has remained very much of a mystery to astronomers. It was discovered as a result of its gravitational perturbations on Uranus and Neptune and cannot be seen with the naked eye, although estimates give its diameter as being approximately 1,430 miles (2,300 kilometers). Pluto is about 700 times fainter than Neptune at opposition and has the most elliptical orbit of all the planets, spending about one-eighth of its orbit inside that of Neptune; at its closest approach to the sun, it comes within 2,749,600,000 miles (4,425,100,000 kilometers). The planet is not known to have an atmosphere, although frozen methane has been detected on its surface, because its mean surface temperature is well below −369° F. (−223° C), a temperature in which most matter exists in solid form. Pluto is probably not dense enough to retain any atmosphere.

In 1978, Pluto was discovered to have a satellite that has a diameter of about one-third that of its parent planet. Charon, as the moon was named, is the largest satellite in our solar system relative to the size of its parent planet,

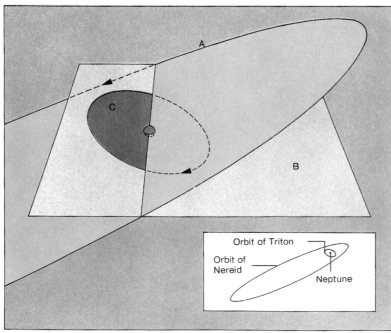

Orbit of Triton

Orbit of Nereid

Neptune

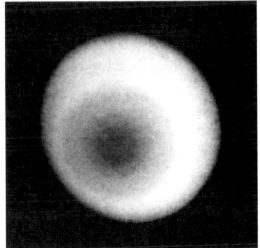

**Jupiter** *(far left)* **and Uranus** *(left)* are two of the four gaseous planets. Uranus' mass is 6 per cent that of Jupiter and its diameter is only 31,763 miles (51,118 kilometers) compared to the giant, which is 88,846 miles (142,984 kilometers) across. Jupiter's patterned surface is due to the turbulence in the dense cloud layers covering it. These layers comprise ammonia crystals and methane ice, and cover a body of liquid hydrogen and helium. Uranus' appearance is blue-green because of the methane in its atmosphere, which absorbs certain wavelengths, and it has some cloud cover.

and Pluto and Charon can therefore be said to be a twin planetary system.

### Planetary properties

The key quantities of a planet are its mass, radius, and rotation period. Using Kepler's Third Law, a planet's mass can be calculated from the observed distances and orbital periods of any satellites it may have. Alternatively, the mass can be determined from the planet's gravitational effect on the trajectories of unmanned probes.

The radius of a planet can be arrived at with trigonometry, using the values for its apparent angular size and its distance from the earth. The radius enables a planet's volume and density to be estimated, which give an indication of the internal composition of the planet. Once the mass and radius have been calculated, a wealth of other data can be computed. By equating Newton's Second Law of Motion with the inverse-square law of gravitation, the acceleration due to gravity can be determined at any point from the planet.

From a knowledge of a planet's gravity, its escape velocity can be calculated (that is, the velocity an object requires to effectively escape the planet's gravitational field). The escape velocity, combined with data on the temperature of gases within the atmosphere of the planet, enables estimates of the composition of the atmosphere to be made. Its rotation rate is another major characteristic of a planet. The centrifugal force on the atmosphere as the planet spins and its mass cause the planet to bulge at its equator, at a right angle to the rotation axis. The extent of this bulging can be used to estimate the relative proportions of materials of different density within the planet.

**The force of gravity** at the surface of a planet depends on its mass and size. On Earth, a mass of 1 pound weighs 1 pound. On the other planets, a mass of 1 pound would have the weights (in pounds) indicated on the diagram; only on Jupiter, Neptune, and Saturn would the weight be heavier than on Earth.

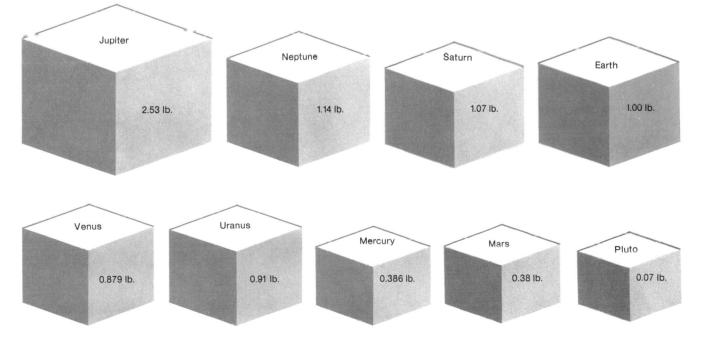

# IS THERE LIFE ON *other planets?*

**S**cientists known as exobiologists *have been searching for evidence of extraterrestrial life for years. Many of these specialists believe that life exists—or may once have existed—on other planets. Let's look at the evidence.*

## The elements of life

Most scientists believe that life on Earth developed gradually through physical and chemical reactions that occurred during Earth's formation and early development. Exobiologists use this theory as a basis in their search for life on other planets. They believe the chances are high that the chemistry of life elsewhere in the universe would resemble the chemistry of life on Earth. However, while they may have similar organic molecules (molecules that contain carbon atoms), extraterrestrial life and life on Earth would have developed in response to different environmental conditions. As a result, extraterrestrial life would almost certainly differ greatly in structure and appearance from life forms on Earth.

So far, scientists have found that organic molecules are surprisingly common in the solar system—in some comets and meteorites, on some planets and moons of the outer solar systems, and in the gases and dust of interstellar space. However, these locations are unlikely habitats for living things. Life appears to need liquid water, which in turn seems to need a planet or moon.

**The spacecraft Galileo** was launched on a mission to Jupiter in 1989 and reached the planet in 1995. Scientific data gathered during Galileo's two-year orbit of Jupiter will provide astronomers with clues about the possibility of life on the giant planet.

## The search for life

Equipped with instruments that could detect signs of life, spacecraft have already explored more than 70 planets, satellites, asteroids, and comets. None has shown compelling indications of extraterrestrial life.

Beginning in the 1960's, for example, the United States and the Soviet Union sent missions to Venus. They found that environmental conditions on the surface of Venus could not support life as we know it.

Mars, the nearest planet whose surface scientists can see, has an atmosphere, polar icecaps, seasonal changes, and a 24-hour-and-37-minute day. Mars seemed to be the most likely place to support life. In 1976, two U.S. space probes, Viking 1 and Viking 2, landed on Mars and performed experiments to test for life. These experiments found no likely signs of life in Martian soil, and a highly sensitive chemical detector failed to detect any organic compounds.

The Vikings' findings suggest that Mars, today at least, is lifeless. But some scientists suggest that about 4 billion years ago, conditions on Mars may have favored life. The planet's surface is covered with evidence of ancient rivers and lakes. In addition, the Martian climate was much warmer and wetter about 4 billion years ago. These facts suggest that life may have once existed on Mars. As a result, a number of scientists agree that any future exploration of Mars should include a search for fossils—evidence of ancient life—in addition to existing life.

A 746-pound probe from the Galileo spacecraft, which was launched in 1989, plunged into Jupiter on December 7, 1995. The probe sent back to Galileo 75 minutes of weather and chemical data. After receiving the data, Galileo entered orbit around Jupiter for two years of study. The mission could give the best view ever of the planet's composition. Scientists believe that Jupiter is primarily made up of the main elements of the primordial mix. Could there be life on Jupiter? Scientists will have to stay tuned.

While scientists wait to find out about Jupiter, they are happy to report that Galileo has made other important contributions. Along its journey, the spacecraft made close-up observations of our own planet. And in December 1990, it detected life on Earth. While this may not seen like news, it is a tremendously significant observation. Galileo's findings proved that remote-sensing spacecraft can detect life at various stages of evolutionary development. These results help assure scientists that their methods would effectively spot signs of life in other parts of the universe. And, since scientists have not yet found such evidence, they can say with some certainty that widespread biological activity, at least today, exists on Earth—and nowhere else.

## Other planetary systems

The findings of the Hubble Space Telescope have suggested to exobiologists that many of the stars in the Milky Way may have planetary systems. And some of those planets may have extraterrestrial life. In January 1996, two scientists revealed that they had evidence of only the second and third planets found to exist outside the solar system. And both seem to be temperate enough to allow liquid water to exist. In addition, the scientists said, the two planets would be close enough to their suns to soak up the rays needed for life. The scientists are looking forward to the installation of a new infrared camera on the Hubble Space Telescope. Planned for 1997, the camera could take pictures of at least one of the newly unveiled worlds.

The first of the two giant planets orbits a star known as 47 Ursae Majoris, 200 trillion miles from Earth in the Big Dipper. It is about twice the size of Jupiter. The second circles the star 70 Virginis in the constellation Virgo, and it is more than six times the mass of Jupiter.

Given today's technology, there is no way to say for sure that life exists on these planets. But if our solar system is an example, giant, volatile planets are likely to be accompanied by small, amicable ones. Giant planets also tend to keep company with giant moons, which too could be well suited for life. Probably the most important conclusion that can be made from the planets' discoveries is that the Milky Way is probably filled with other worlds waiting to be discovered. And NASA has unveiled plans to further search for those worlds. Known as the Origins project, the plan is to build a new generation of space telescopes.

Some scientists are now using radio telescopes, sophisticated receivers, and modern data analysis to detect communication signals from distant civilizations. These methods will only prove successful, however, if our extraterrestrial neighbors include intelligent beings capable of communicating with humans across the vast reaches of space. Known as the Search for Extraterrestrial Intelligence (SETI), this ongoing effort has taken many forms. The most recent is BETA (Billion-channel Extra-Terrestrial Assay), which consists of an 84 foot, dish-shaped antenna. The antenna sweeps across the sky, capturing radio waves. Funded by NASA until 1993, SETI is now privately funded.

A few unmanned spacecraft carry greetings from planet Earth, so that if one is found some day by another civilization, its origin will be more obvious. Pioneer 10 and Pioneer 11 each carry a small metal plaque that shows a man and woman offering greetings and also describes graphically the location of Earth. Voyager 1 and Voyager 2 each carry a 12 inch disk containing digitized images and sounds specially selected to portray the diversity of life on Earth.

**Clouds and ozone** were detected in Mars' atmosphere by the Hubble Telescope. Their presence indicates that the planet's climate has changed since the 1970's. Such climate changes suggest that Mars may once have been a very different place than it is today. In fact, astronomers believe that about 4 billion years ago, conditions on Mars may have been capable of supporting life.

# Asteroids, meteors, and comets

In addition to the sun and the planets (with their satellites), the solar system contains many smaller objects: asteroids, or minor planets; meteors, some of which collide with the surface of the earth as meteorites; and comets. Asteroids, or more accurately, planetoids, are relatively small planetary bodies.

## Asteroids

Various theories have been proposed about the origin and position of asteroids. One theory suggests that a substantial body was smashed by a planetary collision to leave the large number of assorted fragments that remain today. Another theory proposes that the asteroids acquired their present forms through the condensation of solar gas in the early stages of the sun's formation.

Apart from most asteroids, which lie in the belt between the orbits of Mars and Jupiter, there are other groups of minor planets, each with its own characteristic orbit. The Trojan asteroids, for example, keep to the same orbital path as Jupiter. There are two separate groups—the Achilles group, located about 500 million miles (800 million kilometers) ahead of the planet, and the Patroclus group, at an average of the same distance behind it—both held in these "Lagrangian" positions by Jupiter's gravitational influence. The Trojans are believed to have been satellites of Jupiter (when it was about 20 times more massive than it presently is) that escaped the planet's gravitational field to fall into the position they now occupy in Jupiter's orbit. These asteroids range in average diameter from 2 to 60 miles (3 to 97 kilometers).

Most asteroids do not remain as close to Jupiter as the Trojans, because the perturbations they receive from their proximity to the planet cause their orbits to change. There are specific distances from Jupiter where few asteroids are found, such as 2.1 and 2.5 astronomical units. These relatively barren areas are called Kirkwood gaps and may be the result of an interaction with Jupiter, because these distances correspond to orbital periods that are rational multiples of Jupiter's orbital period.

Another group of asteroids that do not lie in the main belt is the Apollo group, which passes within the earth's orbit for a short period as their orbits take them closer to the sun. The Apollo-Amor group of asteroids appear to be remnants of comets whose volatile material has been consumed through repeated interaction with the inner solar system. All that is left of them are their dark, solid nuclei orbiting the sun.

Chiron, the asteroid discovered by Charles Kowal in 1977, may herald a group of remnants from the outer solar system. For much of its orbit, Chiron stays between the orbits of Saturn and Uranus, but for about one-sixth of the time it orbits closer to the sun than Saturn.

Most asteroids appear to be irregular in shape. Variations in the light reflected by several of them indicate that they are elongated bodies that tumble in orbit. The rotation periods of irregular asteroids can be determined by plotting their light curves. One asteroid known to be irregular in shape is 433 Eros, discovered by Carl Witt in 1898. Eros makes close approaches to earth, and at one such approach (in 1931), its elongated shape was observed telescopically by the astronomers Finsen and van den Bos.

Another explanation for the variability in light is the suggestion that some asteroids have satellite companions, such as 532 Herculina—a binary asteroid. It was observed that in 1978, Herculina occluded a star, and shortly afterward there was a second dimming of the star, which indicated that Herculina has a companion.

The brightness of an asteroid depends on its size and its *albedo,* or the fraction of sunlight it reflects. The amount of light reflected in turn depends on the composition of the asteroid. Two basic compositions of asteroids are known: the larger group consists of dark objects and are assumed to be composed of carbonaceous chondrites. The second, smaller group is brighter and reddish in color. This type is rich in silicates.

Ceres, the biggest asteroid, has been calculated to be about 600 miles (970 kilometers) across.

## Meteors and meteorites

The breakup of a comet produces a swarm of particles spread out along its orbital path. If one of these particles, or any of the millions of dust grains orbiting the sun, strays too close to the earth, it is pulled down by gravity through the atmosphere and generally burned up, destroyed by friction with the air. The usual result is a brilliant streak of light moving across the night sky—known as a meteor, or more commonly, a shooting star. Meteors are not stars, however, and only their appearance has given rise to their common name.

Meteor particles (meteoroids) orbit the sun in elongated orbits, often in random planes. Earth passes through these orbital paths at certain times of the year, when meteor showers can be seen. Due to the effect of perspective, each meteor in a shower appears to radiate from the same point in the sky, called the radiant, usually named after the constellation

**Few meteorites** leave noticeable evidence of their impact on earth, but the iron meteor that struck northeast Arizona about 15,000 to 50,000 years ago left a crater 4,150 feet (1,265 meters) across and 570 feet (174 meters) deep.

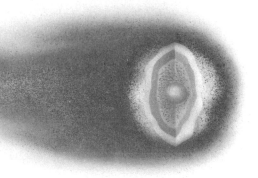

in which the point is located. For example, the Leonid shower radiant is in the constellation of Leo. All the meteors in a particular shower travel in parallel paths.

Those meteors that are not members of a meteor shower are known as sporadics and are visible at any time of the year, because they orbit around the sun in the same direction as the planets and near the ecliptic plane.

Most meteoroids disintegrate completely, but some are sufficiently large to partly survive the fall to the earth. These objects are known as meteorites, and certain features on the surface of the earth bear testimony to past meteoric impacts. One of the best-known examples is the large meteorite crater in northeast Arizona, which was created by an impact that occurred many thousands of years ago.

Meteorites are classified into two major types: iron (siderite) and stony (aerolite). Iron meteorites are thought to be remnants of the metallic core of a planet that has broken up. Stony meteorites are made up of various rocks and minerals. The mineral composition of these meteorites suggests that they may once have formed part of the outer layers of a planetary body.

## Comets

Awesome though comets are, they are fairly unimportant members of the solar system. A typical comet is made up of three main parts: the nucleus, coma, and tail. Most of the comet's mass is concentrated in the nucleus, which comprises a mixture of the ice and snow of various frozen materials, together with a large proportion of dust. The vaporization of matter from the nucleus results in the appearance of the coma.

Most comets form several tails containing both dust and plasma. They always point away from the sun and can reach lengths of more than 100 million miles (160 million kilometers).

Comets are classified according to their orbital periods. Short-period comets have periods that range from 3 to 25 years. About 80 of these have been observed on repeated occasions.

Intermediate-period comets have periods of between 25 and 200 years. The most notable example is Halley's Comet. It has a period of 76 to 79 years, and recorded observations of it go back as far as 240 B.C. In this century, it was seen in 1910 and in 1986.

Long-period comets have very elongated orbits that carry them up to 10,000 astronomical units from the sun. Some 450 examples have been observed.

In 1950, Jan Oort put forth the theory that a great number of comets originate in a vast, spherical cloud surrounding the solar system. Comets are released from the cloud and pushed toward the inner regions of the solar system by the gravitational perturbations of passing stars. Astronomers cannot actually observe the cloud, however, and its existence is based only on theory. Another suggestion is that in its orbit, the sun encounters clouds of gas and dust and when going through these clouds, its gravitational pull attracts particles from the cloud that follow it in its orbit. These particles accrete to form the nucleus of a comet.

**A comet** consists of its nucleus, coma, and tails. The nucleus—usually less than 10 miles (16 kilometers) in diameter—stores gas and dust in a mixture of ice and snow. It vaporizes as it approaches the sun to form the coma, and matter spread out behind the comet makes up the tails.

# Earth as a planet

Earth is the fifth largest planet in the solar system and the third out from the sun. Its position relative to the sun is such that the overall surface temperature is neither too hot nor too cold for life to exist upon it. Also, its mass and gravity are of the right size to provide a layer of gases, the atmosphere, which screen out harmful solar radiation.

The earth itself is basically a slightly flattened sphere, although satellite observations have shown its shape to be somewhat more complex, with the polar radius being 26 miles (42 kilometers) less than the equatorial radius. It rotates on its axis once every 23.9 hours and orbits the sun once every 365 days, 6 hours, 9 minutes, and 9.54 seconds; the axis is tilted by 23.44° to this orbit. The earth's atmosphere reflects back into space about 25 per cent of the light it receives from the sun, so that to an observer near the sun, the earth would appear as a point of light to magnitude −3.8.

Only 30 per cent of the earth's surface crust is visible, the rest being covered by liquid water. The rigid crustal layer is composed mainly of oxygen and silicon and is segmented into a number of plates. These are only about 20 miles (32 kilometers) thick, but thousands of square miles in extent. They are in constant motion, "floating" on the underlying mantle. Seismic evidence and the existence of a weak magnetic field around the earth suggests that its center consists of a nickel-iron core.

### The atmospheric zones

The earth's atmosphere is composed of a mixture of gases and can be considered as a series of layers that extend from the surface up to a nominal height of about 1,000 miles (1,600 kilometers). Its overall chemical composition is 78 per cent molecular nitrogen and 21 per cent oxygen, the balance being made up of traces of gases such as carbon dioxide and water vapor. Although vast in extent, the low density of the atmospheric constituents implies that its mass makes up only one-billionth of the earth's total mass.

The lowest level, in which our weather occurs, is the troposphere, which varies in depth from less than 6 miles (10 kilometers) near the poles to 10 miles (16 kilometers) at the tropics. Above this layer is the stratosphere, which contains the ultraviolet-absorbing ozone layer. The temperature in this layer is about −67° F. (−55° C) near the tropopause, at a height of around 6 miles (10 kilometers) above the earth's surface, but rises to nearly 28° F. (−2° C) at about 50 miles (80 kilometers) above the surface, in the mesosphere. Above the mesosphere, from an altitude of about 50 miles (80 kilometers), are the rarefied layers of the thermosphere, so called because of the higher temperature of this zone. Ionization takes place at these heights; it is caused by the most energetic photons from the sun, such as X rays, being absorbed by gas molecules and releasing free electrons. This results in the observed rise in temperature. The free electrons in the ionosphere, between about 150 and 450 miles (240 and 720 kilometers) above the earth's surface, are capable of reflecting radio waves of more than a few meters in wavelength, and this phenomenon permits radio transmissions over large distances on the earth.

### The surface and interior of the earth

The surface layer of the earth, the crust, has an average thickness of 20 miles (32 kilometers) over the continental areas. But it is much thinner (only about 5 miles [8 kilometers]) in the regions under the oceans. The crust is composed chiefly of igneous rocks, with an average density of about 190 pounds per cubic foot, which is about 40 per cent less than that of the underlying layer, the mantle. Details of the earth's interior have been deduced by seismological studies that indicate the existence of a boundary between the crust and mantle known as the Mohorovičić discontinuity. Below this boundary, the density steadily increases to about 300 pounds per cubic foot. Although solid, the mantle is also reasonably plastic. There is a region known as the asthenosphere that may well be fluid enough to transport, by means of convection currents, some of the heat produced within it by radioactive decay. These currents may, in turn, be responsible for the movement of the crustal plates over the surface, in the process called plate tectonics.

The mantle comes to an abrupt end at the Weichert, or Gutenberg, discontinuity, which lies at a depth of 1,800 miles (2,900 kilometers). At this level, the density suddenly increases to 625 pounds per cubic foot, which marks the boundary of the earth's outer core. Seismic

**Seen from space,** Earth appears as a blue planet, with parts of it obscured by swirling white clouds.

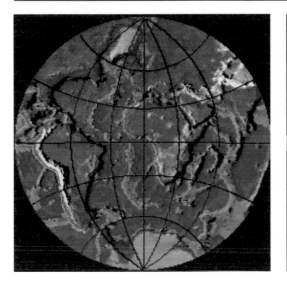

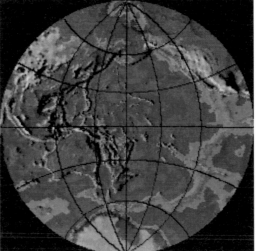

Earth's topography can be presented as a false-color map, similar to those compiled for Venus and other planets using radar scanning. The dark blue areas correspond to the ocean depths, with high mountains represented in white. The smallest details discernible are about 60 miles (100 kilometers) across.

data indicate that it is composed of an extremely dense liquid. Finally, the innermost central core of the earth occurs at a depth of around 3,200 miles (5,150 kilometers) from the surface and is thought to consist of solid nickel and iron with a temperature of around 9000° F. (5000° C).

### The earth's magnetic field

The most likely process responsible for the earth's weak magnetic field is called the self-exciting dynamo effect. It is generally believed that a combination of the earth's rotation and the convective currents within it provide a means whereby the molten iron outer core can generate electric currents. These produce the observed magnetic field. The magnetic field has, however, shown substantial changes over geological time. Analyses of ocean-floor igneous rocks reveal that the north magnetic pole and the south magnetic pole periodically reverse over a time scale of a few hundred thousand years. On a shorter time scale, in the order of a few centuries, the magnetic poles "wander" slightly and change position. It is postulated that the liquid nature of the outer core may also be responsible for these motions.

### Radiation belts

The earth's magnetic field also affects highly charged particles from deep space called cosmic rays. These particles are trapped by the magnetic field, forming two barrel-shaped regions. The boundaries of these belts are not

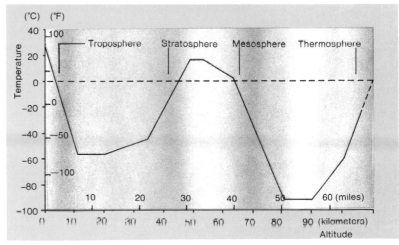

sharp but the inner one extends from about 600 miles (1,000 kilometers) to 3,000 miles (5,000 kilometers) above the earth, and the outer one extends from about 9,300 miles (15,500 kilometers) to about 15,000 miles (25,000 kilometers). They are called the Van Allen belts, after the scientist who discovered them in 1958.

The pressure of the particles from the sun squashes the earth's magnetic field into a hemispherical cap on the sunward side, trailing it off on the opposite side into a long tail that stretches back beyond the moon's orbit. This region is known as the magnetosphere, and it is only beyond this protective sheath that interplanetary space begins.

The temperature of the earth's atmosphere varies with altitude. In the troposphere, temperature falls rapidly up to a height of about 6 miles (10 kilometers). It rises again in the upper stratosphere, only to fall to less than −150° F. (−100° C) in the mesosphere, at 50 miles (80 kilometers) altitude. In the thermosphere and beyond, the temperature rapidly increases.

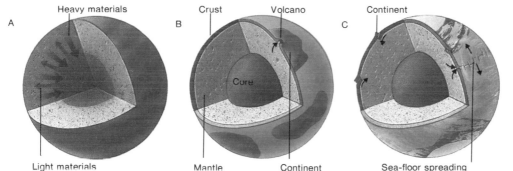

Early in the earth's history (A), when it was less than 100 million years old, light materials rose toward the surface and heavy ones sank. The light ones formed the crust (B) and the heavy ones the core. The crust then broke into plates (C) that "drift," carrying the continents.

# The moon

The moon is the nearest celestial object to earth and the only one on which a manned spacecraft has landed. For these reasons, scientists today probably know more about the moon than any other heavenly body.

In the entire solar system, the moon is the second largest satellite in terms of mass relative to its parent planet: its mass is about $\frac{1}{81}$ of the earth's. In comparison, the proportionally largest satellite is Charon, which is about $\frac{1}{6}$ as massive as its governing planet, Pluto. (Ganymede, the most massive satellite in absolute terms, has a mass only about $\frac{1}{12,800}$ that of Jupiter.) The moon's equatorial diameter is 2,160 miles (3,476 kilometers), more than a quarter that of earth.

Because of the moon's low absolute mass, its gravity (and, therefore, escape velocity) is also low—about $\frac{1}{6}$ that of the earth. As a result, the moon has virtually no atmosphere—except for minute traces of hydrogen, helium, argon, and neon. The lack of an atmosphere—and of water—means that the lunar terrain has been (and still is) shaped by forces other than the forces of erosion (wind and rain, for example) that constantly change the earth's surface features. Instead, the moon's surface has been fashioned principally by volcanic activity and by the impact of meteorites. Because the

moon lacks an appreciable atmosphere, these meteorites are not burnt up as they approach the planet—unlike the meteors that enter the earth's atmosphere.

### The origin of the moon

Despite the American Apollo and Soviet Lunokhod missions to the moon in the late 1960's and early 1970's, and the many centuries of detailed scientific investigations carried out from terrestrial observatories, the origin of the moon remains a mystery.

According to one theory, the fission hypothesis (which was first put forward in 1879 by the British astronomer Sir George Darwin), the moon was originally part of the earth. In the early phases of the development of the solar system, while the planets were still hot and fluid, the primordial earth was rotating so rapidly that it became distended and eventually threw off a spherical globule, which became the moon. Although not part of the original theory, it has even been suggested that the present-day Pacific Ocean represents the enormous hollow left when the moon broke away from the earth. There are, however, several problems with the fission hypothesis. Scientists have calculated that for fissioning to occur, the primordial earth would have had to spin about eight times faster than it does at present, which is generally thought to be impossible. Furthermore, the earth and moon have different densities and chemical compositions, factors that make a common origin extremely unlikely.

The binary accretion hypothesis—similar in some respects to the fission theory—maintains that particles spun off from the rapidly-rotating, primordial earth and later condensed to form the moon. The objections to this hypothesis are basically the same as those to the fission theory. The primordial earth is unlikely to have been spinning fast enough to eject particles, and the different compositions and densities of the earth and moon indicate that they originated separately (although analysis of lunar rocks suggests that the earth and moon were formed at about the same time).

A more probable related origin theory is the precipitation hypothesis. According to this theory, energy released by the condensation of the primordial earth heated the thick cloud of dust that then surrounded the planet, simultaneously transforming the dust into various

**Moon's statistics**
Equatorial diameter:
    2,160 miles (3,476 kilometers)
Mass: 0.0123 (Earth = 1)
Mean relative density: 3.34
Surface gravity: 0.17 (Earth = 1)
Escape velocity: 1.5 miles (2.4 kilometers) per second
Distance from Earth
    farthest: 252,711 miles (406,699 kilometers)
    nearest: 221,456 miles (356,399 kilometers)
    mean: 238,857 miles (384,403 kilometers)
Orbital period:
    27d., 7h., 43min.
Rotational period:
    27d., 7h., 43min.
Inclination of orbit to ecliptic: 5°

**The moon orbits the earth** which, in turn, orbits the sun (A); as a result, the moon also orbits the sun (B). In fact, the moon's primary orbit is around the sun because the gravitational attraction between the sun and moon is greater than that between the earth and moon. The moon orbits the earth once every 27.3 days; therefore, it moves through $\frac{1}{6}$ of a complete revolution approximately every $4\frac{1}{2}$ days (B, 1 to 7). But while the moon is orbiting the earth, the latter is also moving around the sun (about once every 365 days), hence the moon traces out an oscillating path around the sun.

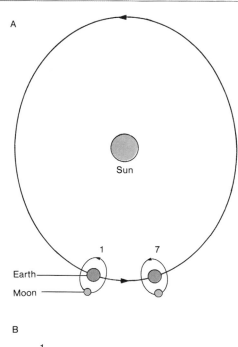

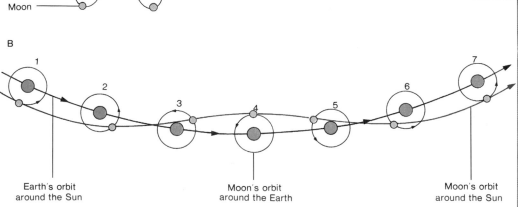

**The near side of the moon** *(far left)*, shown with north at the top, is the only face visible from earth. It has many large maria (the dark regions), mostly in the Northern Hemisphere; the rayed crater in the Southern Hemisphere is Tycho. On the *near left* is a satellite photograph showing part of the near side (to the left of the picture) and part of the normally unobservable far side.

metals and metal oxides—a process that explains the density and composition differences between the earth and moon. Shortly afterward, the transformed dust cooled and condensed to form the moon.

The fourth main lunar origin theory ignores the exact process by which the moon was formed and concentrates instead on explaining how the earth acquired its satellite. According to this last theory—the lunar capture hypothesis—the primordial earth and moon condensed into planets in different parts of the solar system (which explains their different densities and compositions). The theory also postulates that the moon's orbit brought it close enough to the earth to be captured (possibly after having been slowed down by passing through the dust cloud then surrounding the earth), thereby becoming a satellite.

Of these four principal theories of the origin of the moon, the last two are the more credible, although none provides an entirely satisfactory explanation.

### The orbit of the moon

The gravitational attraction between the sun and moon is about twice as strong as that between the earth and the moon. The overall effect of these two forces is that the moon has a primary orbit around the sun, superimposed on which is its elliptical orbit around the earth. The sun also influences the shape and orientation of the moon's secondary orbit around the earth. One of the most marked of these effects is the periodic rotation of the entire lunar orbit, which moves around the earth (in the same direction as the earth's rotation) with a period of 8.85 years.

The moon always presents the same "side" toward the earth. This is because the moon's rotation is synchronous—that is, the time taken for it to complete one rotation about its axis is the same as that taken for it to orbit once around the earth. But because the moon's axial rotation rate is constant, whereas its orbital speed is not (a phenomenon caused by the elliptical shape of its orbit), and because its orbit is inclined at 5° to the plane of the earth's orbit, it is possible to see about 59 per cent of the moon's total surface area from earth. The other 41 per cent remained unknown until 1959,

when the Soviet spacecraft *Luna 3* took the first photographs of the moon's far side.

### The surface of the moon

The lunar surface can be divided into two main regions: highlands, which cover about 85 per cent of the moon's total surface area, and plains (called maria), which cover the remaining 15 per cent. The formation of these two types of terrain is intimately connected with the evolution of the moon itself.

About 4.6 billion years ago, the moon was a hot, fluid mass. As it cooled, relatively low density matter rose to the surface and solidified, forming a primordial crust. After the crust had been formed, it was heavily bombarded by meteorites and other celestial debris (of which there was a much larger amount in the solar system than there is now), which gave rise to the impact craters and other surface features characteristic of the rugged highland terrain.

The era of heavy bombardment ended about 3.9 billion years ago and was followed by a period of intense volcanic activity, during which the maria were formed. Some of the earlier bombardments created vast basins, which became flooded with lava from the lunar volcanoes. When the lava in the basins cooled, it left large, smooth plains—the maria.

After the volcanic activity, which ended

**The moon** is seen in different phases as it orbits the earth. From new moon (1), when it cannot be seen, our satellite waxes successively through crescent (2), first quarter (3), gibbous (4), and full moon (5), then wanes through gibbous (6), third, or last, quarter (7), crescent (8), and back to new moon.

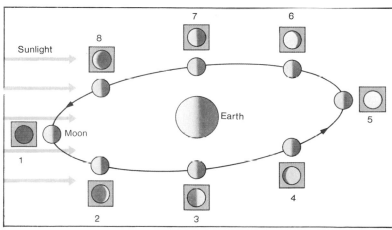

**Part of the Southern Hemisphere** of the moon's far side is shown in this color-composite image taken by the Clementine probe. The large dark red-gray region is the South Pole-Aitken Basin, a multiring basin several billion years old. A multiring basin is formed when a violent impact from a large asteroid or other object folds the surface into several circular mountain ranges centered on the point of collision. The Aitken Basin is enormous, extending about 1,700 miles (2,700 kilometers) from rim to rim.

about 3.2 billion years ago, the lunar surface appeared much as it does today, apart from craters formed by subsequent meteorite impacts.

### The interior of the moon

Although the lunar surface shows no obvious signs of activity, the interior of the moon is still hot (a discovery made by means of heat-flow experiments carried out by the American *Apollo 15* and *Apollo 17* missions) because of the presence of subsurface radioactive material. The Apollo missions also found that about 3,000 tremors ("moonquakes") occur every year. By investigating these moonquakes, selenologists (who specialize in studying the moon) have determined the moon's inner structure.

The crust extends to a depth of about 31 miles (50 kilometers) on the near side of the moon and to about 40 miles (65 kilometers) on the far side. It consists of several layers. Down to a depth of a few miles is the regolith, comprising the shattered remnants of bedrock that

was broken up by meteorite bombardment. The thickness and composition of this region varies from highlands to maria; the highlands are composed mainly of anorthesite, whereas the maria are chiefly basaltic.

At about 12 miles (20 kilometers) below the surface, the upper crust's composition changes, becoming similar to that of the surface highlands. Below the crust is a layer of denser material that extends to a depth of about 90 miles (150 kilometers), where the lithosphere begins. Moonquakes originate within this region, at a depth of about 600 miles (1,000 kilometers). Under the lithosphere is the asthenosphere, the partly-molten outer core. Finally, at the center of the moon, is the molten inner core, which is about 900 miles (1,500 kilometers) across.

An interesting feature of the moon's interior was discovered in 1968 as a result of unexpected variations in the orbital velocity of the American probe *Orbiter 5*. The cause was found to be localized subsurface areas of abnormally high density. Called mass concentrations, or mascons, these regions may have formed as a result of lava from the outer core rising through cracks in the lithosphere (these cracks possibly having resulted from a large meteorite impact early in the moon's history) and then solidifying into localized high-density masses just below the surface.

### The moon and the tides

It has been known since antiquity that the tides on earth and the positions of the moon are related in some way. However, scientists were not able to explain the phenomenon until Isaac Newton published his theory of gravitation in 1687. It was then found that both the moon and the sun play a part in producing the tides: the moon produces about 54 per cent of the tide-raising effect, and the sun, the remaining 46 per cent.

The tides are probably best explained by considering the earth to be a solid sphere covered by a layer of water. The moon's gravita-

**In the formation of an impact crater** (*right, top*), a meteorite hits the surface (A) and explodes violently, ejecting surface material at great speed. Then heavier, slower-moving particles from the bottom of the crater are thrown up (B). Finally, the ejected material falls back to the surface (C), forming a raised ring around the crater. Volcanic craters (*right, bottom*) were created when hot magma forced its way upwards, cracking the surface layers (D). Hot gases then escaped through the cracks (E), as a result of which the magma cooled and receded, leaving a subsurface cavity. Lacking support, the surface collapsed (F), thereby forming a crater.

Impact crater formation

A          B          C

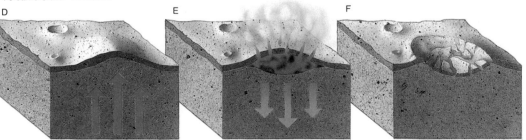

Volcanic crater formation

D          E          F

**Man first landed on the moon** in July 1969, when two astronauts on the American Apollo 11 mission set foot on our satellite. Conditions on the surface are harsh; there is neither water nor an appreciable atmosphere, and temperatures vary between about 260° F. (127° C) during the day and −280° F. (−173° C) at night. The terrain is stark, virtually colorless, and rugged, being covered with numerous craters, vast dusty maria, and mountainous highlands.

tional attraction is greatest on the water on the part of the earth facing the moon. This attraction causes the water to bulge slightly toward the moon—a high tide. On the opposite side of the earth, the moon's gravitational attraction is at a minimum. But the solid earth, being nearer the moon, is attracted more than the water, which is therefore "left behind"; the effect is to produce a second bulge (and thus another high tide) on the opposite side of the earth.

During the earth's daily rotation, the tidal bulges move with the moon so that one bulge is always at the part of the earth nearest the moon and the second is directly opposite. The overall effect is to cause a high tide—and a low tide—every 12.42 hours. The tides do not recur at exactly 12-hour intervals because, in addition to the earth's rotation, the moon is orbiting the earth and is not in the same position on consecutive days. The sun also produces two tidal bulges that move around the earth approximately every 24 hours; these tides are

about half the amplitude of the lunar tides because of the sun's lesser tide-raising effect. When sun, moon, and earth are directly in line—at every full and new moon—the solar and lunar tides reinforce each other, producing larger than average tides (called spring tides). The sun's tidal influence is at its least during the first and third quarters of the moon, when the moon is at right angles to the line of the earth and sun. In this situation, the solar and lunar tides partly cancel each other, producing smaller than average tides (neap tides).

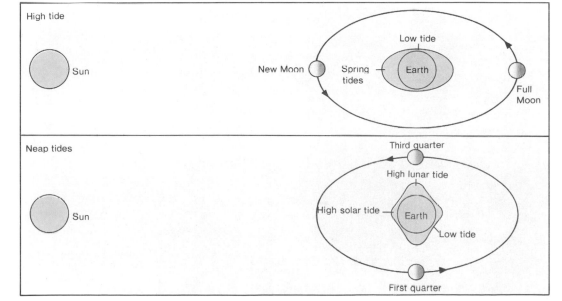

**The earth's tides** are caused by the gravitational attractions of both the moon and sun. Larger than normal (spring) tides *(left, top)* are produced when the sun, moon, and earth are in line (at every full and new moon) because the tide-raising effects of the sun and moon reinforce each other. Smaller than normal (neap) tides *(left, bottom)* occur at the first and third quarters of the moon, when the sun and moon's tide-raising effects partly cancel each other.

# Eclipses

An eclipse occurs when a celestial body becomes totally or partly darkened. The sun is eclipsed when the moon comes between it and the earth. The moon is eclipsed when it passes into the shadow cast by the earth.

### Solar eclipses

By a fortunate coincidence, unique in the solar system, the moon appears to be the same size as the sun, so it can completely obscure the sun when it passes directly between the earth and the sun. There are three types of solar eclipses: total, partial, and annular eclipses. Which of these is seen depends on the position of the earth (and of the observer on earth) in relation to the moon's shadow.

The moon's orbit is elliptical, hence its apparent size varies as its distance from earth changes. Similarly, the apparent size of the sun varies as a result of the earth's elliptical orbit. A total eclipse is possible only when the apparent sizes of the sun and moon are such that the moon is large enough to completely obscure the bright disk of the sun (called the photosphere). But the area of the main shadow cone (the umbra) cast by the moon is relatively small, so a total eclipse is visible from only a limited area of the earth. As the moon orbits the earth and the earth rotates on its axis, the umbra passes across the earth, sweeping out a narrow band (the belt of totality) from which the total eclipse is visible. The belt of totality is widest (up to a maximum of 170 miles (274 kilometers) across) when the moon is closest to earth and the sun is at aphelion (its greatest distance from earth).

On either side of the belt of totality is a second region, from which a partial eclipse can be seen. This area is the zone swept out by the penumbra of the moon's shadow and is considerably larger than the belt of totality. A partial eclipse can also occur without a total eclipse. This happens when the sun, moon, and earth are not exactly in line, so that only the moon's penumbra passes across the earth, the umbra missing our planet entirely.

An annular eclipse occurs when the earth lies beyond the tip of the moon's umbra. In this situation, the moon is too small to completely obscure the sun's photosphere, which therefore appears as a bright ring around the moon.

Several impressive phenomena can be seen during solar eclipses. During totality (which lasts for a maximum of eight minutes, and is usually much shorter), the glare of the photosphere is concealed and the sun's atmosphere—the corona, which is normally invisible—appears as a spectacular halo. Just before totality, the thin crescent of the photosphere suddenly becomes broken up by the irregular surface features at the "edge" of the moon, thereby making the sun's crescent look like a series of bright beads—a phenomenon called Baily's beads. And, as the sun slowly reappears from behind the moon, there is a brief, dramatic flare of light from one side— the "diamond ring" effect.

### Lunar eclipses

Lunar eclipses occur when the earth passes directly between the sun and the moon. The length of the earth's umbral shadow cone is more than three times the average distance between the moon and the earth, so the shadow is relatively wide at the point where the moon crosses it. As a result, lunar eclipses last a comparatively long time (totality may last up to a maximum of 1 hour 40 minutes).

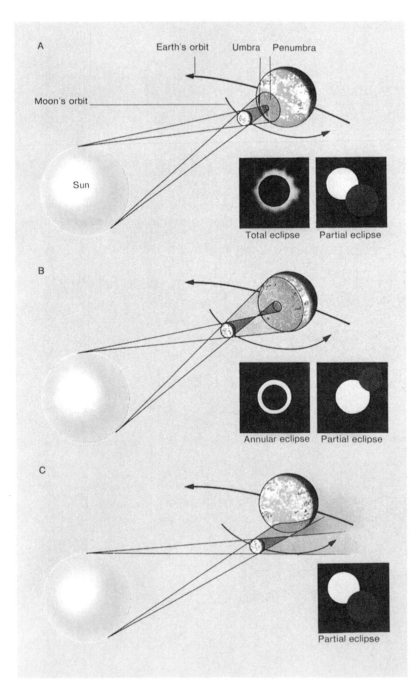

A — Earth's orbit — Umbra — Penumbra — Moon's orbit — Sun

Total eclipse — Partial eclipse

B

Annular eclipse — Partial eclipse

C

Partial eclipse

**Solar eclipses** are of three main types. In A, the moon's umbra reaches the earth and an observer within it sees a total eclipse; to each side (in the penumbra) there is a partial eclipse. In B, the umbra falls short of the earth, resulting in an annular eclipse; there is a partial eclipse in the penumbra. In C, only part of the penumbra reaches earth, resulting in a partial eclipse.

Three types of lunar eclipses are possible, depending on the orientation of the moon's orbit relative to the earth's shadow. A total lunar eclipse occurs when all of the moon passes through the umbra (it also passes through the penumbra both before and after totality). In a partial eclipse, the entire moon passes through the penumbra, but only part of it passes through the umbra. And in a penumbral eclipse, the moon passes through only the penumbra.

The moon is not invisible during an eclipse, even during totality, because the earth's atmosphere refracts light from the sun into the umbra and on to the lunar surface. Atmospheric conditions on earth affect the amount and color of the refracted light, but generally, the moon is clearly visible and is a red-brown color during totality.

depending on the number of leap years) 8 hours. This is called the Saros cycle and can be used to predict both solar and lunar eclipses. The periodicity occurs because the sun, moon, and earth return to almost the same relative positions after every Saros period. But because the positions are not identical, every sequence of eclipse types ends after about 1,300 years, and a new sequence begins; at any one time, however, there are about 40 overlapping sequences. Because the Saros cycle is not an exact number of days, the successive eclipses in a sequence are not visible from the same place on earth.

### Occurrence of eclipses

Solar eclipses are more common than lunar eclipses, there being at least two solar eclipses every year (and as many as five in an exceptional year). In contrast, there are usually between zero and three lunar eclipses (most years have two) each year. At a given location, however, lunar eclipses are more frequent because every lunar eclipse is visible from the entire hemisphere of the earth facing the moon, whereas solar eclipses can be seen from only a very limited area. From any one point, a solar eclipse is visible only about once every 360 years.

Eclipses can occur only at new moon (for solar eclipses) and full moon (for lunar eclipses), but they do not occur every month because the moon's orbit is inclined to the ecliptic (the plane of the earth's orbit). Thus, seen from the earth, the moon usually passes above or below the sun (which precludes a solar eclipse) and similarly, passes above or below the earth's shadow (thereby precluding a lunar eclipse). Only when the moon is in the plane of the ecliptic, therefore, are eclipses possible.

It has been known since the time of the Babylonians that eclipses of the same type recur at an interval of 18 years 10 days (or 11,

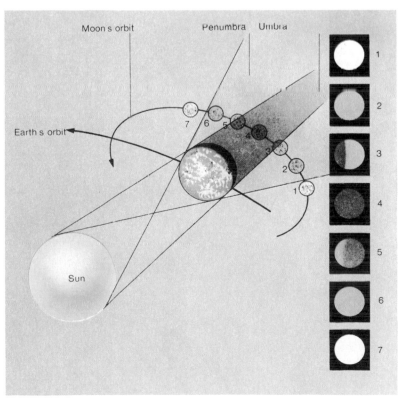

# Mercury

Mercury is the closest planet to the sun and the second smallest in the solar system. It has an extremely elliptical orbit, rivaling that of Pluto. Mercury's farthest distance from the sun (at aphelion) is 43,400,000 miles (69,800,000 kilometers), but at closest approach (perihelion), it is only 28,600,000 miles (46,000,000 kilometers) away—Earth, in comparison, orbits at three times that distance from the sun. Like Venus, Mercury shows phases.

### Observing Mercury

Because it is so close to the sun, the planet is difficult to see with the naked eye, appearing like a twinkling light near the horizon as a morning or evening star. Mercury is usually best seen in the Northern Hemisphere in the west at twilight in May, or just before sunrise in the east in November. These are the times at which Mercury reaches maximum elongation—the point farthest from the sun at the extreme east or west position in its orbit. But even at maximum elongation, the planet is never more than 28° from the sun. If favorably placed, Mercury can be seen during daytime through a telescope with an aperture of at least 3 inches (75 millimeters).

Mercury can also be observed when it crosses the sun's disk, when it is said to be in transit. Transits are relatively rare because Mercury's orbit is inclined appreciably (7°) to the ecliptic. They occur every 3 to 13 years, always in May (near perihelion) and November (near aphelion). November transits occur twice as frequently as those in May, although the May transits are longer, lasting almost nine hours. The first prediction of a transit of Mercury across the sun was made by Johannes Kepler for November 7, 1631. It was then observed by Pierre Gassendi in Milan. On Earth, an observer sees Mercury start crossing the sun's disk 43 seconds later than the actual event because the sun's gravitational field bends the light rays reflected from the planet. It was because of this fact that predictions of the transit were found to be several seconds late. This apparent discrepancy puzzled astronomers until 1915, when Albert Einstein proposed his general theory of relativity, in which he explained the effect of gravity on light rays.

### Mercury's rotation

In 1965, radar waves bounced off Mercury provided the first accurate measurement of

## Mercury's statistics

Equatorial diameter:
  3,031 miles (4,878 kilometers)
Mass: 0.056 (Earth = 1)
Mean relative density:
  5.42 (water = 1)
Surface gravity:
  0.386 (Earth = 1)
Escape velocity: 2.6 miles (4.2 kilometers) per second
Distance from sun:
  farthest: 43,400,000 miles (69,800,000 kilometers)
  nearest: 28,600,000 miles (46,000,000 kilometers)
  mean: 35,980,000 miles (57,900,000 kilometers)
Closest approach to Earth:
  57,000,000 miles (91,700,000 kilometers)
Orbital period:
  87.97 earth-days
Rotational period:
  59 earth-days

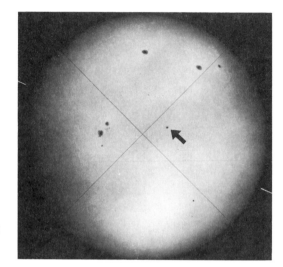

Mercury appears as a small black dot near the center of the sun's disk in this transit, which took place in 1970.

Mariner 10 was launched on a double space probe on November 3, 1973, to view Venus and Mercury. Mariner had to be programmed to pass near Venus to use its gravitational force to accelerate the probe into an elliptical orbit around the sun.

Mercury's orbit around the sun takes about 88 earth-days, during which time it rotates on its axis one-and-a-half times. Its "day" (from sunrise to sunrise) lasts about 176 earth-days, during which it makes three axial rotations and orbits twice around the sun. In the 180 days it took Mariner 10 to orbit once around the sun, Mercury had orbited twice.

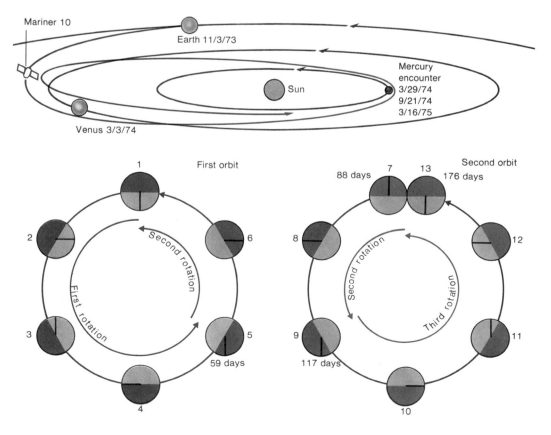

the planet's period of rotation. It was found to be 59 earth-days—19 days shorter than previously believed. During this time, it travels two-thirds of its orbit around the sun. All of the planet thus receives sunlight at some time; before this discovery, astronomers had for 75 years thought that Mercury had a captive rotation and always presented the same face to the sun, with one side of the planet in perpetual darkness. This was supposed to be due to the planet's proximity to the huge mass of the sun with its high gravitational attraction. It is now known that Mercury's "day" (from one sunrise to the next) lasts about 180 earth-days—a product of its comparatively slow rate of rotation and relatively swift orbit.

### Mariner 10's discoveries

In 1974, the United States launched Mariner 10 on a space probe to observe Mercury and Venus. The close-up photographs showed Mercury's surface for the first time, revealing it to be similar to the lunar landscape with a heavily cratered crust and lava-flooded plains. The argument as to whether these features were caused by meteoric bombardment or by volcanic activity remains unresolved.

The main impact feature is the Caloris Basin, or Caloris Planitia—similar in appearance to the moon's large maria. The Caloris Basin is so called because it is near a "hot pole" (one of two) in a region of the highest temperatures, around 650° F. (345° C). It is 800 miles (1,287 kilometers) in diameter and is ringed by smooth mountains that rise to about 6,600 feet (2,000 meters). On the opposite side of the planet from Caloris is a region of chaotic terrain, possibly formed by shock waves that resulted from the same impact that cre-

ated the Caloris Basin. Ray craters are also present; the largest—more than 25 miles (40 kilometers) in diameter—is the Kuiper Crater. These craters have bright streaks formed of surface deposits that radiate from the center to the walls of the crater. Other features include scarps (dorsa), possibly created as Mercury's core cooled and contracted, causing the silicate-rich crust to wrinkle.

One surprising discovery of Mariner 10 was that Mercury has an atmosphere, albeit a very tenuous one. A deep atmosphere would not be expected because Mercury has a low surface gravity—only about one-third that of Earth. Any atmospheric gases would long since have escaped into space. Mercury's "atmosphere" consists of gases, mostly helium, trapped from the passing solar wind by the planet's magnetic field. There are also minute traces of neon and argon, which could cause auroral displays in Mercury's night skies.

Because it has so little atmosphere, Mercury experiences extremes of temperature. Night temperatures can fall as low as −279° F. (−173° C), and day temperatures at perihelion can rise to more than 801° F. (427° C)—hot enough to melt tin and lead.

The discovery that Mercury has a magnetic field also came as a surprise. But the strength of this field is only about one per cent that of Earth. Mercury also has a magnetosphere, a region of magnetic influence in space that deflects the solar wind, causing it to curve around the planet. There are two magnetic poles, one at each end of the rotational axis.

**The surface of Mercury,** photographed by Mariner 10 on March 29, 1974, shows a similarity to that of the moon. The distribution of the craters resembles generally the pattern of those on the lunar surface. They tend to appear in pairs, groups, or lines, and some have central peaks. This view shows Mercury's northern hemisphere and was taken 48,350 miles (77,800 kilometers) from the planet. The "tear" along the horizon was caused by some data being lost in the composition of the photograph.

# Venus

As the second planet outward from the sun and the one that comes closest to earth, Venus superficially appears to be the twin of Earth. It has a similar mass and a similar radius to the earth. But that is the full extent of any similarity; Venus must be one of the most hostile environments of the whole of the solar system.

The planet's highly reflective atmosphere, together with its relative proximity to the sun, causes Venus to be the second brightest object in the night sky (next to the moon), with a magnitude of −4.4. Furthermore, because it is closer to the sun than is the earth, when viewed from the earth it exhibits a series of phases (like those of the moon), being "full" when it is farthest from us.

### The mysterious planet

Venus has been known since ancient times, but at first it was identified with two different objects, the Morning Star (Phosphorus) and the Evening Star (Hesperus). Later, it was recognized as a planet and named after the Roman goddess of love and beauty, equivalent to the Greek goddess Aphrodite. But only

since the explorations by Soviet and American space probes has much been revealed about the surface of the planet itself. The reason for this quickly becomes apparent when Venus is viewed through a low-powered telescope: it is completely shrouded in a dense, pale yellow layer of cloud. In an attempt to study the hidden structure of Venus, astronomers have used radio and radar observations and sent space probes to fly by, orbit, and even land on the planet. Because of its close approach to the earth, it was the first to which unmanned spacecraft were sent, the first fly-by being made by the American *Mariner 2* probe in 1962.

### Surface and atmosphere

Radio observations revealed that the surface of Venus must be very hot, a fact confirmed by the Soviet Venera probes. It is now thought that it has the hottest surface of any planet, at 864° F. (462° C). Early probes that attempted to land on the planet's surface were both scorched by the heat and crushed by the enormous atmospheric pressure of about 1,323 pounds per square inch (93 kilograms per square centimeter), 90 times that of Earth's atmosphere. In addition, Venus's atmosphere absorbs about 99 per cent of the sunlight that strikes the top of the clouds, 50 miles (80 kilometers) above the surface. Any sunlight that does reach the surface, however, is absorbed and re-emitted, heating up the clouds from below and producing a "greenhouse" effect, which leads to opacity of the atmosphere.

The atmosphere is made up almost entirely of carbon dioxide, with nitrogen and argon forming most of the remainder. Water vapor, hydrogen chloride, and hydrogen fluoride have also been detected. The clouds themselves are composed of droplets of concentrated sulfuric acid which, together with the high temperatures at the surface, seems to be the principal cause of erosion on the planet. Surface wind velocities are only a few miles per hour on average, although high in the

## Venus's statistics
Equatorial diameter:
7,521 miles
(12,104 kilometers)
Mass (Earth = 1): 0.815
Mean relative density: 5.25
Surface gravity: 0.879
(Earth = 1)
Escape velocity: 6.4 miles
(10.3 kilometers)
per second
Distance from sun:
farthest: 67,700,000 miles
(108,900,000 kilometers)
nearest: 66,800,000 miles
(107,500,000 kilometers)
mean: 67,230,000 miles
(108,200,000 kilometers)
Closest approach to Earth:
25,700,000 miles
(41,400,000 kilometers)
Orbital period:
224.7 earth-days
Rotational period:
243 earth-days
(retrograde)

**The thick cloud layer** that covers Venus can be clearly seen in the photograph (taken in ultraviolet). The curved dark trails indicate the great turbulence in the clouds, which rotate around the planet about once every four days.

**Venus,** seen from Earth, passes through different phases and also appears to change in diameter. When nearest to earth (A), Venus is "new" and invisible. As it orbits the sun (in an almost circular path), the distance between Venus and Earth first increases (A to E), reaches a maximum (E), then decreases (E to A); during this sequence, Venus appears in different phases. It is brightest when at the crescent phases (B and H) because it is close to Earth, and relatively dim when "full" (E) because it is farthest from Earth.

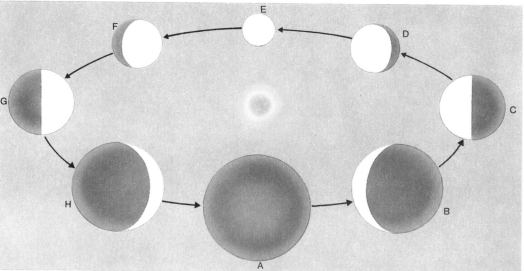

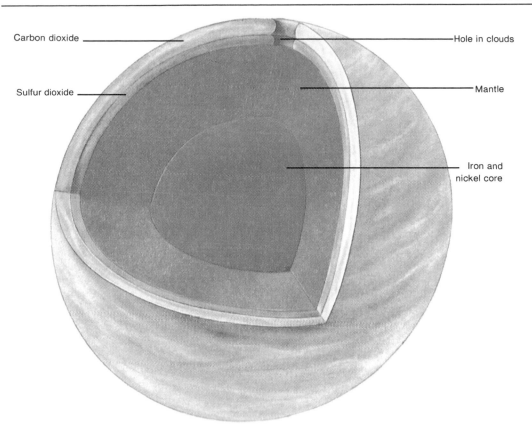

Carbon dioxide

Sulfur dioxide

Hole in clouds

Mantle

Iron and
nickel core

**The inner structure of Venus** is believed to resemble that of the earth, with a dense iron and nickel core surrounded by a mantle that is covered, in turn, by a thin crust. Above the surface, the lower atmosphere consists of sulfur dioxide, on top of which is a layer of carbon dioxide (the principal atmospheric constituent). Over the north pole, there is a hole in the clouds caused by a vortex in the circulation of the atmosphere.

atmosphere the velocities are much greater, and they follow the retrograde (clockwise) direction of the planet's rotation as a whole.

Radar observations have revealed important information about the general form of the planet's surface. There seems to be fairly extensive cratering, some of which may have been caused by meteors that have penetrated the atmosphere of Venus, and some by volcanic activity. Indeed, there is a large volcano, 185 miles (300 kilometers) wide and less than one mile high, and this may be one source of the carbon dioxide and nitrogen discovered in the planet's atmosphere. Mountain ranges and a 900-mile (1,500-kilometer) trench (near the Venusian equator) have also been found. On a smaller scale, photographs sent back from the surface of Venus by the Soviet probes *Venera 9* and *Venera 10* in 1975 show that it is probably strewn with stones averaging a few feet in size, although general conclusions are difficult to draw from the scant information available. The soil seems to have a chemical composition and density corresponding to basalt. Lava flow has also been detected by radar.

### Orbit and structure

Radar observations from earth indicate that Venus rotates very slowly on its axis (as well as in the opposite direction to most planets), completing one "day" every 243 earth-days. As a result, Venus is the only planet whose day is longer than its year (its orbital period being 225 earth-days). It is believed that this long rotation period results from the gravitational effect of the earth.

Such a long period of rotation rules out a "dynamo" mechanism as the source of Venus's magnetic field, which is about one one-thousandth the strength of the earth's field. It is

possible that the magnetic field, like that of the moon, results from permanent magnetism, although a complete explanation is lacking. But the planet does possess an ionosphere like that of the earth.

Under its harsh surface, Venus becomes similar in structure to the earth. Present models suggest that there is a dense iron and nickel core with a radius of 1,850 miles (2,980 kilometers), surrounded by a mantle. With a size and structure similar to those of the earth, and volcanic features on its surface, it seems that the crustal layer is split up into plates that interact and give rise to the Venusquakes and fold mountains.

**A computer-enhanced image** of the crescent Venus shows the "airglow," a phenomenon that occurs when sunlight hits the atmosphere and causes the gases to ionize

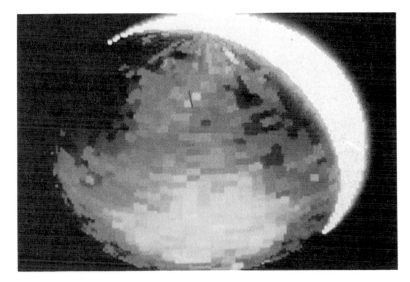

# Mars

Of all the planets, Mars has fascinated human beings the most. Its fiery orange-red hue makes it a distinctive sight in the night sky and has earned it the name of the Red Planet. The Romans named it after Mars, their god of war.

Although much smaller than the earth, Mars shows many similarities to our own planet. It has seasons, and its day is a little over 24 hours long. There is also an atmosphere, although a very slight one, and icecaps at the poles.

Mars has two satellites, discovered by Asaph Hall in 1877, and named by him Phobos and Deimos (Fear and Terror). The origin of these satellites is unknown, although their composition and small size—Phobos is about 14 miles (23 kilometers) across and Deimos 6 miles (10 kilometers)—have led to suggestions that originally they might have been asteroids that were "captured" by Mars.

In the late 1800's, astronomers began observing Mars closely with ever more powerful telescopes. In 1877, the Italian astronomer Giovanni Schiaparelli reported seeing "channels" on the surface of the planet. Astronomers also noted the so-called "wave of darkening" that sweeps over the planet in spring. These observations suggested to many people that Mars must be inhabited by intelligent creatures. One of the most avid supporters of this theory in the 1890's was the American astronomer Percival Lowell, who built an observatory at Flagstaff, Arizona, specifically to observe Mars and its surface features.

As time went on and more powerful instruments were trained on Mars, it became less

**Mars's statistics**
Equatorial diameter:
 4,223 miles
 (6,796 kilometers)
Mass: 0.107 (Earth = 1)
Mean relative density:
 3.94 (water = 1)
Surface gravity:
 0.38 (Earth = 1)
Escape velocity: 3 miles
 (5 kilometers)
 per second
Distance from sun:
 farthest: 154,800,000 miles
 (249,200,000 kilometers)
 nearest: 128,400,000 miles
 (206,600,000 kilometers)
 mean: 141,600,000 miles
 (227,900,000 kilometers)
Closest approach to Earth:
 approx. 48,700,000 miles
 (78,390,000 kilometers)
Orbital period:
 686.98 earth-days
Rotational period:
 24 h., 37min.
Satellites: 2
 (Phobos, Deimos)

**Large volcanoes** dominate the northern face of Mars in this photograph of the planet taken in 1976 from the American space probe *Viking 2.* The four biggest volcanoes, which are situated on the prominent Tharsis Ridge, are huge by earth standards, the highest rising to over 12 miles (20 kilometers). Near the south pole can be seen the frost-filled Argyre Basin, a vast depression some 500 miles (800 kilometers) across that was formed eons ago by a massive meteorite. Absent are the famous Martian "channels"; the detailed photographs sent back by Viking did not show these features, noted by Giovanni Schiaparelli in 1877. Their absence, together with the failure to find evidence of life on the planet's surface, finally disproved the myth that Mars was once inhabited by civilized beings.

and less likely that the planet could support life of any kind. When spacecraft began observing the planet close-up from 1965 onward, the prospects of life virtually vanished. In 1976, Viking spacecraft soft-landed on Mars and sent back television pictures of a barren, waterless landscape. They also searched for signs of life by sampling the soil, but they searched in vain. They could find no traces of any kind of organic matter.

### Rhythm of the seasons

Mars comes closer to Earth than any other planet, except Venus. At times of most favorable oppositions, it approaches to about 48,700,000 miles (78,390,000 kilometers) away from Earth and shines with a magnitude of −2.5, rivaling even Jupiter in brightness. But at most oppositions, which occur every 26 months, Mars is much farther away because of the eccentricity of its elliptical orbit around the sun.

This eccentricity is responsible for the unequal length of the seasons on Mars, which are caused by the inclination of the planet's axis of rotation. It is also responsible for the variation in temperature between the Martian hemispheres from season to season. Thus, the southern summer is shorter than the northern summer, which explains the difference in behavior of the polar icecaps. The southern cap disappears almost completely at southern midsummer, whereas the northern cap remains quite large, even in the middle of the northern summer.

Temperatures—low by earth standards—vary widely over the planet. At noon in midsummer they may rise to −63° F. (−17° C) for a time; in winter at the poles, however, temperatures fall to below −225° F. (−143° C). There is also a wide variation in daily temperatures, and at night, temperatures fall rapidly because the atmosphere is too thin to retain much of the daytime heat.

### The Martian atmosphere

A haze can often be seen over the icecaps, showing that the planet has at least some atmosphere; elsewhere on the planet, clouds can also occasionally be distinguished. Sometimes features on the planet's surface are obscured by huge dust storms.

Measurements by spacecraft instruments have shown that the atmosphere is less than one one-hundredth as dense as the earth's and is made up mainly of carbon dioxide. There are also traces of nitrogen, argon, carbon monoxide, and even some oxygen and water vapor; in addition, hydrogen has been detected in the upper atmosphere. The polar caps are made up of a mixture of frozen carbon dioxide ("dry ice") and frozen water. The clouds in the tenuous atmosphere appear to be water-ice clouds.

### Surface features

From the earth, we can distinguish a variety of dark markings on Mars that rotate with the planet. Particularly prominent is the region called Syrtis Major near the Martian equator. The size and shape of the markings are not

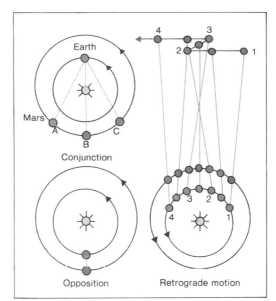

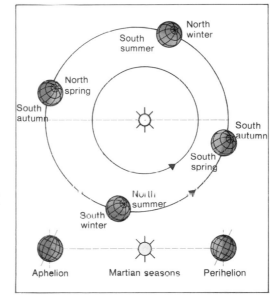

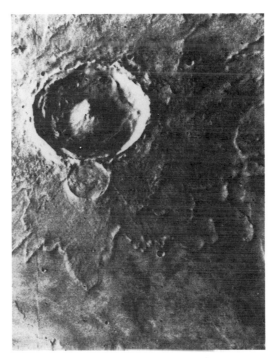

**Conjunction** occurs when Mars appears in the same part of the sky as the sun because it has traveled to the sun's far side. At exact conjunction (B), when Mars is perfectly aligned with the sun, the planet is totally hidden. Shortly before conjunction (A), Mars appears as an evening star in the western part of the sky. After conjunction (C), Mars rises in the east, just before dawn. Usually Mars appears to move from west to east (1 to 2); however, as the faster-orbiting Earth overtakes it, Mars appears to change direction (2) and moves from east to west—a phenomenon called retrograde motion. As Earth continues to overtake Mars (3), it reverts to west-to-east motion (3 to 4).

**Mars's axis** is tilted and so the planet experiences four seasons in the same way as does Earth. Moreover, Mars's orbital speed varies—fastest at perihelion (the closest approach to the sun) and slowest at aphelion (the farthest point)—so its seasons are of different lengths. About one-fifth of an orbit past perihelion, Mars's south pole reaches the optimum combination of maximum tilt toward the sun and near approach to the sun. At this point the south experiences summer, which lasts for 156 days. It then passes through the other seasons as the combinations of tilt and distance from the sun change: autumn (194 days long) near aphelion; winter (177 days); and spring (142 days) near perihelion. In the north, the seasons are reversed.

**The crater of Yuty** was photographed by *Viking 1* as it orbited Mars in 1976. The crater, which is typical of those found on the planet's surface, is about 11 miles (18 kilometers) across and was probably formed as the result of a meteorite impact. The fingerlike projections consist of layers of broken rocks that were thrown out of the crater by the shock of the meteorite impact.

**Various-sized rocks** litter the landscape in this photograph of the Martian surface taken during the winter by the *Viking 2* lander at its touchdown site on Utopia Planita (which is near the north pole). Surrounding the bases of the rocks are patches of frost, which probably consist of frozen carbon dioxide ("dry ice"). The photographs sent back by the *Viking 1* lander, which touched down farther south, showed a similar rock-strewn terrain with vivid orange-red soil.

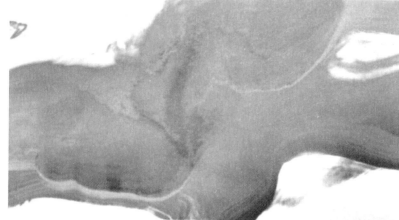

**The icecap** at Mars's north pole never melts completely, even in midsummer. But as summer approaches, the icecap does recede from the lower latitudes to reveal the underlying terrain. This photograph (which is a computer-produced color composite of three black-and-white photographs taken through different colored filters) shows strata in the exposed orange-colored part of the terrain. These strata consist of alternate layers of dust and ice which, over the ages, have been repeatedly eroded, then overlain by more ice.

constant, however. Close-up observations by spacecraft have failed to correlate all of the dark markings with topographical features, and it is thought likely that they are often caused by some differences in the appearance of the surface as dust blows and drifts in the wind. Transport of dust on a global scale is most certainly the explanation of the dark regions known as maria (seas).

Winds are generally light on Mars, but occasionally gust to 75 miles (120 kilometers) per hour or more. Evidence of wind activity is everywhere. In the desert regions around the north polar icecap, the surface dust is whipped into vast undulating dunes; dunes also occur in canyons and craters. In addition, dust-laden wind modifies the landscape everywhere by eroding the rocks.

Close-up television pictures reveal various different features on the generally rust-colored surface. In the southern hemisphere in

particular, there are extensive cratered regions, reminiscent of a lunar highland landscape. In contrast, the northern hemisphere has vast, lightly-cratered plains, like the mare regions on the moon.

Within the cratered southern hemisphere, two huge basins stand out—Hellas, which is more than 1,000 miles (1,600 kilometers) across, and Argyre, which is about half the size of Hellas. They are circular areas of dusty desert containing a few craters and were formed as a result of the impact of huge meteorites eons ago. The floor of Hellas is some 2.5 miles (4 kilometers) below that of the surrounding landscape.

The most prominent feature of the northern hemisphere is a vast volcanic ridge called Tharsis, which has four massive volcanoes. The biggest, called Olympus Mons, rises to a height of about 16 miles (25 kilometers) from a base 375 miles (600 kilometers) in diameter. The other three volcanoes stand in a row to the southeast of Olympus Mons.

To the east of the Tharsis Ridge and just south of the Martian equator is a great gash in the surface, which has been called the Grand Canyon of Mars, but is more properly known as Valles Marineris (after *Mariner 9,* the American spacecraft that discovered it). It extends for some 2,500 miles (4,020 kilometers), reaches a maximum width of about 250 miles (400 kilometers), and is as much as 4.5 miles (7 kilometers) deep.

### Abundant water

In Valles Marineris—and in many other places on the planet—there are what appear to be dried-up water channels. Studies of the direction and flow patterns of the channels make it almost certain that they were in fact made by flowing water many millions of years ago. In some places, there is evidence of flash floods, which probably occurred when water-ice in the long-frozen ground was suddenly melted, either by meteorite impact or by volcanic activity. In such regions, the surface rocks have collapsed, leaving behind them what is termed chaotic terrain.

The water that once flowed on Mars was probably released from the interior of the planet during the volcanic eruptions that helped to shape the Martian landscape millions of years ago. (Water vapor and carbon dioxide are released in huge quantities during volcanic eruptions on Earth.)

There is no free water on Mars today, but there is probably subsurface water almost everywhere, locked in the ground as ice. And water-ice also makes up most of the permanent north polar ice-cap. This cap has a fascinating spiral pattern, shaped partly by the prevailing winds. When the cap melts and shrinks as summer approaches, interesting layered terrain is uncovered that shows how alternate layers of ice and dust are laid down and eroded year after year.

### The Martian soil

The Viking landers, although they touched down at different locations (Chryse and Utopia), pictured a similar landscape and reported similar soil types at each site. The soil is soft

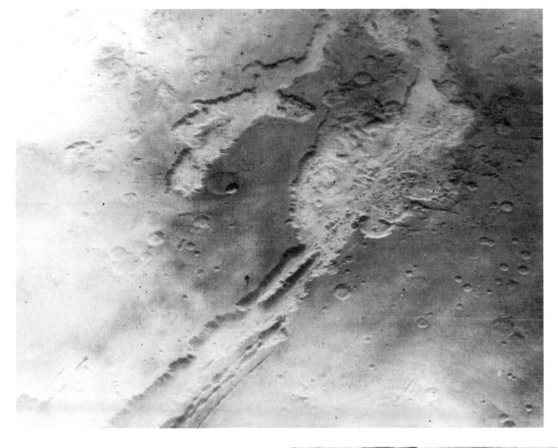

**Valles Marineris,** sometimes called the Grand Canyon of Mars, is a major feature of the planet's southern hemisphere. Situated just south of—and running approximately parallel to—the equator, the canyon is about 2,500 miles (4,020 kilometers) long and up to 250 miles (400 kilometers) wide. Its resemblance to a rift valley has been taken as evidence that there was previous tectonic activity on the planet, with its crustal plates slowly moving and forming the Valles Marineris and also the huge volcanoes in the Tharsis Ridge area.

**Eroded channels** have been photographed in many places on Mars. Detailed analysis of the photomosaic shown here indicates that this channel was probably formed by a flash flood in which water-ice in the ground was suddenly melted—either by volcanic activity or a meteorite impact. Near the beginning of the channel is the chaotic terrain normally associated with flash flood channels.

and a vivid orange-red in color. Rocks of many shapes and sizes litter the landscape to the horizon. Most of the rocks are pitted and appear porous, probably as a result of outgassing during their formation or of wind erosion.

Automatic analysis of the soil at the landing sites showed that it contains mainly silicon and iron, together with magnesium, aluminum, cerium, calcium, and titanium. There is more sulfur than there is on average in the earth's crust, but less potassium. The rusty color of the Martian soil is undoubtedly caused by the presence of iron oxides, probably much like terrestrial hematite or the magnetic magnetite.

The soil appears to be similar in many respects to an iron-rich clay found on earth, called nontronite. It is formed when volcanic basalt rock breaks down under the action of the weather, and scientists believe that a similar process, involving liquid water, must have been at work on Mars to produce this type of soil.

# Jupiter

**Jupiter's statistics**
Equatorial diameter:
88,846 miles
(142,984 kilometers)
Mass: 317,892 (Earth = 1)
Mean relative density: 1.33
Surface gravity: 2.53
(Earth = 1)
Escape velocity: 37 miles
(60 kilometers) per
second
Distance from sun:
farthest 507,000,000 miles
(816,000,000 kilometers)
nearest: 460,200,000 miles
(740,600,000 kilometers)
mean: 483,600,000 miles
(778,400,000 kilometers)
Closest approach to Earth:
390,700,000 miles
(628,760,000 kilometers)
Orbital period:
approximately 12
earth-years
Rotational period:
9h., 55 min.
Satellites: 16

Jupiter was known to the ancient astronomers and was aptly named after the ruler of the Roman gods. It is by far the largest of all the planets, having a mass 318 times that of the earth, and is vast enough to contain more than 1,300 globes the size of our planet. Of the total extrasolar mass in the solar system, more than 70 per cent is contained within this one planet. Despite these statistics, however, Jupiter's density is only 1.33 times that of water, a reflection of the fact that the planet's composition differs radically from that of the earth; it is a gaseous, hot terrestrial planet.

Through the telescope, Jupiter appears as a yellow, oblate disk, crossed with orange-red bands that often show signs of turbulence. Observation of the movement of atmospheric features, such as the Great Red Spot, reveals the rapid axial rotation of this massive planet: Jupiter has the fastest rotation period of any planet. This is the reason for the relatively large ellipticity shown by the disk—the equatorial radius is 44,685 miles (71,900 kilometers) and is 2,670 miles (4,300 kilometers) greater than the polar radius.

Bursts of radio emission from the planet were detected in 1955, and steady synchrotron emission at shorter wavelengths was picked up a few years later. Because synchrotron radio emission results from charged particles moving at high speeds within a magnetic field, it was proposed that Jupiter itself must be trapping electrons in its own magnetic field. Not until *Pioneer 10,* the American Jupiter probe, flew past Jupiter in December 1973 was this idea proved to be true. Jupiter has the

most intense magnetic field of any planet—about five times the strength of the earth's field. When it was passing through the planet's radiation belts, *Pioneer 10* was exposed to radiation levels 400 times the lethal dose for humans from the electrons trapped there.

**The Jovian atmosphere**

Before the Pioneer and Voyager expeditions to Jupiter, it was thought from spectroscopic observations that the planet's atmosphere contains methane, ammonia, and hydrogen as well as other gases in much smaller quantities. It is now believed that Jupiter's atmosphere consists of about 84 per cent hydrogen and 15 per cent helium. The latter has been calculated not on the basis of direct observation, but on determinations of molecular weights.

Such a chemical composition is intriguingly similar to that of the sun. In fact, it has been estimated that if Jupiter had been formed from material that was dense enough for the planet to have fifty times its present mass, fusion reactions may well have started up within it and it would have evolved into a star. The solar system would then have been a binary star system.

The clouds that lie within Jupiter's atmosphere are stacked mainly at three different levels. Each is at a different temperature, and so has a different chemical composition, which determines its color. Uppermost, with a temperature of $-234°$ F. $(-148°$ C), are the white clouds, probably composed of solid ammonia; the intermediate clouds at $-40°$ F. $(-40°$ C),

**The energy Jupiter emits** is twice the amount it absorbs from the sun, which indicates that the planet has an internal heat source. This infrared photograph shows bright spots on Jupiter's equator where holes in the upper cloud layers let through heat from the deeper, hotter levels.

**Jupiter** is one of the five planets known to human beings for centuries. It is the brightest planet apart from Venus and is also the largest and most massive planet in the solar system. The colored, parallel bands on Jupiter's "surface" are the top layers of its atmosphere.

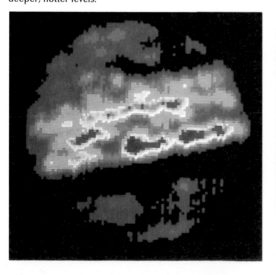

are tinged brown by polymerized ammonium hydrosulfide; the lower visible levels are so deep that the atmosphere above scatters their light to make them appear blue—just as Earth's daytime sky looks blue.

The Great Red Spot, the most prominent of Jupiter's features, remains a mystery despite the observations made by the Pioneer and Voyager space probes. A number of theories have been put forward that suggest how this feature, measuring about 25,000 miles (40,200 kilometers) by 20,000 miles (32,000 kilometers), could have survived for at least the century over which it has been observed. (It is at least 300 years old if seventeenth-century observations refer to the same spot.) The periphery of the Spot rotates counterclockwise and, as it is in the southern hemisphere of the planet, this rotational direction indicates that the Spot is a high-pressure zone. The red color is probably due to phosphorus, which is produced when phosphine (brought up from below) is dissociated by sunlight.

The Great Red Spot and smaller white ovals lie between zones where the wind blows in opposite directions. These winds have speeds of up to about 300 miles (500 kilometers) per hour. The zones adjacent to them have speed differences of up to 400 miles (650 kilometers) per hour. The zones themselves correlate with the position of the colored bands, and remain relatively fixed in latitude. The spots are rotated by the shear between adjacent wind-flows, in a movement similar to rollers turning beneath a moving load.

### The internal structure of Jupiter

Earth-based observations have been important in determining the internal structure of Jupiter, by giving values for the size, shape, and mass of the planet. For example, the mass of Jupiter's gas relative to that of its solid core can be estimated from observations of the planet's satellites.

These satellites respond to the gravitational attraction of the whole planet. The flattening of the globe due to its rotation rate results in a torque that causes the whole orbit of a satellite to revolve, or precess, around the planet. From observations of the precession rate, astronomers can calculate the invisible gravitational flattening of the whole planet, whereas direct observation of Jupiter reveals the flattening of only the outer, gaseous layer. This layer is affected by the centrifugal force result-

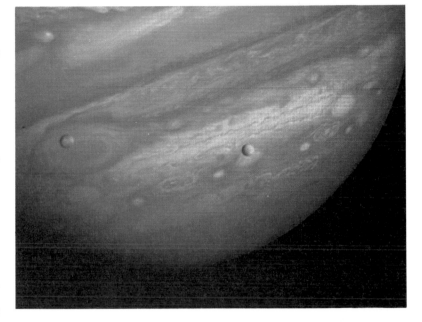

**Jupiter's clouds** and two of its satellites are shown here, photographed by *Voyager 1* at a distance from the planet of 12 million miles (20 million kilometers). Io is on the left and Europa on the right. The predominant movement of circulation in the bands is from east to west, but small eddies can be seen in and between the bands.

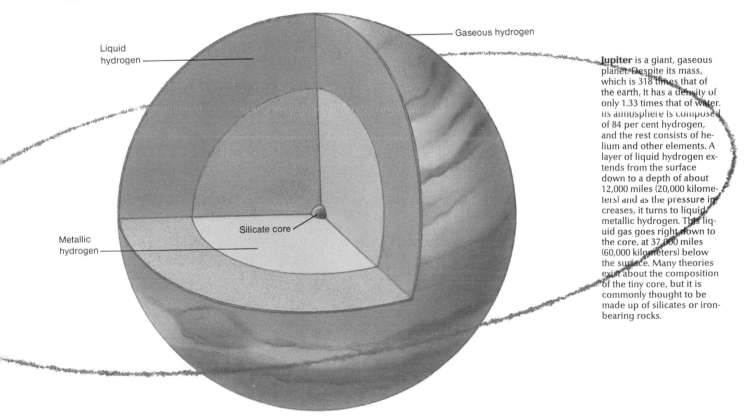

Liquid hydrogen

Gaseous hydrogen

Metallic hydrogen

Silicate core

**Jupiter** is a giant, gaseous planet. Despite its mass, which is 318 times that of the earth, it has a density of only 1.33 times that of water. Its atmosphere is composed of 84 per cent hydrogen, and the rest consists of helium and other elements. A layer of liquid hydrogen extends from the surface down to a depth of about 12,000 miles (20,000 kilometers) and as the pressure increases, it turns to liquid metallic hydrogen. This liquid gas goes right down to the core, at 37,000 miles (60,000 kilometers) below the surface. Many theories exist about the composition of the tiny core, but it is commonly thought to be made up of silicates or iron-bearing rocks.

**In July 1994, pieces of the disintegrated comet** Shoemaker-Levy 9 plunged into Jupiter's atmosphere. The impacts caused huge, fiery explosions on the planet. In this color-composite image, taken with the Hubble Space Telescope's Planetary Camera, eight impact sites are visible. From left to right are the E/F complex (barely visible on the edge of the planet), the star-shaped H site, the impact sites for tiny N, Q1, small Q2, and R, and on the far right limb the D/G complex. The D/G complex also shows extended haze at the edge of the planet.

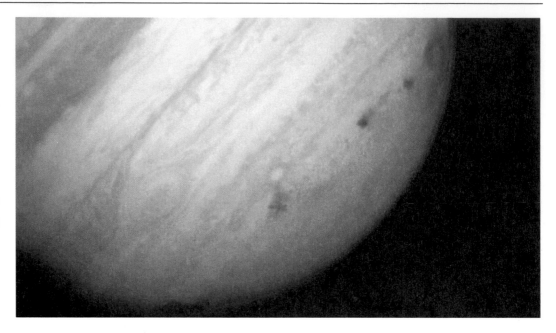

ing from Jupiter's rapid rotation to a greater extent than is the underlying solid core. The relative masses of the two regions can be calculated from the precessing orbits of the satellites and from the observed degree of flattening of the planet.

Earth-based observations have revealed another important clue to the internal structure of Jupiter, which is that the planet emits about twice the amount of heat it receives from the sun. Convection is assumed to be the process by which this heat is transported from the interior of Jupiter to the surface layers. Theoretical models demonstrate that most of the planet is composed of hydrogen, and that only the uppermost few thousandths of Jupiter are gaseous. Moving down the atmosphere toward the center of the planet, the hydrogen becomes liquid as the temperature rises 34,000° F. (19,000° C) at a depth of about 8,080 miles (13,000 kilometers). The temperature continues to rise toward the core until at a depth of about 37,000 miles (60,000 kilometers), at the outer layer of the silicate core, the temperature reaches 43,000° F. (24,000° C).

**Jupiter's atmosphere** is dominated by extremely strong latitudinal air currents that flow against each other. These winds generally blow eastward but those with negative velocities blow westward. The average wind speed is 165 feet (50 meters) per second. Both hemispheres of the planet each have about five of the two counterflowing currents. These winds have not changed markedly in position for more than fifty years. Their pattern follows that of the colored parallel bands on the planet's surface. These bands change in appearance but on the whole remain arranged in alternate light and dark striations. The dark bands are the belts and the bright ones are the zones.

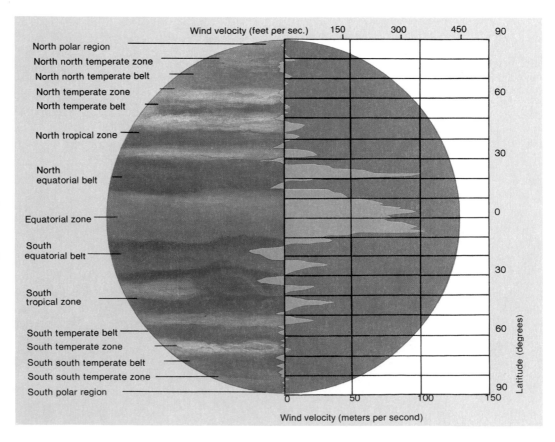

## Jupiter's magnetic field

The source of Jupiter's intense magnetic field is probably an internal dynamo, driven by the planet's fast rotation and its high-temperature regions that conduct heat. Jupiter's magnetic field is in the opposite direction to the earth's, so a terrestrial compass would point south rather than north.

The strong magnetic field, combined with the relative weakness of the solar wind near the planet—Jupiter is 5.2 astronomical units from the sun—endows the planet with a very large magnetosphere, with a magnetotail that extends away from the sun to at least the distance of Saturn.

The outer region of the magnetosphere, which is influenced by plasma pressure and rotation-induced centrifugal forces, is disk-shaped. All of the Galilean satellites, especially Io, are deeply embedded in this field. In addition, Io seems to be eroded by interaction with the high-energy particles within the field and it is also the source of the plasma that inflates the magnetosphere.

Before the Voyager missions to Jupiter, 13 satellites were known to orbit about the planet, extending from the innermost one, Amalthea, at 112,590 miles (181,200 kilometers) from Jupiter, to Sinope, which, at a distance of 14,900,000 miles (24,000,000 kilometers), takes 758 days to complete a single orbit.

## The ring system

The probes found three more satellites close in to the planet, but one of the most surprising discoveries, made by *Voyager 1*, was the detection of a faint ring around Jupiter, split into three bands. This discovery makes Jupiter the nearest planet to the earth to exhibit a ring system.

Composed mostly of micron-sized particles and extending from about 1.7 to about 1.8 of a Jupiter radius, the principal ring is relatively thick, 18 miles (29 kilometers), with a width of 4,000 miles (6,400 kilometers), and is encapsulated in a much thicker halo. Furthermore, there appears to be a tenuous sheet structure that extends down from the main ring to the upper layers of the planet's atmosphere. A ring system such as Jupiter's must have a constant supply of new material, because particles are continually lost by atmospheric and other drag

effects. Astronomers believe that there is a population of boulderlike objects inside the ring. These objects are broken up by micrometeoroid impacts and so replenish the supply of ring material. Two satellites, in the form of extra-large boulders, have been seen to orbit just outside and just within the ring. They may have a gravitational influence on the particles that maintains the structure of the ring system.

The origin of the ring around the planet may lie in the breakup of a satellite whose unstable orbit brought it close enough to Jupiter to enter the Roche limit—a point from the planet beyond which material condenses to form satellites. Satellites that orbit within the Roche limit are subjected to a tidal stress from the parent planet that is greater than the gravitational force holding the satellite together. Satellites are torn apart if they wander within this orbital distance. Alternatively, any material in this region can never accrete to form a satellite, and the rings may be the residue from the unsuccessful accretion of primordial material. From observations, astronomers have found that all the rings so far discovered around Jupiter lie within the Roche limit.

**The Great Red Spot** is Jupiter's most prominent feature. It lies in the south tropical zone and rotates once every six days, moving between faster-flowing vortices. It also has a lower temperature than the surrounding clouds and is about 5 miles (8 kilometers) above them. This enormous feature is almost as wide as the earth—the depth of the photograph covers an area of about 15,000 miles (24,000 kilometers)—and is thought to have existed for 300 years. The oval below it is one of three that appeared in 1938 and that have remained there. The most commonly accepted explanation of the Great Red Spot is that it is the vortex of a storm.

**Jupiter's rings** are extremely faint and only when *Voyager 1* approached the planet in 1979 were they discovered. The main ring is about 35,750 miles (57,520 kilometers) above Jupiter's surface and is 4,000 miles (6,400 kilometers) wide. The distinct shape of the rings is possibly maintained by satellites that orbit on either side of them.

# Saturn

**Saturn's statistics**
Equatorial diameter:
74,898 miles (120,536 kilometers)
Mass: 95.184 (Earth = 1)
Mean density:
0.69 (water = 1)
Surface gravity:
1.07 (Earth = 1)
Escape velocity:
22.1 miles
(35.6 kilometers)
per second
Distance from sun:
farthest: 937,600,000 miles
(1,508,900,000 kilometers)
nearest: 838,800,000 miles
(1,349,900,000 kilometers)
mean: 888,200,000 miles
(1,429,400,000 kilometers)
Closest approach to Earth:
762,700,000 miles
(1,277,400,000 kilometers)
Orbital period:
29.50 earth-years
Rotational period:
10 h., 39 min.
Satellites: 18

Saturn was the outermost of the six planets known to ancient astronomers (the other five being Mercury, Venus, Earth, Mars, and Jupiter). The Greeks named it after the god Cronus, whose Roman equivalent was Saturn. It remained the most distant planet known until William Herschel discovered Uranus in 1781. Saturn is not much smaller than Jupiter, although it appears to be much fainter because it orbits nearly twice as far away from the sun, at a distance of 888,200,000 miles (1,429 million kilometers). Saturn appears to the naked eye as a very slow-moving, pale yellow star—even at favorable oppositions, its magnitude seldom exceeds +0.7. It takes nearly 30 earth-years to complete its orbit.

Seen through a telescope, Saturn is the most beautiful of all the planets. It is circled by a large, shining, flat ring, which larger tele-

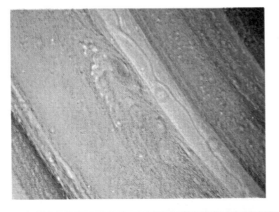

scopes show to be made up of three separate concentric rings. Through telescopes, up to 10 satellites can be seen orbiting the planet, including the giant Titan, which is nearly half the size of the earth.

These telescopic views do not, however, do full justice to this jewel of a planet. When viewed close-up from space (as they were by the American Voyager space probes in 1980 and 1981), the three main rings can be seen each to consist of hundreds of separate ringlets. It is also now known that many more moons orbit the planet; by 1982, at least 17 had been detected.

**The appearance of the planet**

Seen from the earth, Saturn's rings appear to change during the time of its orbit. This apparent variation is due to the inclination of the planet's axis (about 27°) with respect to the plane of its orbit. In 1980, the rings were almost edge-on to our line of sight and they virtually disappeared from view; they did so again in 1995. In 2003, however, they will present their most open aspect and be seen at their best from earth.

Telescopes also reveal that Saturn is primarily a gaseous body that is rotating rapidly. This movement can be inferred from the distinctly oblate appearance of the disk—it bulges outward at the equator and is noticeably flattened at the poles. The diameter is 8,000 miles (13,000 kilometers) greater at the equator than at the poles. From its mass and volume, its

**Saturn,** regarded as the outermost planet by the ancients, is the second largest planet in our solar system and is the most massive after Jupiter. Saturn's northern hemisphere was photographed by *Voyager 1* in 1981. This false-color photograph shows a bright blue band just north of the equator, which is thought to be a region of deeper atmosphere that is not covered by the gaseous haze that obscures lower regions of the planet's atmosphere. The cloud belts *(above)* covering Saturn's surface have been photographed in false colors. The large blue oval is really a brown spot. It occurs in the northern hemisphere. The wave structures north of the oval are moving east at 150 yards per second (540 kilometers per hour).

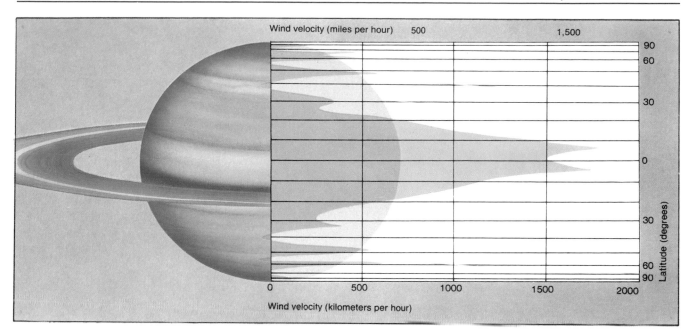

Wind velocity (miles per hour)    500    1,500

Wind velocity (kilometers per hour)

average relative density has been calculated to be only about 0.69, which means that it could float in water. It is thus by far the least dense of all the planets.

## Saturn's cloud belts

Like Jupiter, Saturn has a disk that is crossed by alternate light and dark bands parallel to the equator; they are known respectively as zones (light) and belts (dark). These bands are formed by thick clouds in the deep atmosphere that are forced to travel in parallel bands by the rapid rotation of the planet. The belts and zones of Saturn are, however, less distinct than those on Jupiter because of the presence of a thick layer of haze above the tops of the clouds.

The winds that drive the cloud belts reach extremely high speeds of up to 1,100 miles (1,800 kilometers) per hour. Away from the equator, in both hemispheres, the winds decrease in speed symmetrically, and in the middle latitudes, they start to deviate from their main easterly course. At the boundaries where the wind streams change direction, the atmosphere experiences extreme turbulence, and violent storms prevail. These disturbances appear as dark and light oval markings similar to, but less distinctive than, the Great Red Spot and white ovals that appear on Jupiter's disk.

The winds and storms on Saturn are generated mainly by the planet's internal heat rather than by heat received from the sun, as happens on Earth. (Saturn receives only about one per cent of the solar heat that Earth does.) Its internal heat is believed to originate in the gravitational separation of, or interaction between, the hydrogen and helium that make up the planet.

At the center of Saturn, there is thought to be a rocky core that may be about twice the size of Earth. Surrounding the core is a layer of highly compressed "metallic" hydrogen, and above that, a layer of ordinary liquid hydrogen mixed with some liquid helium. The outermost layer comprises a very deep atmosphere of gaseous hydrogen and helium.

Temperatures at Saturn's cloud tops are about −288° F. (−178° C). They would be even lower were it not for the heat generated from inside the planet, which causes it to release nearly twice as much heat as it receives from the sun.

## Aurorae and radiation belts

The rotation of a massive iron core could account for Saturn's powerful magnetic field, whose existence was confirmed only in 1979. The strength of this field is about 1,000 times greater than that of the earth. It extends for several million miles into the space around the planet to form a huge, magnetic "bubble," or magnetosphere, shaped like a teardrop with the broad end facing the sun. The exact size and shape of the magnetosphere varies according to the strength of the solar wind. Unlike Earth, Jupiter, and the sun, in which the magnetic and geographic poles are some 10° apart, Saturn's magnetic poles nearly coincide with its geographic poles.

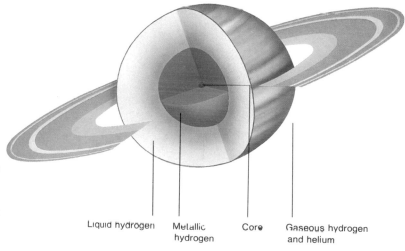

Liquid hydrogen    Metallic hydrogen    Core    Gaseous hydrogen and helium

Saturn's rings are shown here in false colors; the A and B Rings are the brightest. The orange-and-green striped band is the B Ring, which is separated from the outer ring (A) by the Cassini Division. The gap in Ring A is the Encke Division. The blue-and-white striped band is the C Ring. The rings consist of particles that have never condensed to form a satellite and are kept in orbit by their angular momentum. The A, B, and C Rings are thought to be composed of particles of water-ice, ranging from microscopic grains to blocks 10 feet (3 meters) in diameter.

The magnetosphere surrounding Saturn was discovered by the Pioneer space probe. The solar wind hits the magnetic field at the bow shock—1,100,000 miles (1,800,000 kilometers) from the planet—at speeds of up to 250 miles (400 kilometers) per second. Titan, one of the outermost satellites, moves near the edge of the magnetosphere, affecting its shape.

The presence of a magnetic field around Saturn gives rise to phenomena similar to those that occur on Earth—aurorae in the polar regions. The magnetosphere is also responsible for the emission of radio waves and for concentrating charged particles into a torus—a ring girdling the planet—analogous to the Van Allen radiation belts that surround the earth.

Saturn's inner radiation belt is composed mainly of hydrogen ions, oxygen ions, and electrons that probably originate in the splitting up of water from the surfaces of two of Saturn's satellites, Dione and Tethys. A major source of particles in the outer belt is the atmosphere of Titan—the largest of Saturn's satellites—which often comes within the planet's magnetosphere. Titan, a moon, is itself surrounded by a torus of neutral hydrogen.

## The ring system

When Galileo first focused his telescope on Saturn in 1610, he reported that the planet looked as though it had "ears," and considered them to be close-orbiting moons. It was Christiaan Huygens, 45 years later, who provided the correct explanation—that Saturn has a ring around it. Over the years, the "ring" was resolved into three rings, A, B, and C. Then came the discovery, or confirmation, by the American space probes *Pioneer 11* (1979), *Voyager 1* (1980), and *Voyager 2* (1981), of D, E, F, and G rings.

The outermost of the classic rings, Ring A, extends to a distance of some 47,000 miles (76,000 kilometers) from Saturn's cloud tops. Within this ring is a narrow gap, known as the

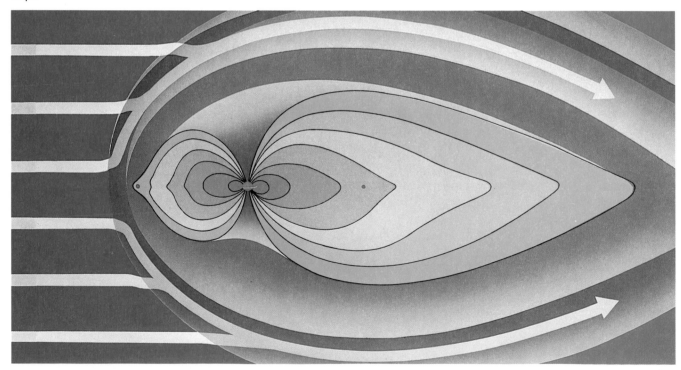

Encke Division. This gap is difficult to see even with high-powered instruments, but may be glimpsed at the extremities (ansae) of the rings. A much broader gap, the Cassini Division, separates the inner edge of Ring A from the outer edge of Ring B. It is visible in telescopes and measures some 2,000 miles (3,200 kilometers) across. Viewed close-up, these "gaps" are not entirely empty, but contain a number of much fainter rings.

Ring B is noticeably brighter than Ring A and about twice as broad. Inside it is the much fainter Ring C, the Crepe or Dusky Ring. Inside Ring C is the very diffuse Ring D, which probably extends right down to Saturn's atmosphere. On the outskirts of Ring A is the narrow Ring F and, even farther out, the faint and narrow Ring G. This ring is itself surrounded by an even fainter, very broad ring, Ring E, which spans the orbits of the moons Enceladus and Tethys.

Space photographs reveal that the classic rings are each made up of hundreds of separate ringlets, which appear to consist of orbiting particles of various sizes. The diffuse Rings E and F seem to be made up mainly of microscopic dust particles, whereas the particles in Ring A may be up to 10 feet (16 meters) or more across. The composition of the particles is unknown, but they are thought to consist of ice and ice-covered rock. The thicknesses of the rings also vary; they appear to be less than 10 miles (16 kilometers) thick.

The structures observed within the ringlet systems are in general transitory, although large-scale features, such as the Encke and Cassini Divisions, appear to be permanent. Transient features, such as the spokes in Ring B, or white spots, may be caused by traveling density waves triggered off by the passage of Saturn's moons. The eccentric, or braided, ringlets observed near clear gaps in the rings may be caused by the presence of undetected moonlets. In a similar way, the braiding of the narrow Ring F appears to be due to the presence of two tiny "shepherd" moons, one on each side.

### Saturn's satellites

Saturn has at least 18 satellites (of which 9 are very large) that have been observed quite attentively, and named. Titan is the largest of the satellites and was also the first to be discovered, in 1665. It was once believed to be the largest satellite in the solar system, but since the Voyager probes, it has been found to be slightly smaller than Jupiter's largest satellite, Ganymede. Enceladus, although one of the smaller satellites, is the brightest and is one of

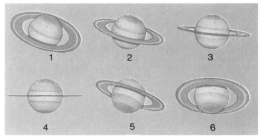

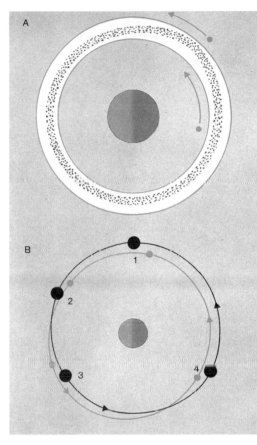

the most reflective bodies in the solar system with an albedo of almost 100 per cent. Tethys is similar to the planet Jupiter in that it has two bodies on its orbital plane, one located 60° ahead, and the other the same distance behind it. This configuration is known as the Lagrangian arrangement. Some minor satellites are "shepherd" satellites and others are co-orbital—their orbits are almost identical, but they periodically overtake each other and interchange their orbits; Epimetheus and Janus are examples of this co-orbital relationship.

**The appearance of Saturn** as seen from Earth seems to change during its orbit because of the varying presentation of the rings. The rings, which are inclined to the ecliptic, change their presentation because of the axial inclination of the planet combined with Saturn's orbital position relative to the earth.

**Guardian satellites** (A), or shepherd moons, are found on either side of Saturn's F Ring. The inner satellite, which moves faster than the outer one, gives energy to the ring particles and kicks them into a higher orbit. The outer satellite slows down the particles, which lose energy and drop toward the planet. Both satellites are small—about 125 miles (200 kilometers) across—but exert sufficient gravitational force to keep the particles in check. The co-orbital satellites (B), Janus and Epimetheus, orbit between Saturn's F and G Rings. Their similarity and the proximity of their orbits—less than 60 miles (100 kilometers)—suggest that they share a common origin. Epimetheus is about 25 by 55 miles (40 by 90 kilometers) in size, and its companion measures about 55 by 62 miles (90 by 100 kilometers). In 1982, Epimetheus was closer to Saturn (1) and moving slightly faster than its companion, as it approaches Janus, the gravitational interaction between them will decelerate the inner satellite (2). The outer one will then accelerate so that eventually they exchange orbits (3). The interchange occurs every 4 years (4), by which time both satellites have orbited more than 2,000 times.

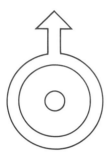

# Uranus, Neptune, and Pluto

The three outer planets in the solar system—Uranus, Neptune, and Pluto—were unknown to astronomers before the late eighteenth century. The planets were discovered following improvements to optical instruments and the subsequent discovery of gravitational effects on the orbit of Uranus.

### Uranus

Uranus was discovered by the German-born British astronomer William Herschel in 1781, using a 6.4-inch (16-centimeter) reflecting telescope. Its distance from the sun is almost exactly where it was predicted by Herschel according to the Titius-Bode law of the positioning of planetary orbits. There is evidence, however, that the planet had been seen by other astronomers before its date of discovery, but its true nature was not recognized. Herschel believed this discovery to be a new comet, and it was not until two months later that the find was considered to be a planet.

A small telescope reveals Uranus to be a faint blue-green disk. More powerful instruments show that the planet is accompanied by 15 satellites, the brightest of which is Oberon, with a magnitude of 14. This satellite, and the satellite Titania, were also discovered by Herschel. The orbital plane of five of the satellites reveals that Uranus' equator is tilted at nearly 98° to the plane of its orbit, which means that the planet lies virtually on its side as it travels around the sun. The axial rotation period (the length of a day on Uranus) is thought to be 17 hours and 8 minutes.

The speed of rotation of Uranus causes the planet to be flattened at its poles, so that the polar radius is 900 miles (1,500 kilometers) less than the 16,200-mile (26,000-kilometer) equatorial radius. Because of the axial tilt, the poles usually point alternately toward the sun. This means that the polar regions alternately remain in light and dark for durations of up to 42 years. Seen from Earth, the direction of rotation of Uranus changes, at times turning clockwise and at others rotating from top to bottom.

Uranus receives little of the sun's heat because it is so far away, and probably has a surface temperature as low as −357° F. (−216° C). In addition, the planet does not seem to have any internal source of heat. Such conditions restrict the type of atmosphere Uranus can have: most substances subjected to such low temperatures turn to a solid state. The blue-green color of the disk is due to the absorption of red light by large quantities of methane in the planet's atmosphere. Molecular hydrogen and helium have also been found in abundance and, although not observed at cloud-top level, ammonia is expected to be present as well. The internal composition of Uranus remains virtually unknown. One model proposes that beneath the atmosphere lies a solid interior, consisting of a rocky core with a radius of about 5,000 miles (8,000 kilometers) covered by a crust of ice.

Astronomers observed an occultation of the star SAO 158687 by Uranus in 1977. To their surprise, the star's light was obscured five times before the main body of Uranus covered it completely, and the "winking" was repeated on the other side of the planet. This observation indicated the existence of a system of 11 sharply defined rings around Uranus, the innermost one lying 28,000 miles (45,000 kilometers) from the planet's center and extending out to about 33,000 miles (53,000 kilometers). The rings are far narrower than those of Saturn, most being only about 6 miles (10 kilometers) in width, and only one, the outermost, Ring E, reaches 60 miles (100 kilometers) wide. This ring varies in width from 12 to 60 miles (20 to 100 kilometers) and this variation is reflected in its changing distance from Uranus—a fluctuation of about 500 miles (800 kilometers). It lies at about 1.95 planetary radii from Uranus. The rings are composed of charcoal-dark icy particles and are almost circular. Their rigid shape is maintained by small satellites.

**Uranus** was the first planet to be discovered that required a telescope for it to be seen clearly. It is the seventh planet out from the sun, and its average orbital distance is twice that of Saturn. Uranus is the third largest planet in the solar system—its diameter is four times that of the earth. Its blue-green color is due to the presence of methane in the atmosphere, which absorbs the red wavelengths. This Hubble Space Telescope image of Uranus reveals the planet's rings, at least five of its inner moons, and bright clouds in the planet's southern hemisphere. (Each of the inner moons appears as a string of three dots in this picture because it is a composite of three images, taken about six minutes apart. When these images are combined, they show the motion of the moons compared with the sky background.)

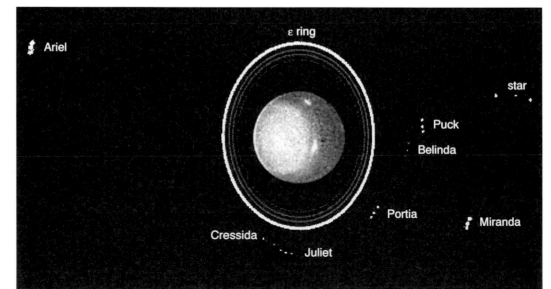

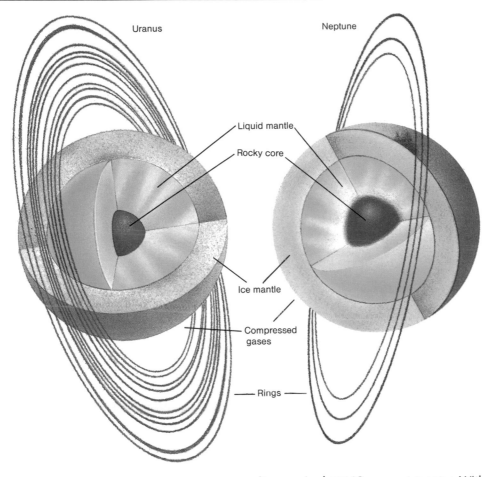

Uranus

Neptune

Liquid mantle

Rocky core

Ice mantle

Compressed gases

Rings

**The compositions of Uranus and Neptune** are not known definitely, with the exception of their atmospheric gases, which have been determined spectroscopically. Both planets are thought to have a rocky core composed of metals and silicates surrounded by a fluid layer containing water, methane, and ammonia. This layer is covered by an icy mantle of frozen gases similar to those in the atmosphere. The outermost layers consist of compressed hydrogen and helium. These gases gradually disperse into the atmosphere. Neptune has a hazy atmosphere that contains ice crystals, whereas Uranus has less of a cloud cover. Neptune also has a heat source which, it has been suggested, results from convective activity in its mantle.

## Neptune

Soon after the discovery of Uranus, astronomers noticed that the planet strayed from the orbit predicted for it if only the sun and the known planets were exerting their gravitational effects. It was suggested that the discrepancy was the result of the gravitational force of an undiscovered planet beyond Uranus' orbit. John Couch Adams, using the Titius-Bode law, attempted to determine the position of this new planet. However, it became apparent that the law did not apply to the body, although it did help to narrow the range of the planet's possible orbits. Adams' findings were met with skepticism in Britain and further research was consequently hindered. As a result, work on the same problem by Urbain Le Verrier in France caught up, and with the help of Johann Galle at the Berlin Observatory, he found the planet in 1846 within one degree of the predicted position. As with Uranus, it was later found that the planet—called Neptune—had been observed before that date but was unrecognized as such. It was calculated that Neptune appeared very close to Jupiter in the sky in January 1613. The most likely person to have observed this event would have been Galileo Galilei. A search through his notes produced drawings that indicated that Galileo had seen Neptune and had observed its movement over the period of a month, but had thought it to be a star and not a planet.

Both Neptune and Uranus are grouped with Jupiter and Saturn as being the giant planets of the solar system. In several ways, Neptune is the twin of Uranus: Neptune's radius is about 5 per cent less than that of Uranus, and

its mass is about 16 per cent greater. With a maximum magnitude of 7.7, Neptune is never visible to the naked eye. Viewed with a telescope, however, the planet appears as a blue-green disk similar to Uranus, and it is also flattened at the poles as a result of its rotation.

Unlike its neighbor, however, Neptune is a world of surprising turbulence. Winds sweep the planet at the rate of 400 miles (640 kilometers) per hour. And a storm system the size of Earth churns counterclockwise around the planet at the rate of 700 miles (1,120 kilometers) per hour. Scientists call this violent hurricane in Neptune's southern hemisphere the Great Dark Spot.

Two of Neptune's satellites, Triton and Nereid, had been detected with the use of a telescope. Six more moons were found when the *Voyager 2* probe flew by Neptune in 1989.

**Uranus has 15 satellites:** Miranda is at a mean distance from Uranus of 80,400 miles (129,400 kilometers), followed by Ariel, Umbriel, Titania, and Oberon. Oberon has a mean distance from Uranus of 362,600 miles (583,500 kilometers). Titania is the largest, being 990 miles (1,590 kilometers) in diameter, but Oberon is the brightest, with a magnitude of 14.1. Ten new satellites were discovered during the *Voyager 2* probe in January 1986.

**Neptune's statistics**
Equatorial diameter:
    30,775 miles (49,528
    kilometers)
Mass: 17.15 (Earth = 1)
Mean relative density: 1.64
Surface gravity:
    1.14 (Earth = 1)
Escape velocity: 14.6 miles
    (23.6 kilometers)
    per second
Distance from sun:
    farthest: 2,824,800,000
    miles (4,546,100,000
    kilometers)
    nearest: 2,774,800,000
    miles (4,465,600,000
    kilometers)
    mean: 2,798,800,000 miles
    (4,504,300,000 kilometers)
Orbital period:
    165 earth-years
Rotational period:
    16 hours and 7 minutes
Satellites: 8

Neptune lies at an average distance from the sun of 2,798,800,000 miles (4,504,300,000 kilometers), with the result that it receives very little heat and its temperature is extremely low—about −353° F. (−214° C). Unlike Uranus, however, Neptune does seem to have an internal heat source. The planet's small size would imply that any heat source would also be small, but Neptune has been observed to give out heat at a rate of 0.03 microwatts per ton of mass. This emission has the effect of heating the planet to about the same temperature as Uranus, even though it is much farther from the sun. Being so far from the sun, Neptune takes nearly 165 earth-years to complete a single orbit. As a result, it will not return to the point at which it was discovered until 2011.

Neptune's atmosphere contains hydrogen, helium, methane, and acetylene. Ammonia may also exist in the lower levels of the atmosphere. A cycle of updrafts and downdrafts pushing methane gas creates cloud formations. Gaseous methane drifts high into Neptune's atmosphere where it freezes into ice particles. The clouds are then dragged down to warmer regions where they are broken up. This process produces cloud cover over almost half of Neptune, including the Great Dark Spot. The clouds help the planet retain sunlight, which is absorbed by the upper atmos-

phere. The absorption of sunlight by methane gives Neptune its blue color.

Auroras spread over a wide area have also been sighted in Neptune's atmosphere. Radiation belts similar to those encircling Earth surround Neptune. Charged particles in these belts appear to plunge into Triton's atmosphere and generate auroras at its equatorial plane. Images taken by *Voyager 2* have revealed that, like the other giant planets, Neptune is encircled by a system of complete rings.

Radio signals have disclosed that Neptune completes one rotation every 16 hours and 7 minutes. The Great Dark Spot, however, takes about 18 hours to complete a rotation. Its strong winds sweep westward against Neptune's rotation. Neptune possesses a magnetic field that is tilted about 50° from the rotation axis. Uranus's magnetic field is similarly tilted. The internal structure of Neptune is also thought to be similar to that of Uranus, with a rocky core covered by a crust of ice.

**Pluto**

In 1930, during a painstaking search among photographic plates of the region of the sky near the constellation Gemini, Pluto was discovered by the American astronomer Clyde Tombaugh. Mathematical predictions of the position of a new planet had been made based on the observed deviations in the orbits of Uranus and Neptune, but it now appears that the closeness of these predictions to the true position of Pluto was a coincidence.

Pluto's orbit is the strangest of all the planets in the solar system. It is the most elliptical and comes inside Neptune's orbit for 8 per cent of the 249 earth-years that Pluto takes to complete one revolution. Because of this, Neptune will be the outermost planet in the solar system until March 1999. Also, Pluto's orbit is highly inclined, at an angle of more than 17° to the ecliptic.

Pluto appears in the largest telescopes as only a tiny, rather fuzzy disk. At its greatest distance from the earth its size is equivalent to that of a small coin seen from a distance of about 6 miles (10 kilometers). Recent estimates of Pluto's diameter suggest that it is about

**On August 24, 1989, *Voyager 2*** came within 3,000 miles (4,800 kilometers) of Neptune. It obtained images of the Great Dark Spot, a violent hurricane the size of Earth that churns around the southern hemisphere of Neptune at the rate of 700 miles (1,120 kilometers) per hour.

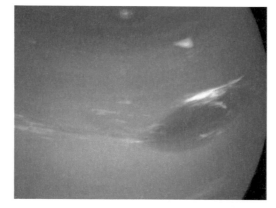

**The orbits of Neptune and Uranus** are almost circular. But Pluto's orbit (inclined at 17° to the ecliptic) is very elliptical; at perihelion it comes within Neptune's orbit.

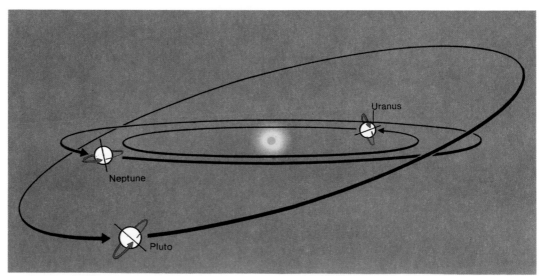

1,430 miles (2,300 kilometers). Pluto is therefore the smallest planet in the solar system. Its small size has made all observations of the planet liable to considerable inaccuracy.

In 1978, Pluto was discovered to have a satellite, Charon. It is about one-third the size of the planet, having a diameter of about 500 miles (800 kilometers). This makes it the largest satellite, relative to its parent planet, in the solar system. Charon's orbital period is 6.39 earth-days, and the satellite orbits about 11,000 miles (18,000 kilometers) from Pluto. Observations of Charon's orbit about its parent planet have revealed that Pluto has a mass of only about 0.002 times that of the earth, which makes it the lightest planet in the solar system. Pluto has a mean relative density of 2.03. With such a low mass, it is unlikely that much of an atmosphere can exist around the planet. Its estimated maximum temperature—-369° F. (-223° C)—also makes the presence of a gaseous atmosphere unlikely. Methane frost was, however, detected on the planet's surface in 1976, indicating a somewhat tenuous atmosphere containing methane. For this atmosphere to be retained, heavier elements (such as neon) must also be present because the planet has such a low density. The icy crust is thought to comprise a layer a few tens of miles thick, below which may lie a solid core consisting of rock and ice.

## Planets beyond Pluto

The latest estimates of Pluto's mass, based on observations of the orbital motion of Charon, are much lower than would account for the deviations of Uranus and Neptune from the orbital paths that they should follow. This raises the question of the existence of another planet, orbiting beyond Pluto, which may be exerting sufficient gravitational force to cause the observed discrepancies. The two methods by which planets outside the orbit of Saturn have been detected were constant observation and mathematical analysis. Neither method will prove practical in the search for a trans-Plutonian planet. This is because a search of magnitudes low enough involves expenditure in precious observatory time, and too many variables exist to enable mathematical analysis to narrow the field down sufficiently. The belief now is that no planet similar to Pluto seems to exist out to a distance of 60 astronomical units from the sun.

**Pluto's statistics**
Equatorial diameter:
  1,430 miles (2,300 kilometers)
Mass: 0.002 (?) (Earth = 1)
Mean relative density:
  2.03 (?)
Surface gravity:
  0.07 (?) (Earth = 1)
Escape velocity: 3.3 miles (5.3 kilometers) per second
Distance from sun:
  farthest: 4,582,700,000 miles (7,375,100,000 kilometers)
  nearest: 2,749,600,000 miles (4,425,100,000 kilometers)
  mean: 3,666,200,000 miles (5,900,100,000 kilometers)
Orbital period:
  249 earth-years
Rotational period:
  about 6 earth-days
Inclination of equator to orbit: 75°
Satellites: 1

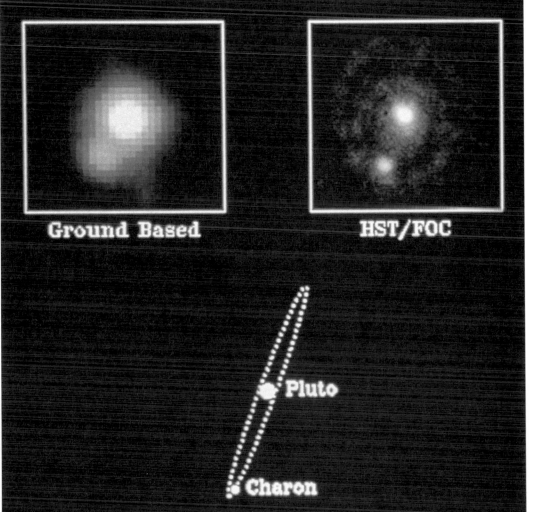

**The separation between Pluto and Charon** can be seen in this image taken by the Hubble Space Telescope *(upper right)* and accompanying diagram *(bottom).* For comparison, the best ground-based image of Pluto and Charon ever taken to date is shown in the upper left.

# Planetary satellites

All the planets in the solar system (except Mercury and Venus) have satellites. At least one asteroid, 532 Herculina, has also been found to have a companion orbiting it. Altogether, there are at least 61 principal planetary satellites, some of which are bigger than the planet Pluto. Most satellites orbit in the same direction as the parent body's axial spin; those that do not were probably captured by the planet after its original satellite system formed. The first planetary satellite to be observed was our moon, but it was not until Galileo's observations in the early seventeenth century that astronomers realized that the earth is not unique in having a companion satellite.

### The satellites of Mars

The two Martian satellites were found in 1877

**The moon** is the earth's only satellite. Its orbit around the earth has an ellipticity of 0.0549, which is sufficient to make the moon's distance from the earth vary from 221,456 miles (356,399 kilometers) at the perigee, to 252,711 miles (406,699 kilometers) at the apogee. The moon's movement around the earth is synchronous with the earth's rotation so that it always presents the same face toward the earth. This satellite is 2,160 miles (3,476 kilometers) across, has a thick crust that extends down to 40 miles (65 kilometers), and covers a mantle 750 miles (1,200 kilometers) thick. This mantle, in turn, surrounds a very dense core with a diameter of about 600 miles (1,000 kilometers). The fractured surface of the moon is pitted with maria and craters, which indicates that it is very old and has been subjected to heavy bombardment. Estimates of the moon's age vary around 4.6 billion years.

by the American astronomer Asaph Hall. Named Phobos and Deimos, after Mars's mythological companions Fear and Terror, they were known only as faint points of light until the 1970's, when the American Mariner probes took measurements of them. The largest dimension of Phobos is 14 miles (23 kilometers), whereas that of Deimos, which is also ellipsoidal, is only about 6 miles (10 kilometers). Both are irregular in shape and deeply pitted with craters. Observations by the Viking orbiter missions of 1975/1976 showed both had undergone considerable bombardment over their lifetimes; the largest crater on Phobos, Stickney, is 6 miles (10 kilometers) across. Their densities are similar, at twice that of water. The irregularity in shape of these two satellites, together with their small size and density, suggests that both are captured asteroids. Phobos is the only satellite in the solar system whose orbital period is less than the rotation period of its parent planet.

### The satellites of Jupiter

In 1610, the four largest Jovian satellites were discovered independently by Galileo and the German astronomer Simon Marius; they are now collectively called the Galilean satellites. In order outward from the planet they are Io, Europa, Ganymede, and Callisto. They range in diameter from 1,942 miles (3,126 kilometers)—the size of Europa, which is slightly smaller than our moon—to 3,278 miles (5,275 kilometers), the diameter of Ganymede, which is larger than Mercury and probably the largest satellite in the solar system.

Io has been described as the nearest one can get to hell in the solar system. When the American probe *Voyager 1* passed by Jupiter in 1979, it discovered that Io's surface is covered in sulfur. The satellite is volcanically active and sends plumes of sulfurous material into space, which forms a torus around Jupiter. The absence of cratering suggests that the surface is regenerated by the volcanic deposition of sulfur over a period of only a million years.

The activity of Io probably results from heat caused by the tidal forces acting on Io generated by Jupiter, Europa, and Ganymede. The whole surface of the satellite heaves up and down by as much as 330 feet (100 meters) every $1\frac{1}{2}$ days. Io is thought to have a molten silicate core, and it is from this central region that plumes of material are shot hundreds of miles above the satellite's surface. The surface is also continually bombarded and eroded by the high-energy particles within Jupiter's magnetosphere.

All the Galilean satellites are embedded in the magnetosphere. By passing through the lines of Jupiter's intense magnetic field, an electric current of 5 million amperes is created. This flows between Io and the planet along a flux tube, which may be responsible for auroral displays on Jupiter.

The next satellite out from Jupiter, Europa, is completely different from the other Galilean satellites and is one of the smoothest objects in the solar system. It has a bright surface covered by a brownish network of fissures, with few craters of more than 30 miles (50 kilometers) across (which implies a relatively young surface). The fissures indicate an expansion of the ice crust that makes up Europa's surface, and it is believed that beneath this crust lies a silicate mantle.

The surface of Ganymede, the third of the Galileans out from Jupiter, appears to be much older, with far more craters in its thick ice crust, which is itself split into tectonic plates. These surface features suggest that the satellite's interior was once more active than now, with considerably more heat in its mantle. The ice crust is frozen to a depth of about 60 miles (100 kilometers), and beneath it may be a layer of convecting water or soft ice surrounding a silicate core.

The outermost of the Galileans is Callisto, which is slightly smaller than Ganymede, being 2,995 miles (4,820 meters) across. It or-

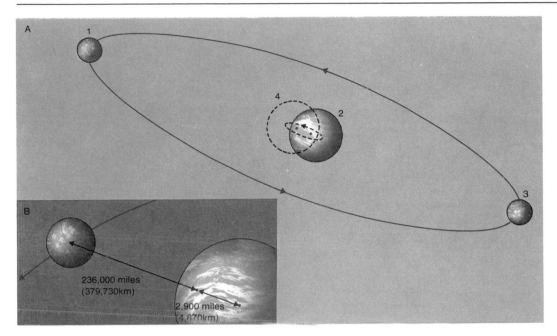

**The moon and the earth**
orbit around their common
center of gravity, just as all
bodies in planetary and stellar systems do. This center
of gravity, called the barycenter, is marked by a solid
dot in the diagram. It lies
1,000 miles (1,600 kilometers) below the earth's surface. Both bodies stay on
opposite sides of the barycenter, so that when the
moon is in position 1, the
earth is at point 2, and when
the moon moves to 3, the
earth shifts in orbit to 4. The
gravitational attraction between them keeps them in
their orbits.

bits at a distance of 1,170,000 miles (1,883,000 kilometers) from Jupiter. Callisto's surface consists of a dark slurry that probably froze on formation, and is now churned up only by micrometeoroid impacts. Callisto seems to have been severely bombarded when it was quite young—one impact has left a crater ring system that is 1,900 miles (3,000 kilometers) in diameter. Since those early impacts, little else has occurred to alter the appearance of the rocky ice crust, which extends to a depth of several hundred miles, and, like Ganymede's, probably covers a convecting water mantle.

The next Jovian satellites were discovered in 1892. Amalthea, Jupiter's innermost moon (excluding smaller bodies found by the Voyager missions), was also photographed by the Voyager craft and found to be a dark red, rocky object resembling an asteroid, with a large crater in the surface. Its red color may be due to the emanations of Io. All the other satel-lites are comparatively minor objects, up to 106 miles (171 kilometers) across. The outermost four orbit Jupiter in a retrograde direction on complex paths greatly affected by the sun. They are all probably captured asteroids. In addition to these major satellites, there are many smaller bodies orbiting Jupiter.

### The satellites of Saturn

The largest member of Saturn's family of 18 satellites, Titan, is 3,190 miles (5,140 kilometers) in diameter and orbits 759,000 miles (1,221,000 kilometers) from the planet. It is the only satellite in the solar system to possess a substantial atmosphere, consisting almost entirely of nitrogen. Because of its distance from the sun, Titan's surface is cold—about −274° F. (−170° C)—and may be covered by oceans of liquid methane. It is also believed that Titan has an icy crust and a mantle that extends to a

**Phobos and Deimos** are
the two satellites that orbit
Mars. Deimos *(below left)* is
the smaller of the two with a
diameter of only 6 miles (10
kilometers)—the lit area
measures about 12 by 5
miles (19 by 8 kilometers). It
is also the outermost of
Mars' satellites. Deimos is
heavily cratered, with its
largest depression measuring nearly a mile across.
Phobos *(below right)* has a
diameter of about 14 miles
(23 kilometers). These two
satellites have spectra similar to those of carbona-
ceous chondrite asteroids,
which suggests that they
were captured by Mars.

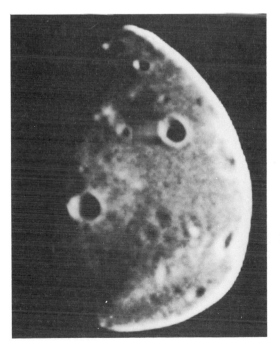

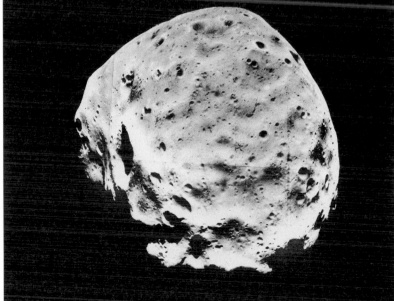

**Io** is the second smallest and the innermost of the Galilean satellites. It is 2,257 miles (3,632 kilometers) across, and its surface is covered with sulfurous material. Io's volcanic activity is evident from the explosion seen here on its limb. Because Io's surface gravity is so low, the ejected material can reach great heights before it drops back slowly to the surface. This plume has reached an altitude of about 60 miles (100 kilometers).

depth of 530 miles (850 kilometers), which covers a core of low-density rock.

Of Saturn's other major satellites, the innermost is Mimas, which is 240 miles (390 kilometers) across and heavily cratered. One impact has left a huge depression in it—almost one-third of its diameter. The next satellite out is Enceladus, which appears as a smooth sphere 310 miles (500 kilometers) across. Tethys appears to have a large gouge across its surface. It is 650 miles (1,050 kilometers) across and seems to be covered in ice mixed with some other, perhaps stony, material.

Dione and Rhea are two of Saturn's satellites that are fairly comparable; Dione is 700 miles (1,130 kilometers) across, and Rhea's diameter is 950 miles (1,530 kilometers). The Voyager probes found them both to be heavily cratered, and both have icy crusts. Rhea's surface is crisscrossed with light streaks of material produced by impact-generated fractures,

and one hemisphere of Dione shows similar features.

Of the outer three satellites—Hyperion, Iapetus, and Phoebe—Iapetus is the most interesting because its brightness varies by a factor of six as it orbits Saturn. The fluctuation results because one hemisphere is covered by much darker material than the other, whose surface is reflective ice. The outermost satellite, Phoebe, orbits a very eccentric path in the opposite direction of Saturn's rotation; it is probably a captured asteroid. Saturn also has nine other satellites that are much smaller.

### The satellites of Uranus

*Voyager 2* circled around Uranus during January 1986, and the planet is now known to have 15 satellites. Most of these are quite small and are believed to orbit around the planet's equatorial plane at a high inclination to the ecliptic (98°). The satellites are named for characters from Shakespeare's plays: Miranda, Ariel, Umbriel, Titania, Oberon, Puck, Portia, Juliet, Cressida, Rosalind, Belinda, Desdemona, Cordelia, Ophelia, and Bianca. Miranda is only 300 miles (480 kilometers) in diameter and therefore very faint (magnitude 16.5). Miranda probably has a density 1.3 times that of water, and consists of a crust of water-ice with a rocky core. Such characteristics are common to Ariel, Umbriel, Titania, and Oberon. The last is at a distance of 362,600 miles (583,500 kilometers) from Uranus. Titania is the largest member, with a diameter of 990 miles (1,590 kilometers). None of these satellites has an appreciable atmosphere, because their masses are too low, and the temperature at that distance from the sun is about −333° F. (−203° C).

### The satellites of Neptune

Uranus has a satellite system that is highly regular, but Neptune's system shows signs of a catastrophe having taken place at some stage in its history.

By far the largest of its eight satellites, Tri-

**Europa,** with a diameter of 1,942 miles (3,126 kilometers), is the smallest of the Galilean satellites. It differs from other satellites and planets in that its surface is relatively smooth and has virtually no craters. This might suggest that the satellite is quite young, and estimates of 100 million years have been made. The surface consists of a thick layer of fissured ice, the cracks in which may have resulted from forces of tension. The reason for them, however, is still not definitely known.

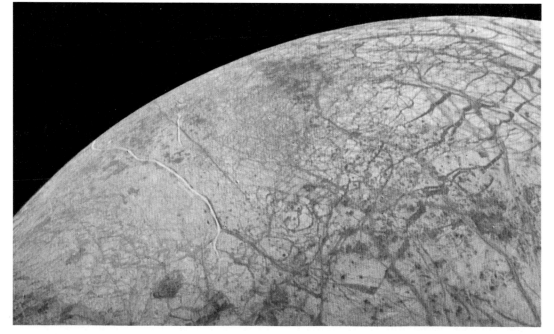

ton has a highly inclined, retrograde orbit that is unstable. The satellite is due to break up as it approaches Neptune closely in a few hundred million years from now. It is about 1,700 miles (2,720 kilometers) across, has a density about twice that of water, and orbits at a distance of 221,750 miles (354,800 kilometers) from Neptune. Triton appears to be the coldest place in the solar system; its surface temperature is about −400 F. (−206 C). *Voyager 2*'s images revealed a bizarre landscape of canyons, peaks, and craters, resembling the skin of a cantaloupe. Some scientists believe this strange geology may be due to violent eruptions of ice volcanoes at Triton's south polar cap. Triton is the only moon in the solar system to have auroras.

Another of Neptune's satellites, Nereid, is an exceptionally faint (19th magnitude) asteroidal body, which was discovered by Kuiper in 1949. It follows the most elongated path of any satellite. Nereid is about 3.4 million miles (5.5 million kilometers) from its parent planet.

### Pluto's satellite

For many years, the physical characteristics of Pluto were largely unknown, because of its distance from earth. The discovery in 1978 of a satellite, Charon, enabled some of the questions to be answered. It appears that Pluto and Charon form the most closely-matched planet-satellite pair in the solar system, with Charon's mass being about one-sixteenth that of Pluto, and its diameter about one-third. Charon has a magnitude of 17. It orbits just 12,500 miles (20,100 kilometers) from Pluto in a retrograde orbit, and its orbital period is the same as the rotational period of Pluto, so the same hemisphere of Pluto always faces Charon. Tidal interactions are also likely to have locked Charon in such a way that it keeps the same face toward Pluto at all times. Pluto and Charon thus form the only known completely synchronous pair in the solar system. Apart from its orbital characteristics, very little is known about the satellite.

**Ganymede** is the largest satellite in the solar system. It is slightly larger than Mercury, but has only one-third its density. This photograph, taken 2,100,000 miles (3,400,000 kilometers) above Ganymede, shows a surface similar to that of the moon. There are dark areas resembling the maria and the bright areas are reminiscent of lunar ray craters. The darker regions are the oldest on Ganymede, possibly 3 billion years old. The grooves crisscrossing the satellite's surface may be due to tensional forces.

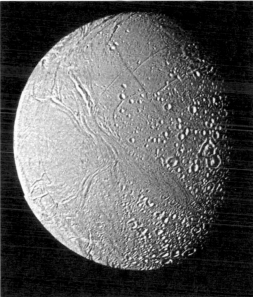

**Enceladus** is a Saturnian satellite that orbits the planet at a mean distance of 149,000 miles (240,000 kilometers). The satellite's surface resembles that of other inner Saturnian satellites in that it is bright and icy, whereas the outer satellites tend to be darker. The lack of prominent surface features indicates that Enceladus undergoes a continual process of resurfacing, because it seems unlikely that it would have escaped the bombardment that has marked the surface of the outer satellites.

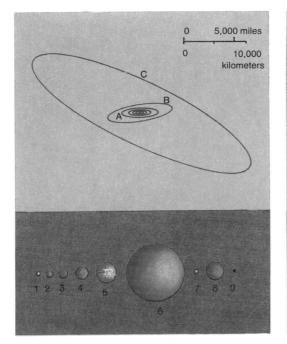

**Saturn's satellites** *(far left)* fall into three groups. The first (A) contains Mimas (1), Enceladus (2), Tethys (3), Dione (4), and Rhea (5). The second group (B) consists of Titan (6), Hyperion (7), and Iapetus (8). Phoebe (9) is the sole member of group C. Jupiter's satellites *(left)* also form three groups. The innermost contains Amalthea (1), Io (2), Europa (3), Ganymede (4), and Callisto (5). Group B consists of Leda (6), Himalia (7), Lysithea (8), and Elara (9). Ananke (10), Carme (11), Pasiphaë (12), and Sinope (13) form group C.

# Astronomy from space

The earth's atmosphere is the sustainer and, to some extent, protector of life on our planet. But to the astronomer, it often seems to be a severe handicap, affecting the quality of telescope images, as well as blocking some parts of the electromagnetic spectrum, and preventing radiation from space from reaching the surface of the earth. It is not surprising, then, that since the early 1960's, much effort has been expended on finding ways of observing the heavens from above the limits of our atmosphere.

## The atmosphere and image quality

The limitations that the earth's atmosphere imposes on ground-based astronomy become apparent even in the optical (visible) region of the spectrum. The atmosphere is completely transparent between wavelengths of 4,000 and 7,000 Å, but observation of very faint sources of light is hampered by the background of natural airglow and interference from man-made sources, such as city lights. The atmosphere is also in a state of constant movement because of temperature and humidity changes, which cause the telescope image to dance around or spread out. The result is that the resolution of a telescope is always less than it should theoretically be. All these factors lead to unfavorable "seeing," or conditions, for observations of a good quality from beneath the atmosphere. "Seeing"—the viewing conditions—limits the useful size of large optical telescopes. The 200-inch (5-meter) Hale telescope on Mt. Palomar is theoretically capable of a resolution of 0.025 arc seconds, but invariably falls well short of this figure because of the "seeing" condition; the resolution is usually around 0.8 arc seconds.

The limitations imposed by the atmosphere were reduced dramatically when the American space shuttle placed the Hubble Space Telescope into an orbit about 380 miles (610 kilometers) above the earth's surface. This telescope has a resolution of 0.066 arc seconds at 6,330 Å wavelength, much better than an earth-based telescope of an equivalent size. It can observe objects 50 times fainter than can be seen using the best telescopes on the ground.

## Absorption of radiation by the atmosphere

Many objects in the sky emit radiation over a range of the electromagnetic spectrum. Due to the absorption of parts of the spectrum by various atmospheric atoms and molecules, however, ground-based observations are restricted to selected regions of the spectrum. The parts of the atmosphere that are transparent to electromagnetic radiation are called "windows," the most important for plant and animal life being the optical window between 4,000 and 7,000 Å—the wavelength range of visible light. (This fact provides the reason why most animals have evolved sight organs that are sensitive to these wavelengths, and these alone.)

The other prominent and astronomically useful windows are in the radio region and in the near infrared region (between 8 and 13μm, and 17 and 20 μm). The ultraviolet, gamma-ray, and X-ray regions of the spectrum are completely absorbed by the earth's atmosphere. Astronomers observing from below the atmosphere are therefore unable to obtain full information on the spectrum of an object in the sky because of the opaqueness of the at-

**The Astrobee 1500 rocket** is one of many such vehicles used to take measurements of the atmosphere above the earth's surface. The Astrobee 1500 was developed to carry heavy scientific payloads to high altitudes and designed to boost a 250-pound (113-kilogram) payload to 750 miles (1,207 kilometers) or a 60-pound (27-kilogram) payload to more than 1,600 miles (2,574 kilometers), with a normal launch elevation of 80 degrees. The payload consists of equipment that measures the temperature and pressure of the atmosphere, as well as its density, composition, and movement. Such rockets provide a relatively simple and inexpensive means of atmospheric research.

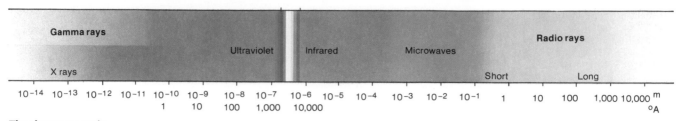

| Gamma rays | | | | Ultraviolet | Infrared | | Microwaves | | Radio rays | | |
|---|---|---|---|---|---|---|---|---|---|---|---|
| X rays | | | | | | | | Short | | Long | |

$10^{-14}$  $10^{-13}$  $10^{-12}$  $10^{-11}$  $10^{-10}$  $10^{-9}$  $10^{-8}$  $10^{-7}$  $10^{-6}$  $10^{-5}$  $10^{-4}$  $10^{-3}$  $10^{-2}$  $10^{-1}$  1  10  100  1,000  10,000 m

1  10  100  1,000  10,000                                                                                     °A

**The electromagnetic spectrum** comprises radio waves, microwaves, infrared, and ultraviolet radiation, X rays and visible light. The waves are measured by wavelength—in meters or angstroms ($10^{-10}$ meters) or frequency (in hertz). Most electromagnetic radiations are absorbed by the earth's atmosphere.

mosphere at certain wavelengths. The advent of rockets, satellites, and space probes has done much to overcome this difficulty and to increase our knowledge of the universe.

### Solving the problem

To minimize the effects on observing conditions, astronomers have built observatories far away from cities to avoid background light, and have sited them at high altitudes where the air is thin, unpolluted, and relatively dry. The last condition is especially important for observations in the infrared region of the spectrum, for which atmospheric absorption depends on the water content of the atmosphere. Some sites, such as those in Northern Europe, are so wet that the 17 to 20μm infrared "window" becomes nearly opaque, making observations impossible. Sites such as Mauna Kea in Hawaii, however, at an altitude of about 13,796 feet (4,205 meters), or the South Pole, are ideal for observations through this "window."

The careful choice of observatory sites may improve the optical quality of the image as well as the transmission of certain regions of the spectrum, but it is not the ideal solution because many spectral regions are completely invisible from the earth. A better solution is to take the observing equipment above the obstructing layers of the atmosphere to a height at which turbulence and atmospheric absorption become negligible.

Before the development of orbital satellites, three methods of observing from above the atmosphere were used—from aircraft, balloons, and sounding (research) rockets. Aircraft observatories can take instruments to altitudes of about 12 miles (20 kilometers)—high enough to open up many more of the "windows" in the

**Far above the atmosphere,** satellites can photograph and measure celestial objects without the distortion that affects ground-based observations. For example, the computer-enhanced X-ray photograph *(right)* of the radio galaxy Cygnus A could have been taken only by satellite.

infrared part of the spectrum. Helium-filled balloons, capable of reaching heights of 30 miles (48 kilometers), enable ultraviolet as well as infrared measurements to be made. Sounding rockets can carry small payloads up to altitudes of 300 miles (482 kilometers), or even higher. At these heights, the experiments are clear of the obstructions of the atmosphere, although observations can be made for only about 12 minutes.

All of these methods are more economical than launching a satellite, but they all also have many drawbacks, the most serious being the limited observing time. Nevertheless, they do enable experiments to be placed at high altitudes quickly (as would be needed for observations of novae or flare stars) if a satellite is not in orbit to undertake the observations. They are also useful as a means of testing equipment before placing it in orbit.

Before the first satellite, *Sputnik 1,* was launched in 1957, most of our knowledge of the universe had come from research with sounding rockets. These carried simple experiments to measure the conditions in the upper reaches of the atmosphere. The real breakthrough in rocket technology came with the work of the Germans in the 1930's, resulting in the development of the A-4 rocket (more commonly called the V-2). This, in turn, became the basis of most subsequent rocket programs. The United States launched 67 V-2's from White Sands, New Mexico, between April 1946 and June 1951, primarily for upper atmosphere research and astronomy. One of these, launched in 1946, carried the first experiment to record the solar spectrum below 3,000 Å, an ultraviolet region that is absorbed by the ozone layer in the earth's atmosphere.

Since these early beginnings, many hundreds of sounding rocket launches have taken place throughout the world. Many of the payloads have been directly intended for astronomical research, such as experiments for recording the spectra of the sun and stars in the ultraviolet and X-ray regions. Sounding rockets still have a useful place in astronomical research, although the real mass of data has come since the advent of satellites in orbit.

### The benefits of using satellites and probes

Apart from improving on the telescope image and observing a greater range of the electromagnetic spectrum, there are other advantages of placing astronomical instruments above the atmosphere that merit the vast amounts of money spent on this aspect of space research. Satellites can provide continuous observing time well above any cloud cover. The advantage of a satellite over sounding rockets is well illustrated by the Orbiting Astronomical Observatory (OAO) launched in 1972. In half a day it furnished data equivalent to that gathered from 40 sounding rockets over a 15-year period.

Satellites also enable scientists to send experiments into a particular environment they wish to study. For example, the *Explorer I* satellite measured belts of intense radiation from particles captured in the geomagnetic field about 600 miles (1,000 kilometers) above the Earth (the Van Allen belts), which were totally unknown from ground-based observations.

### The disadvantages of satellites

Satellites and probes have to operate with a high degree of reliability, because after being launched, they are "connected" to the ground control only by a radio link. All on-board systems must therefore function efficiently—and continue to function—for the mission to be a success. The space environment is very hostile, and satellites are subjected to extremes of temperature, intense solar radiation, and bombardment from micrometeorites and fast particles. The satellite engineer, therefore, has to design the satellite to function for many years without fail in this environment. The extensive development and rigorous "space" testing of a satellite prior to its launch means that the cost of building one is very high—as much as $50 to $60 million—which does not include the cost of the launch.

### Communicating with spacecraft

The communication package on a spacecraft or rocket payload is possibly its most important feature, because without it, the mission would be virtually useless. Communicating with a spacecraft is a two-way process: ground control sends up commands to alter the status of the spacecraft, such as pointing it at different parts of the sky or controlling the start and end of a particular experiment; the spacecraft, conversely, sends back information called telemetry data to the ground station. This information can take the form of scientific data from an experiment, or data on the status of the spacecraft, such as temperature measurements.

The communication payload of the Voyager spacecraft (1979) is a fine example of a system developed for the transmission of large amounts of data over vast distances of space. It also illustrates many of the problems that communication engineers face when designing spacecraft systems. The transmitter on board the Voyager craft had a maximum output of only 23 watts (about the same power as a refrigerator light bulb). It could, however, transmit information accurately and at very high speed over 435 million miles (700 million kilometers) back to earth (40 minutes journey time). This meant that the power at the receiving dish of the satellite tracking station was exceptionally small (about $10^{14}$ watts/m²), and therefore required the most sensitive ground equipment.

The system was designed to transmit information at the rate of one complete picture every 48 seconds. This translates into about 107,000 bits per second. One picture consists of 800 by 800 picture elements, or "pixels," each one being an eight-bit binary number that indicates the light intensity level of that part of the picture. This rate of sending back data is 14,000 times faster than the *Mariner IV* mission to Mars in 1964, when only 20 pictures were sent back to Earth in 7 days. Voyager's communication system, like all those of scientific and communications satellites, was designed to transmit data with a high degree of accuracy, because the information was of such vital importance. The error rate for Voyager was one bit in 10,000, or 0.01 per cent. If it were possible to use the information capacity of the Voyager spacecraft on a commercial communication satellite, it would enable every American citizen to speak to a Soviet counterpart simultaneously—more than 500 million telephone conversations. A typical astronomy satellite is able to transmit data at a rate of 20,000 bits per second—about one-fifth the rate of the Voyager system—over a distance of roughly 18,500 miles (30,000 kilometers).

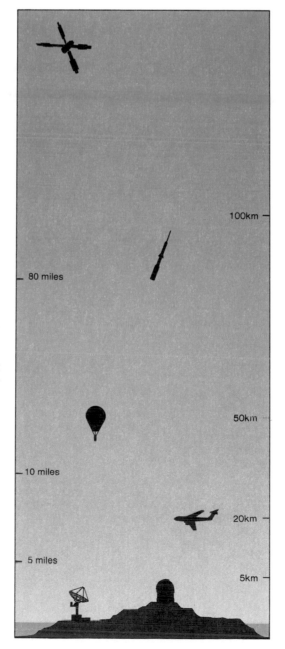

**Data has been collected** on the X-ray, ultraviolet, and gamma-ray regions of the space above earth since it has been possible to lift research instruments above the earth's atmosphere. Observatories sited at dry altitudes can sometimes see into the infrared regions of the atmosphere, but normally, "seeing" is restricted to the visible wavelengths. Aircraft that carry telescopes can fly at a high enough altitude for more extensive information on the infrared to be collected. Farther above the earth's surface, helium-filled balloons transport measuring instruments into the ultraviolet areas. Sounding rockets, flying at 60 miles (100 kilometers) and beyond, penetrate into the X-ray regions, and satellites can carry instruments high enough to record data of all the wavelengths in the electromagnetic spectrum.

# Satellite astronomy

Early results from sounding rockets indicated the enormous potential of astronomical observations from above the earth's atmosphere—a potential that began to be realized with the successful launches of the Soviet Sputnik and American Explorer satellites in the late 1950's. Since these early launches, thousands of satellites have been placed into orbit. Those designed for astronomical research have yielded much information about the heavens that could not have been obtained from ground-based observatories, principally because the earth's atmosphere absorbs almost all forms of radiation apart from visible light and radio waves.

### The early astronomical satellites

Following the launch of the world's first artificial satellite, *Sputnik 1,* on October 4, 1957, the Soviet Union's space effort was devoted mainly to lunar and planetary exploration. Nevertheless, the Soviet Union did launch a few satellites designed for purely astronomical research, such as *Sputnik 3* (launched on May 15, 1958), which carried detectors for cosmic rays, X rays, and ultraviolet radiation. And more sophisticated scientific satellites ap-

peared with the nation's Cosmos series (which began on March 16, 1962 with *Cosmos 1*), such as *Cosmos 51* (launched December 10, 1964), which was equipped with cosmic and ultraviolet radiation experiments, and *Cosmos 166,* a solar X-ray satellite.

The United States, on the other hand, initiated an extensive series of scientific space probes with the launching of its first satellite, *Explorer 1,* on January 31, 1958. One of the series, *Explorer 42* (also called Uhuru, the Swahili word for freedom), was the first satellite devoted primarily to studying celestial X-ray sources. Launched in December 1970, it produced an X-ray map of the heavens and, after six months of observations, had discovered more than 170 discrete X-ray sources—five times as many as were previously known. It also pinpointed the location of Cygnus X-1 (so-called because it was the first X-ray source discovered in the constellation of Cygnus), which is now thought to be a black hole.

Following the lead of the Soviet Union and the United States, other nations began to build satellites, including Britain, Italy, West Germany, Canada, France, Japan, China, and India.

### What is a satellite?

Satellites are complex structures, consisting of many thousands of individual components, designed to operate in the harsh environment of space. They are of various shapes and sizes, and each is designed specifically for the mission it has to perform. Nevertheless, the structure of any satellite can be divided into a number of discrete sections—called subsystems—each having a particular function, such as supplying power or providing communications. All of a satellite's subsystems must work perfectly because it is usually impossible to rectify any fault that may occur after a satellite has been launched.

**Sputnik 1,** a model of which is shown *(right),* was the first artificial satellite. Launched by the Soviet Union on October 4, 1957, it went into an elliptical orbit around the earth, remaining there until early 1958, when it fell back and burnt up in the atmosphere.

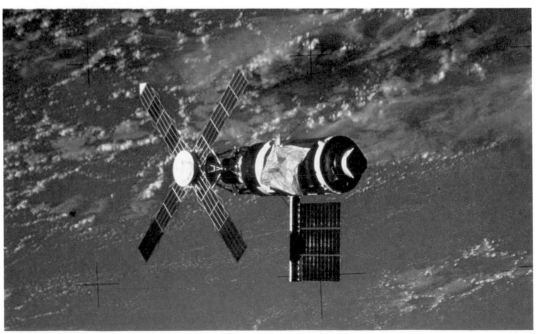

**Skylab,** shown in orbit above the earth, was launched on May 25, 1973. The craft—which was designed to accommodate three astronauts and carried an extensive array of scientific equipment—was slightly damaged during the launch but was repaired by the first group of astronauts who occupied it. Two other three-man teams later spent long periods (60 and 84 days, respectively) in Skylab, where they carried out many valuable experiments. It reentered the earth's atmosphere and burnt up over Australia in July 1979.

## The power subsystem

Although a satellite requires all of its subsystems in order to function properly, the power subsystem is probably the most important, because all others ultimately depend on it. Most satellites are powered by solar cells that convert sunlight into electricity. On average, a scientific satellite requires about 200 watts of power (equivalent to two domestic light bulbs), which is supplied by 10,000 or more solar cells.

There are, however, problems associated with solar cells. They generate electricity only when exposed to light and so do not operate if the sun's rays are prevented from reaching the spacecraft, as when it is in the earth's shadow. For this reason, satellites also carry batteries. Solar cells are also very inefficient; at best, only about 10 per cent of the sun's energy is converted into electricity. Moreover, the constant bombardment of a cell by sunlight tends to reduce its efficiency, and after many years in orbit it can decrease to less than 10 per cent.

Spacecraft on missions that take them away from the sun, where solar cells would receive too little sunlight to provide a useful amount of electricity, need alternative power supplies. For example, the Voyager 1 and 2 probes to the outer planets carried small nuclear generators to provide the necessary power.

## Satellite payloads

From the scientist's point of view, the payload is the most important part of a satellite. It comprises the experiment module, carefully developed and extensively tested on the ground and, if the mission proceeds as planned, the device that will gather important astronomical data.

Astronomical payloads are extremely varied, designed according to the tasks they have to perform. They can range from simple aluminum foil sheets for the detection of small micrometeoroids, to a complex telescope assembly. Although, varying greatly, astronomical payloads have one factor in common: they are all detectors.

The function of most detectors is to investigate part of the electromagnetic spectrum—X rays, gamma rays, ultraviolet radiation, and so on—and the structure of a detector therefore depends on the part of the spectrum being studied. In the visible part of the spectrum, the simplest form of detector is a photographic plate or film. To detect gamma rays, X rays, ultraviolet, infrared, or radio wavelengths, however, it is necessary to use other forms of detectors.

## The observation of X rays

The detection of X rays presents unique problems, mainly because they cannot be reflected and focused by the same types of mirrors used in normal reflecting telescopes. They can, however, be reflected when the incidence angle (the angle at which the X ray hits a mirror's surface) is very small (less than 2°). It is this property that has been used to construct X-ray telescopes, which focus the rays onto special detectors. X-ray telescopes are diffi-

**The Solar Maximum Mission** (SMM or Solar Max) satellite—shown here just before its launch on February 14, 1980—was designed to study the sun during a period of maximum solar activity. Before it reentered Earth's atmosphere and burned in December 1989, the SMM observed more than 12,500 solar flares.

**The SMM's modular construction** increased its lifetime by allowing it to be repaired while it was in orbit. In 1984, astronauts aboard the space shuttle Challenger replaced blown fuses and other damaged components, then successfully relaunched the satellite. The principal parts of the SMM are shown below—control systems in blue, structural components in green, power systems in yellow, scientific instruments in pink, and communications systems in brown.

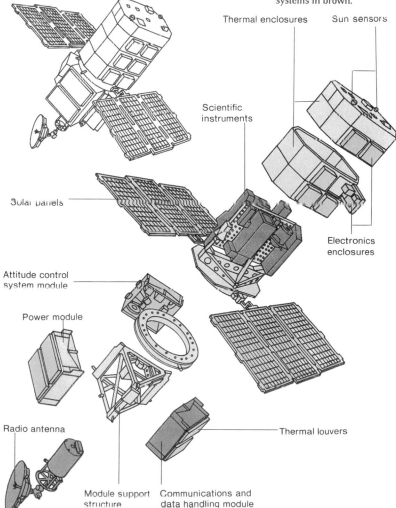

Thermal enclosures

Sun sensors

Scientific instruments

Solar panels

Electronics enclosures

Attitude control system module

Power module

Radio antenna

Module support structure

Communications and data handling module

Thermal louvers

**The Wolter Type I X-ray telescope** has two mirrors (one paraboloid in shape, the other hyperboloid) around its circumference to focus incoming X rays, which are then detected by special instruments at the focal point. The unusual design of this type of telescope is necessary because X rays are reflected only when they hit mirrors at very small angles.

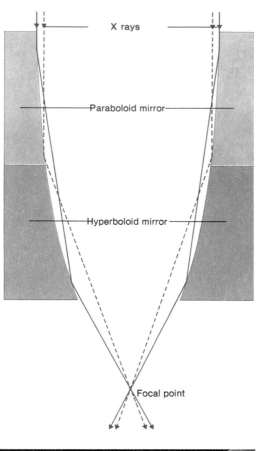

X rays

Paraboloid mirror

Hyperboloid mirror

Focal point

**The Hubble Space Telescope** launched by the Space Shuttle is more than 42 feet (13 meters) long and has an aperture of 7.9 feet (2.4 meters). One of its functions is to detect extremely faint celestial objects, for which purpose a special camera—the Faint Object Camera—has been developed.

cult to build, and for this reason the early models did not use mirrors but rather other mechanisms for channeling the X rays into the detector. The simplest of such channeling mechanisms is the collimator, which consists of an array of thin metal plates. A typical collimator of this type cannot locate X-ray sources very precisely, but more complicated designs, such as modulation collimators (which have fine mesh grids instead of metal plates), are considerably more accurate.

To achieve still greater positional accuracy requires the use of a telescope in which the X rays are reflected by the polished surfaces of extremely accurately shaped mirrors. One of the most common of this type is called the Wolter Type I. A very large X-ray telescope was carried by the Einstein High Energy Astronomy Observatory (HEAO-2), launched in late 1978. It had four Wolter Type I telescopes, mounted one inside the other to increase the collecting area.

Once the X rays have been collimated, or focused, they must be detected with some form of counter; X-ray telescopes often have interchangeable detectors. The most commonly used detector is the gas-filled proportional counter, which is suitable for the detection of low-energy X rays. These enter through a large window made from a thin sheet of beryllium or other light (that is, of low atomic number) metal. Inside the main part of the detector, which is filled with gas, are a series of anodes at a high positive potential (about 2,000 volts). Each X ray entering the window collides with atoms of the gas, causing them to release electrons (called photoelectrons). These electrons then move rapidly towards the anode and, in turn, liberate more electrons, causing an "avalanche" of electric charge. The charge is then measured electronically, which gives an indication of the incoming X ray's wavelength. Proportional counters such as these have been used successfully on the Uhuru, Ariel V, and Einstein satellites.

Other forms of detectors have been developed, all of which rely on the general principle of converting X rays into other, more easily measurable forms of energy. One alternative type is the scintillation detector, which usually consists of a crystal of sodium iodide or cesium iodide. The crystal responds to X rays by generating flashes of light, which are then detected by a photomultiplier tube. Another form of detector is the microchannel plate, which comprises an array of small-channeled electron multipliers. This last type was used on the Einstein satellite to obtain high-resolution images.

### The observation of other radiation

The Infra-Red Astronomical Satellite (IRAS), launched in January 1983, was the first satellite designed specifically to survey the sky at infrared wavelengths, a task hitherto undertaken only by special ground-based telescopes. The satellite's 24-inch (60-centimeter) telescope mirror focused infrared radiation onto photoconductive detectors, which converted the radiation into an electric current. The entire telescope assembly (including the detectors) was surrounded by a dewar vessel (similar to a vacuum flask) containing 154 pounds (70 kilograms) of liquid helium at a temperature of about 2 K, 2° above absolute zero. This extremely low temperature was essential because if the telescope was not cooled, its own infrared (heat) radiation would obscure the relatively weak radiation emitted by celestial sources. In addition to its main task of the sky survey, another function of the IRAS was to record the spectrum of unusual infrared sources.

Other types of unmanned astronomical spacecraft are the International Ultraviolet Explorer (IUE) and various gamma-ray satellites (notably Cos-B). The IUE, a joint American and European project, was launched on January 26, 1978. Orbiting at an altitude of more than 18,500 miles (30,000 kilometers), the IUE carried an 18-inch (45-centimeter) reflecting telescope, remotely controlled from earth, with a special ultraviolet radiation detector linked to a television camera. Cos-B, launched in 1975, was designed to investigate celestial gamma-ray sources. Among the data it sent back was evidence to support the idea that there are two main gamma-ray sources.

### Space Telescopes

From the experience gained from its Orbiting Astronomical Observatory (OAO) satellites—especially from OAO-3 (commonly called Copernicus), which was launched in 1972 and carried a 32-inch (81-centimeter) telescope for ultraviolet observations—NASA launched a 94-inch (2.4-meter) diameter telescope into space in April 1990 using the Space Shuttle. Orbiting about 380 miles (610 kilometers) above the earth, the Hubble Space Telescope is sensitive to a wide range of wavelengths—from 1,100 to 10,000,000 Å (1 millimeter)—and can detect celestial objects 50 times fainter than those observable from earth.

### Astronomy from manned spacecraft

Man's outstanding quality, as compared to electronic and mechanical systems, is his ability to make decisions, based on both experience and intuition, that a machine cannot.

**The space shuttle** was finally launched—after many postponements—on April 12, 1981. Unlike all previous space hardware, most of the shuttle is reusable. Moreover, it is extremely versatile; one of its important functions is to place satellites in orbit using a remote manipulator arm. The satellites can then be tested immediately and, if they malfunction, can be retrieved by the shuttle and returned to earth. Here, the space shuttle Atlantis is about to dock with Russia's Mir space station.

# Probes to the moon

After the successful launching of the first artificial satellites, the Soviet Union's *Sputnik 1* in October 1957 and the United States' *Explorer 1* in early 1958, these two countries began launching probes to the moon. Initially, the Soviet Union was the more successful in its lunar space program, but the most spectacular achievement was made by the United States in July 1969, when Neil Armstrong and Edwin Aldrin became the first men to set foot on the lunar surface.

### The Soviet Luna missions

The Soviet Union began its lunar program with the launch of *Luna 1* on January 2, 1959. Weighing about 790 pounds (360 kilograms), it

*Luna 9* (an exhibition model of which is shown *right*) was launched on January 31, 1966 and made the first successful soft landing on the moon. This Soviet probe used a special landing technique *(below)* whereby its instrument capsule was automatically released when a hinged arm on the main craft hit the lunar surface. Weighted at the bottom, the capsule assumed an upright position after rolling across the surface, and its petal-like panels then opened to expose cameras and other instruments.

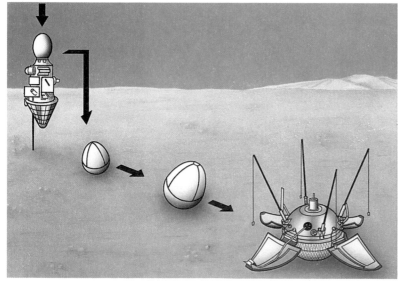

carried instruments to measure magnetic fields and solar and cosmic radiation and passed within 3,700 miles (6,000 kilometers) of the moon. Nine months later, the next Soviet lunar probe, *Luna 2,* hard-landed on the moon's surface, thereby becoming the first probe to reach another world. And shortly afterward, in October 1959, *Luna 3* made the first circumlunar flight and sent back the first photographs of the far side of the moon—during a period in which the United States was experiencing a series of failures in its lunar probe program.

Following the success of the first three Luna missions, the Soviet Union devoted much of its space effort to Mars and Venus probes. In 1963, however, it launched *Luna 4,* which attempted a soft landing on the moon. But the probe by-passed the moon on April 6, 1963 and went into orbit around the sun. After four further attempts, the Soviet Union achieved the first successful soft landing with *Luna 9,* which landed on the moon on February 4, 1966 and began transmitting close-up pictures of the lunar surface.

Three years later *Luna 15* was launched—on July 12, 1969 ($3\frac{1}{2}$ days before *Apollo 11*)—with the intention of soft landing on the moon, taking a soil sample, and returning to earth. The Soviet probe was successfully placed in lunar orbit—where it remained during the Apollo flight—but crashed on the moon during its descent to the surface. *Luna 16,* however, was successful. Launched on September 12, 1970, it soft-landed on the moon, where its automatic drilling rig bored down to a depth of just over a foot and extracted some 0.2 pound (100 grams) of rock and soil. This sample was then placed in a sealed container and launched back to earth, where it was recovered and its contents analyzed.

### The first robot lunar explorer

*Luna 17,* launched on November 10, 1970, was a great technical success for the Soviet space program. The unmanned craft landed safely on the moon and, after checks by its television cameras, one of its two ramps was lowered on command from ground control on earth. Off the top of the craft rolled *Lunokhod 1*—an eight-wheeled robot vehicle which, under guidance from earth, was capable of moving about on the moon's surface. Warmed by the circulation of heated gas, it withstood the extremely cold lunar nights—during which the temperature typically falls to below −200° F. (−130° C)—and remained functional for more than 10 months. In this period, it traveled nearly 7 miles (11 kilometers), testing the soil at points on its path and sending back many television pictures of the surface. In January 1973, the Soviet Union repeated this success with the *Luna 21* mission, which carried *Lunokhod 2.* This second "moonwalker" traveled about $3\frac{1}{2}$ times the distance of its predecessor and also sent back television pictures of the surface.

The Soviet Union, by this time surpassed by the United States in the field of lunar exploration, thereafter devoted much of its space effort to sending probes to the planets, such as Venus.

### The first American lunar probes

Shortly after the success of its first earth satellite, *Explorer 1,* the United States launched three small moon probes—*Pioneer 0, Pioneer 1,* and *Pioneer 2.* Each weighed 84 pounds (38 kilograms) and was equipped with a camera, a micrometeorite detector, and a magnetometer, and they were intended to go into orbit around the moon. All three failed in their objective but valuable experience was gained for future missions. Moreover, before falling back into the southern Pacific Ocean after a 43-hour flight, *Pioneer 1* recorded the extent of the Van Allen radiation belts in the earth's atmosphere, previously discovered by *Explorer 1.*

The next two American lunar probes, *Pioneer 3* (launched in late 1958) and *Pioneer 4* (launched in early 1959), were even smaller, weighing only 13 pounds (6 kilograms). The aim of their missions was to fly past the moon at close range. Again, neither probe was completely successful, the closest approach being achieved by *Pioneer 4,* which passed within about 37,000 miles (60,000 kilometers) of the moon but failed to transmit pictures back to earth.

With the development of the powerful Atlas launching rockets, a new series of Pioneer probes was planned. These probes were more sophisticated than the previous Pioneers, each being a 39.5-inch (100-centimeter) sphere with four solar paddles and hydrazine propulsion units. Four probes were launched between September 1959 and December 1960, but all failed disastrously because of problems with the rocket booster. Meanwhile, Soviet Luna probes had photographed 70 per cent of the moon's far side.

### The Ranger spacecraft

The American moon program began to achieve a measure of success with the introduction of the Ranger spacecraft. They were stabilized in all three axes, had a high-gain antenna pointing at the earth, and an array of instruments directed toward the moon. Despite the effort put into the project, all of the first six missions failed to perform perfectly.

*Ranger 1* and *Ranger 2,* intended as test vehicles, achieved only a low orbit above the earth. *Ranger 3, Ranger 4,* and *Ranger 5* were prepared for attempts to hard-land a capsule on the moon's surface and then transmit seismic and meteorite data back to earth. The plan was to release a small capsule 13 miles (21 kilometers) above the moon, allow it to fall toward the surface then, by firing retrorockets, slow down the capsule to zero velocity at a height of about 1,100 feet (335 meters), from where it would free-fall, and finally hit the surface at about 120 miles (190 kilometers) per hour. On impact, the capsule was designed to right itself so that its aerial pointed toward the earth. But this ingenious device was never put to the test because all three missions malfunctioned. However, *Ranger 4* did reach the moon, becoming the first American probe to land on the lunar surface (it crash-landed on the far side in April 1962).

At about this time there was a marked change in emphasis of the American lunar

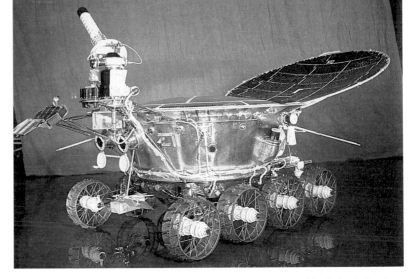

*Lunokhod 1* landed with the Soviet probe *Luna 17* in November 1970. The first vehicle on the moon, *Lunokhod 1*—remotely controlled from earth—traveled over the lunar surface, collecting data and transmitting television pictures back to earth.

The American unmanned probe *Orbiter 4* took this photograph of the lunar surface in 1967; it shows part of Mare Orientale, which spreads onto the moon's far side. The five Orbiter probes undertook a comprehensive survey of the moon. They used a special scanning technique to convert the photographs into transmittable form and for this reason the images have a striped appearance.

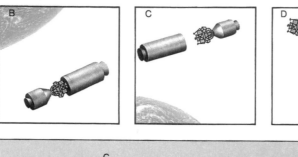

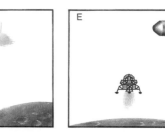

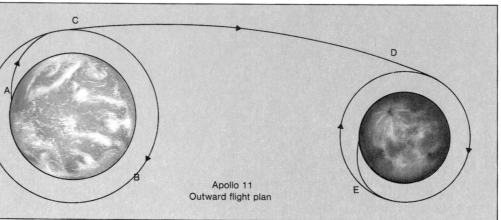

*Apollo 11* was launched (A) on July 16, 1969. In earth's orbit, the Command Module and its attached Service Module turned and docked (B) with the Lunar Module. The remaining rocket stage fired to put the craft into moon trajectory and was then jettisoned (C). Near the moon, the Service Module's main engine fired (D) and the craft entered lunar orbit. During the 12th orbit, the Lunar Module separated from the main craft (E) and, carrying two astronauts, descended to the lunar surface.

Apollo 11
Outward flight plan

program, stimulated by President John Kennedy's declaration in 1961 that the United States' space effort should be directed toward landing a man on the moon.

The first step was to replace the early seismic-capsule Rangers with a new series of Ranger probes equipped with an extensive array of cameras. *Ranger 6,* the first of the new models, was launched in early 1964, en route for a hard landing on the moon. But although it landed on target, its cameras failed to transmit pictures.

The next (and final) three Ranger missions were successful, however. Launched between July 1964 and March 1965, *Ranger 7, Ranger 8,* and *Ranger 9* relayed more than 17,000 high-resolution pictures back to earth. Surface features, 1,000 times smaller than any visible from earth, could be clearly seen in some of the

photographs; *Ranger 9*'s final series of pictures, for example, were taken from about 5,000 feet (1,500 meters) above the lunar surface and showed details as small as one foot across.

### The Surveyor probes

The next logical step for the United States was to attempt a soft landing on the moon, which was achieved in May 1966 with the *Surveyor 1* mission (four months after *Luna 9*'s touchdown on the surface). Launched by an Atlas-Centaur rocket, *Surveyor 1* landed successfully near the lunar equator after a 63-hour flight. As it approached the lunar surface, retrorockets decelerated the craft until it was nearly stationary at a height of about 12 feet (4 meters), from which it free-fell to the surface. Shock-absorbers on the legs softened the impact. Designed to withstand the extremes of lunar temperature, *Surveyor 1* was equipped with a television camera capable of rotating through a complete circle. Over a six-week period, this camera relayed more than 11,500 photographs of the lunar surface.

The next three successful missions, *Surveyor 3, Surveyor 5,* and *Surveyor 6,* also landed near the equator, whereas *Surveyor 7,* the final one in this series, landed outside the rim of the crater Tycho in the Southern Hemisphere. Each of these probes carried a mechanical scoop to carry out investigations of the lunar soil. *Surveyor 3* dug 7 inches (18 centimeters) into the lunar soil and sent back photographs of the results. *Surveyor 5* carried special equipment to analyze the chemical composition of the lunar soil—the first time this had been done. The analysis showed that the moon's soil is reasonably similar to terrestrial basaltic soil. More importantly perhaps, the Surveyor probes proved that the technology existed for a manned landing on the lunar surface.

**The first men on the moon**—the Apollo 11 astronauts Neil Armstrong and Edwin Aldrin—spent about 21½ hours on the lunar surface before rejoining Michael Collins in the orbiting Command Module. On the moon, Armstrong left the Lunar Module about 6¼ hours after touchdown, and Aldrin joined him shortly afterward. The two men stayed outside the module for more than 2 hours, collecting rock and soil samples and setting up various scientific instruments.

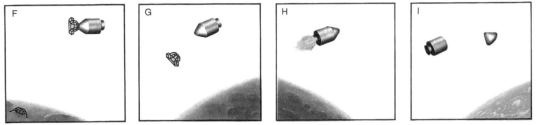
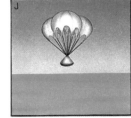

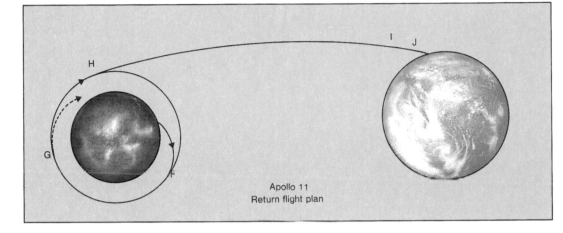

Apollo 11
Return flight plan

**The return part of the Apollo 11 mission** began with the ascent of the top part of the Lunar Module to rendezvous with the orbiting craft (F). The Lunar Module astronauts joined their colleague in the Command Module, and the Lunar Module was jettisoned (G). The Service Module's engine was then fired (H) to put the craft into earth trajectory. On nearing the earth, the Service Module was jettisoned (I) and the three astronauts descended in the Command Module, which splashed down (J) in the Pacific Ocean on July 24.

### The Orbiter probes

Having established the feasibility of landing a man on the moon, the United States launched another series of unmanned probes with the object of assessing potential landing sites for the future manned Apollo missions. In the year following August 1966, five Orbiter probes were put into low orbits around the moon. They photographed more than 3 million square miles (5 million square kilometers) of potential Apollo landing areas. They also made the first complete photographic survey of the far side of the moon.

An interesting feature of the Orbiter spacecraft was the way in which they recorded photographic images. Unlike the Ranger and Surveyor craft, which used conventional television cameras, the Orbiters took photographs on film. The photographs were developed on the craft and the resultant images electronically scanned, the information then being relayed to earth. The scanner examined each photograph in small strips, and for this reason the Orbiter photographs have a faintly striped appearance.

### Manned landings on the moon

The successes of the unmanned Ranger, Surveyor, and Orbiter programs—and of the early manned Apollo missions—prepared the way for landing men on the moon. The United States achieved this goal at the first attempt, the *Apollo 11* mission (launched on July 16, 1969). After going into lunar orbit, Neil Armstrong and Edwin Aldrin transferred to the Lunar Module (the landing craft), leaving Michael Collins in the Command Module, which continued to orbit the moon. On July 20, the Lunar Module landed safely on the moon. The two astronauts spent more than 21 hours on the surface (including about two hours outside the Lunar Module), after which they returned

to their module, took off, and rejoined the orbiting Command Module. On July 24, the three astronauts landed back on earth, splashing down in the Pacific Ocean.

In November 1969, *Apollo 12* made another successful manned moon landing, but the next attempt, *Apollo 13* (launched on April 11, 1970), was a failure. During the outward journey, an explosion caused a total loss of the main power supplies. The planned lunar landing was canceled, and only by using the Lunar Module's air and power was a disaster averted. The three astronauts returned safely to earth on April 17.

There were four further Apollo missions to the moon, all successful; *Apollo 17*, launched on December 7, 1972, was the last in the series. After the Apollo missions, the United States concentrated on developing the reusable Space Shuttle.

**The *Apollo 11* Lunar Module** photographed as it returned to the orbiting Command Module on July 21, 1969; in the background, the earth can be seen rising above the moon's horizon.

# Probes to the planets

Although the planets of our solar system have been extensively studied from earth, most of our present knowledge about them has come from the discoveries made by interplanetary probes. Since the first successful "fly-by" of Venus, by *Mariner 2* in 1962 (only about five years after the launching of the first artificial satellite), great progress has been made in the unmanned exploration of the planets. Probes have soft-landed on Venus and Mars, for example, and the Pioneer and Voyager missions have sent back much new information about the outer planets.

### Venus fly-bys

Following one American and three Soviet failures to fly spacecraft close to Venus, the American probe *Mariner 2* was successful in 1962, when it passed within 21,600 miles (34,760 kilometers) of the top of the Venusian atmosphere. During its 35-minute period of collecting data, *Mariner 2* relayed much new information back to earth. The spacecraft carried various instruments, including radiometers to measure temperatures deep within the dense clouds that surround Venus. The results were surprising; the radiometers indicated that temperatures near the surface are greater than 800° F. (425° C), hotter than the melting point of lead. *Mariner 2* also carried a magnetometer to measure the strength of the magnetic field near the planet and in interplanetary space, as well as a solar plasma detector to measure the concentration and intensity of the solar wind.

Two other fly-by missions (both American) have since taken place: *Mariner 5* (closest approach, 2,480 miles (3,991 kilometers) on October 19, 1967) and *Mariner 10* (closest approach, 3,000 miles (4,828 kilometers) on February 5, 1974). The latter craft was similar to the successful *Mariners 6, 7,* and *9* that were sent to Mars between 1969 and 1971. *Mariner 10* carried two cameras sensitive to visible and ultraviolet light and returned the first close-up pictures of Venus.

After bypassing Venus, *Mariner 10* continued for a rendezvous with Mercury in March 1974. The craft flew past the planet—sending back detailed photographs of the surface—then went around the sun, returned for a second rendezvous with Mercury, and relayed more high-quality pictures of the planet.

### Venus landers

The dense clouds around Venus limit the usefulness of the remote sensing techniques used by fly-by spacecraft. As a result, the Soviet Union and the United States planned missions to land probes on the planet's surface.

Most of the early craft were Soviet. *Venera 3* (launched on November 16, 1965) reached Venus and impacted on the surface, thereby becoming the first man-made craft to reach another world (apart from the moon). Unfortunately, however, it did not return any data. *Venera 4* successfully entered the Venusian atmosphere on October 18, 1967 (one day before the *Mariner 5* fly-by of the planet). At a height of 28,000 miles (45,000 kilometers) above the surface, the parent craft released a spherical probe which, slowed by a parachute, descended through Venus's atmosphere. The probe transmitted data for more than $1\frac{1}{2}$ hours, but it is believed that the transmissions ceased before it reached the surface, at an altitude of about 15 miles (25 kilometers). Slowing the probe's rate of descent by using a parachute was successful and was employed on later Venera missions.

The *Venera 5* and *6* probes also ceased transmitting before they reached the surface, because they could not withstand the tremendous temperatures and pressures deep in Venus's dense atmosphere. As a result of the experience gained from these early missions, *Venera 7* (launched on August 17, 1970) was more robustly constructed. It successfully soft-landed on Venus and sent back the first transmissions from the planet's surface. It found that the surface temperature is about 885° F.

**The Soviet probe**
*Venera 3,* a model of which is shown *right,* became the first spacecraft to reach another world when it crashed on Venus's surface in 1966.

**The U.S. space probe Magellan** used radar waves to pierce Venus's clouds. It provided data that a computer used to construct this image of the planet's surface, *below.*

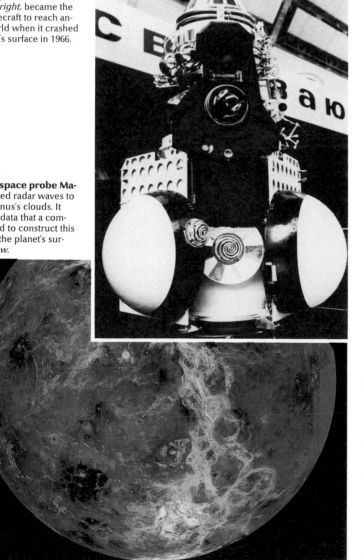

(475° C) and that the atmospheric pressure at ground level is approximately 13,000 pounds per square inch (900,000 kilograms per square meter)—about 90 times that at sea level on earth. The *Venera 7* probe was built to withstand temperatures up to 980° F. (530° C) and continued transmitting for 20 minutes on the planet's surface. *Venera 8* was the first craft to return information about the light levels at the surface, as well as data on the soil's density and composition.

The first photographs of the Venusian surface were sent back by the *Venera 9* and *Venera 10* craft, which landed in October 1975. The pictures were of surprisingly high quality considering the extremely severe conditions on the planet's surface. *Venera 13* and *Venera 14* transmitted the first color pictures of the surface in 1982. They used a special photographic technique in which three black-and-white photographs, each taken through either a red, blue, or green filter, were combined to produce color images. These landers also performed the first detailed analyses of Venusian soil samples.

In 1983, two additional Soviet spacecraft mapped most of the northern hemisphere of Venus. *Venera 15* finished its mapping in July 1984; *Venera 16*, in April 1984. The two probes provided clear images of features as small as 0.9 mile (1.5 kilometers) across.

Five years after the *Mariner 10* mission, the United States sent two other probes to Venus. *Pioneer Venus 1* was launched on May 20, 1978 and was designed to orbit the planet and collect information about its atmosphere. *Pioneer Venus 2*, launched about 11 weeks later, carried four probes for making a detailed analysis of the atmosphere as they descended to the surface. Both missions were successful; among the findings were a larger than expected proportion of argon in the atmosphere and the fact that cloud-top temperatures on the night side of Venus are higher than those on the day side. *Pioneer Venus 1* also made the first detailed map of the planet's hidden surface by using radar.

The U.S. space probe *Magellan* was launched on May 4, 1989 and began orbiting Venus on August 10, 1990. Radar images received from the probe show details of features as small as 330 feet (100 meters) across.

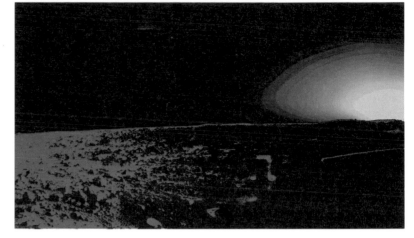

The *Viking 1* lander took this photograph of a sunset over Chryse Planitia on Mars. In addition to photographing the surface, the *Viking 1* and *Viking 2* landers carried out many scientific experiments including (with inconclusive results) a search for life.

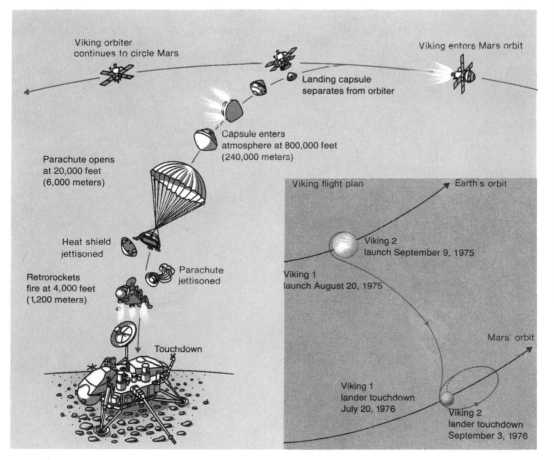

Viking orbiter continues to circle Mars

Viking enters Mars orbit

Landing capsule separates from orbiter

Capsule enters atmosphere at 800,000 feet (240,000 meters)

Parachute opens at 20,000 feet (6,000 meters)

Heat shield jettisoned

Parachute jettisoned

Retrorockets fire at 4,000 feet (1,200 meters)

Touchdown

Viking flight plan

Earth's orbit

Viking 2 launch September 9, 1975

Viking 1 launch August 20, 1975

Mars' orbit

Viking 1 lander touchdown July 20, 1976

Viking 2 lander touchdown September 3, 1976

The two Viking Mars missions were almost identical. The craft (which were of the same basic design) followed similar flight paths and used the same landing technique. As each probe approached Mars, its rockets fired to enter into orbit around the planet. After selection of a landing site, the landing capsule separated from the parent craft (which continued to orbit Mars) and began to descend, maneuvering into the correct attitude for atmospheric entry at an altitude of about 790,000 feet (240,000 meters). Its parachute opened at about 20,000 feet (6,000 meters) and the heat shield was jettisoned. After drifting downward, the lander then jettisoned the parachute and fired its retrorockets to decelerate sufficiently for a soft landing.

## Mars orbiters

The first close-up pictures of Mars were returned from television cameras on board the American *Mariner 4* spacecraft, which passed within 6,118 miles (9,846 kilometers) of the planet in 1965. Other successful Mars missions followed in 1969 with *Mariners 6* and *7,* which sent back more than 200 pictures of the Martian terrain.

The *Mariner 9* craft (launched on May 30, 1971) became the first object from earth to become an artificial satellite of another planet. Carrying a narrow-angle camera capable of resolving features as small as 325 feet (100 meters) across, *Mariner 9* remained operational for 349 days, during which it relayed more than 7,000 high-quality images of Mars and its two moons, Phobos and Deimos. *Mariner 9* also carried an infrared radiometer to measure the temperature of the surface of Mars. The results indicated a range of more than 300° F. (150° C) between the equator and the poles.

## Mars landers

The *Viking 1* spacecraft was launched on August 22, 1975 and, after a 300-day-journey, went into orbit around Mars. It then began sending back pictures of the Martian surface in order to locate a suitable site for the lander part of the spacecraft. After 16 days, a good site was found, and on July 20, 1976, *Viking Lander 1* separated from the Viking orbiter and successfully soft-landed on the surface of Mars (in Chryse Planitia). While the lander analyzed the soil and transmitted close-up pictures of the surface, the parent craft remained in orbit, acting as the communication relay between the lander and earth. *Viking 2* was launched shortly after *Viking 1,* and its lander touched-down on September 3, 1976, in Utopia Planitia, about 4,600 miles (7,400 kilometers) from the *Viking 1* site.

Both of the landers were comprehensively equipped with instruments for analyzing the atmosphere and soil. The tasks they performed included a survey of the chemical composition of the soil, the detection of seismic tremors, and, perhaps most important, the search for life on the surface. Soil for the life-detection experiment was scooped up by a mechanized arm on the side of the lander and divided into three portions, each of which was placed in one of three biology experiments. The fully automatic equipment then tried to incubate the soil samples with sunlight, water, and nutrients, simultaneously testing for signs of life. (The experiments were designed on the assumption that any forms of life would ingest and excrete certain basic chemicals). The results were inconclusive.

Each of the Viking landers had two cameras positioned at a height equivalent to the average human eye level. Remotely controlled from earth, the cameras were capable of performing a complete 360° scan of the surrounding landscape. They could also be operated as a pair to provide stereoscopic views. The cameras used a small mirror that scanned a narrow vertical strip of the landscape, reflecting the image to a photocell that converted the light into an electrical signal that was transmitted back to earth. The camera was then rotated by a small amount and another vertical line scanned, the entire process being repeated until a complete view had been obtained. At the control center on earth, the signals were processed to produce photographs.

## Probes to the outer planets

The exploration of the outer solar system has been dominated by the achievements of American spacecraft. The first probe to the outer planets, *Pioneer 10,* was launched on March 2, 1972, the start of a 21-month journey to Jupiter. During its flight, the craft passed through the asteroid belt, a potentially hazardous zone because collision with even an extremely small asteroid might disable the probe. Fortunately, *Pioneer 10* (and all later long-distance probes) passed through unscathed. *Pioneer-Saturn* was launched about a year later, on April 6, 1973, destined for both Jupiter and Saturn. The probes were identical, each carrying scientific instruments to study both interplanetary space and their destination planets. In addition, each probe had a large dish antenna—8 feet (2.4 meters) in diameter— for communicating with earth. The cameras on board the spacecraft worked in basically the same way as those on the Viking landers, scanning narrow vertical strips and converting the image into digital form for sending back to earth.

After the successes of the Pioneer missions, the United States sent two other probes to the outer solar system—*Voyager 1* (launched on August 20, 1977) and *Voyager 2* (launched on September 5, in the same year). The two craft were identical, and their scientific instruments were more complex than those of any previous unmanned probes. One aspect of their design was given special attention: the radiation-shielding of the electronic components. Pioneer had found that the radiation field around Jupiter was much stronger than expected and so the two Voyagers had thicker shielding of their sensitive microelectronic components. Moreover, the Voyagers' camera systems were different from those on the Pioneer crafts. On the Voyagers, the scanning platform was designed so that it could be rotated to any angle in space. Each probe carried two video cam-

*Voyager 1* photographed Jupiter's satellite Io in March 1979, when the probe passed within about 535,750 miles (862,200 kilometers) of the satellite. *Voyager's* pictures revealed that Io is volcanically active (the circular feature at the center of Io is an active volcano), the first time that such activity had been observed in the outer solar system.

eras, one with a wide-angle lens, the other with a narrow-angle lens; the cameras were remotely controlled from earth. Each camera had a rotating filter wheel in front of its lens, and color pictures were obtained by combining three black-and-white images, each taken through a blue, green, or orange filter—a similar system to that later used on the Soviet *Venera 13* probe. The images were then converted into digital form for transmission back to earth. Another pair of instruments recorded ultraviolet and infrared radiation, which can provide important clues to atmospheric composition or the surface chemistry of solid objects. Other detectors searched the interplanetary space for magnetic fields, charged particles, radio discharges, and cosmic rays. Communication with earth was through a bowl-shaped antenna 12 feet (3.6 meters) across.

*Voyager 1* came closest to Jupiter on March 5, 1979. In the images, scientists found the faint trace of a ring never before seen.

On July 9, 1979, *Voyager 2* arrived at Jupiter and reobserved the planet's ring, Io's volcanoes, and other revelations made during the previous fly-by. Europa was examined closely during the second encounter.

When *Voyager 1* reached Saturn, it encountered the planet and its large moon Titan. Titan's atmosphere is so thick with haze that the spacecraft could not record any features. *Voyager 1* came closest to Saturn on November 12, 1980. *Voyager 2* did not reach the planet until nearly a year later, on August 25, 1981. The spacecraft's observations of Saturn and its satellites were spectacular.

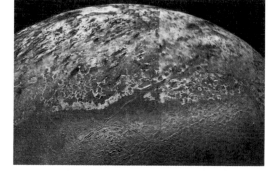

*Voyager 2* **encountered one of Neptune's moons,** Triton, on August 24, 1989. The spacecraft passed within about 24,000 miles (38,400 kilometers) of the satellite. The images obtained showed that Triton has a strange landscape of canyons, peaks, and craters resembling the skin of a huge cantaloupe.

By directing *Voyager 2* on an extremely precise trajectory past Jupiter and Saturn, NASA engineers preserved an opportunity to send the probe past both Uranus and Neptune. On January 24, 1986, *Voyager 2* functioned perfectly as it passed within 51,000 miles (81,600 kilometers) of the cloud tops of Uranus. The space probe discovered two more rings and ten more moons around the planet. And on August 24, 1989, the spacecraft soared about 3,000 miles (4,800 kilometers) over Neptune and passed within about 24,000 miles (38,400 kilometers) of its large moon Triton. The images *Voyager 2* took revealed more about Neptune than had been learned since its discovery in 1846.

After this last planetary encounter, the Voyagers headed for interstellar space, which they should reach around 2015. In the meantime, they will continue communicating information about the stars they pass.

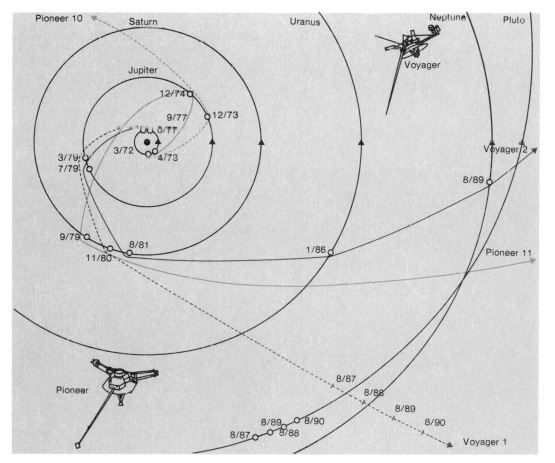

**The trajectories** of four missions to the outer planets are shown *left,* with the dates of the probes' closest approaches to each planet. With the exception of *Pioneer 10* (which encountered only Jupiter), the probes' flight paths were carefully calculated so that the gravitational attraction of each planet was used to swing the craft into the correct trajectory for the next planetary encounter.

# Astronomical Data

## Planetary Satellites—Comparative Data

| | | Mean Distance from Parent Planet In miles | In kilometers | Diameter of Satellite In miles | In kilometers | Year of Discovery |
|---|---|---|---|---|---|---|
| Earth | Moon | 238,900 | 384,500 | 2,160 | 3,476 | — |
| Mars | Phobos | 5,800 | 9,400 | 13 | 21 | 1877 |
| | Deimos | 14,600 | 23,500 | 8 | 12 | 1877 |
| Jupiter | Metis | 79,500 | 128,000 | 25 | 40* | 1979 |
| | Adrastea | 80,200 | 129,000 | 16* | 25* | 1979 |
| | Amalthea | 112,000 | 180,000 | 106* | 170* | 1892 |
| | Thebe | 138,000 | 222,000 | 60* | 100* | 1979 |
| | Io | 262,200 | 422,000 | 2,256* | 3,630* | 1610 |
| | Europa | 416,900 | 671,000 | 1,951* | 3,140* | 1610 |
| | Ganymede | 664,900 | 1,070,000 | 3,268* | 5,260* | 1610 |
| | Callisto | 1,170,000 | 1,885,000 | 2,983* | 4,800* | 1610 |
| | Leda | 6,903,000 | 11,110,000 | 9 | 15* | 1974 |
| | Himalia | 7,127,000 | 11,470,000 | 115* | 185* | 1904 |
| | Lysithea | 7,275,400 | 11,710,000 | 22 | 35* | 1938 |
| | Elara | 7,294,900 | 11,740,000 | 47* | 75 | 1905 |
| | Ananke | 13,173,000 | 21,200,000 | 19 | 30* | 1951 |
| | Carme | 14,509,000 | 23,350,000 | 25 | 40* | 1938 |
| | Pasiphae | 14,500,000 | 23,330,000 | 31 | 50* | 1908 |
| | Sinope | 14,540,000 | 23,400,000 | 22 | 35* | 1914 |
| Saturn | Titan | 759,000 | 1,221,000 | 3,200 | 5,150 | 1655 |
| | Iapetus | 2,213,000 | 3,561,000 | 900 | 1,440 | 1671 |
| | Rhea | 327,000 | 526,000 | 950 | 1,530 | 1672 |
| | Dione | 235,000 | 378,000 | 700 | 1,120 | 1684 |
| | Tethys | 183,000 | 295,000 | 660 | 1,060 | 1684 |
| | Enceladus | 148,000 | 238,000 | 310 | 500 | 1789 |
| | Mimas | 116,000 | 187,000 | 240 | 390 | 1789 |
| | Hyperion | 920,000 | 1,481,000 | 220† | 360† | 1848 |
| | Phoebe | 8,053,000 | 12,960,000 | 120 | 200 | 1898 |
| | Janus | 94,000 | 151,000 | 60† | 100† | 1980 |
| | Epimetheus | 94,000 | 151,000 | 55† | 90† | 1980 |
| | Helene | 235,000 | 378,000 | 20 | 30 | 1980 |
| | Telesto | 183,000 | 295,000 | 22* | 35* | 1980 |
| | Calypso | 183,000 | 295,000 | 22* | 35* | 1980 |
| | Pandora | 88,000 | 142,000 | 55 | 90 | 1980 |
| | Prometheus | 86,000 | 139,000 | 60 | 100 | 1980 |
| | Atlas | 85,000 | 137,000 | 19 | 30 | 1980 |
| | Pan | 83,000 | 134,000 | 12 | 20 | 1990 |
| Uranus | Oberon | 362,500 | 583,400 | 963 | 1,550 | 1787 |
| | Titania | 271,100 | 436,300 | 1,000 | 1,610 | 1787 |
| | Umbriel | 165,300 | 266,000 | 739 | 1,190 | 1851 |
| | Ariel | 118,600 | 190,900 | 720 | 1,160 | 1851 |
| | Miranda | 80,700 | 129,900 | 301 | 485 | 1948 |
| | Puck | 53,400 | 86,000 | 96 | 155 | 1985 |
| | Portia | 41,100 | 66,100 | 68 | 110 | 1986 |
| | Juliet | 40,000 | 64,400 | 53 | 85 | 1986 |
| | Cressida | 38,400 | 61,800 | 40 | 65 | 1986 |
| | Rosalind | 43,500 | 70,000 | 37 | 60 | 1986 |
| | Belinda | 46,800 | 75,300 | 42 | 68 | 1986 |
| | Desdemona | 38,900 | 62,600 | 37 | 60 | 1986 |
| | Cordelia | 30,900 | 49,800 | 25 | 40 | 1986 |
| | Ophelia | 33,400 | 53,800 | 19 | 30 | 1986 |
| | Bianca | 36,800 | 59,200 | 28 | 45 | 1986 |
| Neptune | Triton | 220,500 | 354,800 | 1,678 | 2,700 | 1846 |
| | Nereid | 3,423,800 | 5,510,000 | 211 | 340 | 1949 |
| | Proteus | 73,100 | 117,600 | 261 | 420 | 1989 |
| | Larissa | 45,700 | 73,600 | 118 | 190 | 1989 |
| | Despina | 32,600 | 52,500 | 93 | 150 | 1989 |
| | Galatea | 38,500 | 62,000 | 99 | 160 | 1989 |
| | Thalassa | 31,100 | 50,000 | 50 | 80 | 1989 |
| | Naiad | 29,800 | 48,000 | 37 | 60 | 1989 |
| Pluto | Charon | 12,000 | 19,100 | 750 | 1200 | 1978 |

*Approximate diameter. †Diameter of long axis.

## Brightest Stars

| Name | Magnitude |
|---|---|
| Sirius (Alpha Canis Majoris) | −1.45 |
| Canopus (Alpha Carinae) | −0.73 |
| Alpha Centauri | −0.1 |
| Arcturus (Alpha Boötis) | −0.06 |
| Vega (Alpha Lyrae) | 0.04 |
| Capella (Alpha Aurigae) | 0.08 |
| Rigel (Beta Orionis) | 0.11 |
| Procyon (Alpha Canis Minoris) | 0.35 |
| Achernar (Alpha Eridani) | 0.48 |
| Beta Centauri | 0.60 |
| Altair (Alpha Aquilae) | 0.77 |
| Betelgeuse (Alpha Orionis) | 0.80 |
| Aldebaran (Alpha Tauri) | 0.85 |
| Alpha Crucis | 0.90 |
| Antares (Alpha Scorpii) | 0.98 |
| Spica (Alpha Virginis) | 1.12 |
| Pollux (Beta Geminorum) | 1.15 |
| Fomalhaut (Alpha Piscis Austrini) | 1.18 |
| Deneb (Alpha Cygni) | 1.26 |
| Beta Crucis | 1.24 |
| Regulus (Alpha Leonis) | 1.36 |
| Castor (Alpha Geminorum) | 1.58 |
| Gamma Crucis | 1.61 |
| Adhara (Epsilon Canis Majoris) | 1.63 |
| Alioth (Epsilon Ursae Majoris) | 1.68 |
| Bellatrix (Gamma Orionis) | 1.70 |
| Shaula (Lambda Scorpii) | 1.71 |
| Avior (Epsilon Carinae) | 1.74 |
| Alnilam (Epsilon Orionis) | 1.75 |
| Al Nath (Beta Tauri) | 1.78 |
| Miaplacidus (Beta Carinae) | 1.80 |
| Atria (Alpha Trianguli Australe) | 1.88 |
| Mirphak (Alpha Persei) | 1.90 |
| Alkaid (Eta Ursae Majoris) | 1.91 |
| Alnitak (Zeta Orionis) | 1.91 |

## Solar Total Eclipses

| Date | Approximate location | Approximate duration |
|---|---|---|
| November 3, 1994 | Central South America, South Atlantic | 4 minutes |
| October 24, 1995 | South Asia, Central Pacific | 2 minutes |
| March 9, 1997 | Central Asia | 3 minutes |
| February 26, 1998 | Central Pacific, Northern South America | 4 minutes |
| August 11, 1999 | North Atlantic, Central Europe, South Asia | 2 minutes |

## Constellations

| Name | Abbreviation | Common name |
|---|---|---|
| Andromeda | And | Andromeda |
| Antlia | Ant | Air pump |
| Apus | Aps | Bird of Paradise |
| Aquarius | Aqr | Water-bearer |
| Aquila | Aql | Eagle |
| Ara | Ara | Altar |
| Aries | Ari | Ram |
| Auriga | Aur | Charioteer |
| Boötes | Boö | Herdsman |
| Caelum | Cae | Sculptor's chisel |
| Camelopardus | Cam | Giraffe |
| Cancer | Cnc | Crab |
| Canes Venatici | CVn | Hunting dogs |
| Canis Major | CMa | Great dog |
| Canis Minor | CMi | Little dog |
| Capricornus | Cap | Goat |
| Carina | Car | Keel |
| Cassiopeia | Cas | Cassiopeia |
| Centaurus | Cen | Centaur |
| Cepheus | Cep | Cepheus |
| Cetus | Cet | Whale |
| Chamaeleon | Cha | Chameleon |
| Circinus | Cir | Compasses |
| Columba | Col | Dove |
| Coma Berenices | Com | Berenice's hair |
| Corona Australis | CrA | Southern crown |
| Corona Borealis | CrB | Northern crown |

| Name | Abbreviation | Common name |
|---|---|---|
| Corvus | Crv | Crow |
| Crater | Crt | Cup |
| Crux Australis | Cru | Southern cross |
| Cygnus | Cyg | Swan |
| Delphinus | Del | Dolphin |
| Dorado | Dor | Swordfish |
| Draco | Dra | Dragon |
| Equuleus | Eql | Foal |
| Eridanus | Eri | River |
| Fornax | For | Furnace |
| Gemini | Gem | Twins |
| Grus | Gru | Crane |
| Hercules | Her | Hercules |
| Horologium | Hor | Clock |
| Hydra | Hya | Water snake |
| Hydrus | Hyi | Little snake |
| Indus | Ind | Indian |
| Lacerta | Lac | Lizard |
| Leo | Leo | Lion |
| Leo Minor | LMi | Lion cub |
| Lepus | Lep | Hare |
| Libra | Lib | Balance |
| Lupus | Lup | Wolf |
| Lynx | Lyn | Lynx |
| Lyra | Lyr | Lyre |
| Mensa | Men | Table |
| Microscopium | Mic | Microscope |
| Monoceros | Mon | Unicorn |
| Musca | Mus | Fly |
| Norma | Nor | Rule |
| Octans | Oct | Octant |
| Ophiuchus | Oph | Serpent bearer |
| Orion | Ori | Orion |
| Pavo | Pav | Peacock |
| Pegasus | Peg | Pegasus |
| Perseus | Per | Perseus |
| Phoenix | Phe | Phoenix |
| Pictor | Pic | Painter |
| Pisces | Psc | Fishes |
| Piscis Austrinus | PsA | Southern fish |
| Puppis | Pup | Poop or Stern |
| Pyxis | Pyx | Box or Compass box |
| Reticulum | Ret | Net |
| Sagitta | Sge | Arrow |
| Sagittarius | Sgr | Archer |
| Scorpius | Sco | Scorpion |
| Sculptor | Scl | Sculptor |
| Scutum | Sct | Shield |
| Serpens | Ser | Serpent |
| Sextans | Sxt | Sextant |
| Taurus | Tau | Bull |
| Telescopium | Tel | Telescope |
| Triangulum | Tri | Triangle |
| Triangulum Australe | TrA | Southern triangle |
| Tucana | Tuc | Toucan |
| Ursa Major | UMa | Great bear, Big Dipper or Plow |
| Ursa Minor | Umi | Little bear |
| Vela | Vel | Sail |
| Virgo | Vir | Virgin |
| Volans | Vol | Flying fish |
| Vulpecula | Vul | Fox |

## Solar System—Comparative Data

| | Equatorial Diameter (miles) | Mass (Earth = 1) | Density (g/cm³) | Orbital Period (Earth days) | Distance from Sun (mean) |
|---|---|---|---|---|---|
| Sun | 865,000 | 33,000.00 | 100.00 | — | — |
| Mercury | 3,031 | 0.056 | 5.42 | 87.97 | 35,980,000 mi. |
| Venus | 7,521 | 0.815 | 5.25 | 224.7 | 67,230,000 mi. |
| Earth | 7,926 | 1.00 | 5.52 | 365.26 | 92,960,000 mi. |
| Mars | 4,223 | 0.107 | 3.94 | 686.98 | 141,600,000 mi. |
| Jupiter | 88,846 | 317.892 | 1.33 | 4,332.7 | 483,600,000 mi. |
| Saturn | 74,898 | 95.184 | 0.69 | 10,759 | 888,200,000 mi. |
| Uranus | 31,763 | 14.54 | 1.27 | 30,685 | 1,786,400,000 mi. |
| Neptune | 30,775 | 17.15 | 1.64 | 60,190 | 2,798,800,000 mi. |
| Pluto | 1,430 | 0.002(?) | 2.03(?) | 90,800 | 3,666,200,000 mi. |

## Units of Measurement

**Astronomical unit** (a.u.), mean distance of the earth from the sun:

$1.49598 \times 10^8$ km

$4.848 \times 10^{-6}$ parsecs

$1.58129 \times 10^{-5}$ light-years

**Parsec** (pc), distance at which 1 a.u. subtends one second of arc:

$3.0856 \times 10^{13}$ km

206,264.8 a.u.

3.2616 light-years

**Light-year,** distance traveled by light in one year:

$9.4605 \times 10^{12}$ km

$6.324 \times 10^4$ a.u.

0.3066 parsecs

**Velocity of light** (c):

$2.998 \times 10^5$ km/sec

By international convention, the science of astronomy generally employs metric units, as used for the weights and dimensions in the tables on these pages. For the benefit of readers who are unaccustomed to metric measurements, dimensions in the main body of this book are expressed also in U.S. customary units.

# Glossary

In the following glossary, small capital letters (for example, METEORITE) indicate terms that have their own entries in the glossary.

## A

**ablation** The burning away of the leading surface of an object, such as a METEORITE or an artificial SATELLITE, by friction as it enters the earth's ATMOSPHERE from space. The ablation shielding on a reentry vehicle, such as the Space Shuttle, is designed to protect against or minimize this.

**absolute magnitude** The absolute magnitude of a STAR is defined as the APPARENT MAGNITUDE that star would have if located at a standard distance of 10 PARSECS. It is therefore a measure of intrinsic brightness. If the APPARENT MAGNITUDE is $M_a$, and the distance of the star is $d$ parsecs, then the absolute magnitude $M_v$ is given by $M_v = M_a + 5 - 5 \log_{10} d$.

**absorption spectrum** The SPECTRUM resulting when light from one source is passed through another material, e.g., a tenuous gas. The result is a series of dark bands crossing the spectrum, known as absorption lines.

**accretion** A process in which many smaller bodies congregate together under the action of forces to produce much larger bodies. Such a force could be, for example, GRAVITATION.

**accretion ring** The ring of hot gas and dust that encircles a BLACK HOLE, formed from material torn off the companion STAR to the black hole. In losing its initial ANGULAR MOMENTUM, the hot material descends into the black hole, friction causing it to reach temperatures high enough to produce X RAYS. It is by the accretion ring emission that the presence of the black hole can be inferred.

**aerolite** The class of stony METEORITE that includes the chondrite and achondrite types, both of which commonly consist of silicate material together with nickel and iron. Whether or not a meteorite is chondritic depends on the presence or otherwise of chondrules.

**airglow** A faint glow in the ATMOSPHERE of a planet resulting from the recombination of the atmospheric atoms that had been broken up by the action of sunlight.

**albedo** The ratio of the amount of light reflected from an object in all directions to the amount of incident light. Thus, an albedo of 1.0 corresponds to a perfect reflector.

**alt-azimuth mount** A way of arranging a telescope mount so that the telescope can move parallel to the horizon (AZIMUTH) and at right angles to the horizon (ALTITUDE). Very easy to mechanize, it is becoming more popular in combination with computer control systems, which can alter the altitude and azimuth angles to follow the path of a STAR as it rises and sets. *See also* EQUATORIAL MOUNT.

**altitude** In astronomy, the angular distance above the horizon, from 0° at the horizon to 90° at the zenith. One of the two coordinates (the other being AZIMUTH) that define a celestial object's position, used with an ALT-AZIMUTH mount.

**angular momentum** The product of the moment of inertia of a body and the angular velocity. Its importance lies in the fact that a body with a large angular momentum needs a considerable force (torque) to slow or stop its rotation.

**annular eclipse** The type of ECLIPSE seen when the moon is too far from the earth at the time of a solar eclipse to completely cover the sun's disk. The result is a bright ring, or annulus, of light encircling the moon.

**aperture** The clear diameter of the light-gathering surface of a telescope. Thus, for a REFRACTOR TELESCOPE it is the diameter of the objective lens, and for a reflecting telescope, the diameter of the primary mirror.

**aphelion** The point in the orbit of a planet, COMET, or other celestial body, at which it is farthest from the sun.

**apparent magnitude** A measure of the brightness of STARS as they appear on the CELESTIAL SPHERE.

**asteroid** *See* MINOR PLANET.

**asthenosphere** The region within a planet, such as the earth, below the LITHOSPHERE, that is fairly plastic and at a temperature high enough to sustain CONVECTION.

**astrology** The study of the relative positions of the sun, moon, and planets in order to estimate their supposed influence on human events.

**astronomical unit** (a.u. or AU) A unit of length equal to the average distance between the earth and sun, i.e., 92,975,680 miles (149,597,870 kilometers).

**atmosphere** An envelope of gas surrounding a planet, STAR, or other celestial body, where the gravitational field is strong enough to restrain the gases.

**aurora** A sheet-like display of color occurring high in the earth's ATMOSPHERE near the poles. It is produced by SOLAR WIND particles interacting with the earth's magnetic field.

**axis** The theoretical line about which an object rotates.

**azimuth** The bearing about a vertical AXIS, measured in degrees from north (0°), clockwise through 360°, to north again. One of the two coordinates (the other being ALTITUDE) that define a celestial object's position, used with an ALT-AZIMUTH MOUNT.

## B

**Baily's beads** The effect seen during a total solar ECLIPSE just before or after totality, when sunlight shines between lunar mountains or down lunar valleys.

**barycenter** The point at which all the mass in a system of masses (e.g., in the earth-moon system) may be considered to be concentrated.

**Big Bang theory** A theory of the origin of the UNIVERSE in which all matter and space originated in a cataclysmic explosion, the remnant of which we see in the present expansion of the universe as a whole.

**binary stars** A pair of stars revolving around a common center of gravity, held together by their mutual gravitational interaction.

**black hole** An object whose matter has become so condensed that its gravitational field is strong enough to prevent light escaping from it. The radius of the black hole resulting from the collapse of an object of mass $M$ is called the Schwarzschild radius $R_s$ and is given by $R_s = 2GM/c^2$, where G is the universal constant of gravitation and c is the speed of light.

## C

**calendar** A means of dividing up the earth's year into convenient units for civil and religious purposes. The Egyptians introduced the $365\frac{1}{4}$-day year, which was superseded in 45 B.C. by the introduction by Julius Caesar of the Julian Calendar. This consisted of 12 months of varying length, with every year that could be divided by 4 being a leap year, and with the second month having one extra day. This calendar was itself modified by Pope Gregory XIII in A.D. 1583, whose Gregorian Calendar makes century-years leap years only if they are divisible by 400 (e.g., 2000).

**Cassegrain telescope** A reflecting telescope which has a mirror at its base with a central hole, allowing light reflected from this primary mirror to pass through it after being reflected by a convex secondary mirror.

**celestial equator** The circle in which the earth's equator meets the CELESTIAL SPHERE.

**celestial latitude** The angular distance between a celestial body and the ECLIPTIC, measured along a line at right angles to the ecliptic, which passes through both CELESTIAL POLES. Symbol $\beta$ (beta).

**celestial longitude** The angular distance between a celestial body and the FIRST POINT OF ARIES, measured along the ecliptic. Symbol $\lambda$ (lambda).

**celestial mechanics** The study of the motion of celestial bodies under the influence of GRAVITATION from one or more other bodies.

**celestial poles** The points at which the earth's rotation axis pierces the CELESTIAL SPHERE. All the STARS appear to ORBIT about this point, whose approximate position in the north is marked by Polaris (the polestar).

**celestial sphere** The imaginary sphere on the inside of which celestial objects appear.

**Cepheid variable** One of a group of highly luminous yellow or orange SUPERGIANT STARS, whose brightness varies in a regular manner as the result of stellar pulsations. The prototype for this group of variable star is Delta Cephei, which has a period of about 5.37 days, the changes in LUMINOSITY being caused by changes in the star's radius (amounting to about 15 per cent). The period of the luminosity changes is also found to depend on the brightness of the Cepheid, this being the PERIOD-LUMINOSITY law. Two different types of Cepheid have been identified: POPULATION I and POPULATION II types, whose members have different characteristic period-luminosity dependencies.

**Chandrasekhar limit** A limiting mass, below which a STAR can become a WHITE DWARF, and above which grav-

ity is capable of continuing the collapse to, say, a NEUTRON STAR.

**charge-coupled device (CCD)** A means of converting the electromagnetic energy of PHOTONS of a particular WAVELENGTH into a digital video signal which can be displayed on a television screen.

**chromosphere** The layer in the sun's atmosphere between the PHOTOSPHERE and the CORONA.

**circumpolar stars** Those stars that are of such a declination that in a particular latitude they never set.

**comet** A collection of gas, dust, and volatile ice that travel around the sun, generally in very eccentric orbits. The source of such bodies may be the OORT CLOUD.

**conic sections** Mathematically, the geometric shapes obtained by slicing a cone at different angles relative to the base of the cone. A circle is formed by slicing the cone parallel to its base, an ellipse by slicing at any angle less than that of the side of the cone relative to the base, and a parabola by slicing parallel to the side of the cone. A hyperbola is formed by cutting the cone at an angle steeper than that of the side. To a good approximation, all celestial bodies within the SOLAR SYSTEM follow orbits that can be represented by conic sections.

**conjunction** The lining up of two celestial bodies so that they lie in the same direction as seen from earth. Superior conjunction occurs when a planet lies on the other side of the sun from the earth. Inferior conjunction occurs when a planet lies on the line joining the sun and earth, and is nearer to the earth.

**constellation** A group of STARS lying in a part of the CELESTIAL SPHERE. The boundaries of the 88 accepted groups have been set by international convention; their positions are described in terms of RIGHT ASCENSIONS and DECLINATIONS.

**convection** The transfer of heat through a fluid by the motion of the fluid itself. Such motion is usually in the form of currents, in which the hotter, less dense material rises to be replaced below by cooler, denser material.

**core** The innermost, central region of a planet, often comprising metallic substances that, through the dynamo effect, produce a magnetic field.

**corona** The hot, outermost layer of the sun's atmosphere, lying above the CHROMOSPHERE.

**cosmic rays** Very high energy nuclei moving at velocities close to that of light which are probably produced by SUPERNOVA explosions. On striking the earth's ATMOSPHERE, they produce cascades of other particles (by collision with nuclei in the atmosphere) called air showers.

**cosmology** The scientific study of the structure and evolution of the UNIVERSE as a whole.

**crust** The topmost layer of the solid body of a planet, extending down to the MANTLE.

## D

**declination** The angular distance between a celestial object (e.g., a STAR) and the CELESTIAL EQUATOR. Symbol $\delta$ (delta).

**density** Mass per unit volume. In astronomy, mean relative density compares a planet's density with the density of water, 62.4 pounds per cubic foot (1 gram per cubic centimeter).

**density wave** A theory to account for the spiral structure of GALAXIES. Supposing that such a wave could be set up in the first place, the theory suggests that the spiral arms mark the positions of regions of higher than average density, which rotate about the galaxy. STARS orbiting the center of the galaxy spend a considerable amount of time in the higher density regions before moving out, with the higher density also favoring the formation of young stars by FRAGMEN-TATION within it.

**diamond ring effect** A phenomenon seen as a flash of sunlight shines down a lunar valley during a total solar ECLIPSE.

**Doppler effect** The apparent shift in the wavelength (or frequency) of ELECTROMAGNETIC RADIATION as a result of the relative motion of the source of the radiation and the observer. If the WAVELENGTH emitted is $\lambda_o$, and the wavelength received by the observer $\lambda$, then the velocity of the source relative to the observer $v$, is given by $\lambda - \lambda_o = v\lambda_o/c$, where c is the velocity of light.

**double star** A pair of STARS that appear close together in the sky only because they lie in the same direction from the earth, and not because they are physically associated BINARY STARS.

## E

**eccentricity** A parameter of a CONIC SECTION that describes how much it deviates from a perfect circle, whose eccentricity is zero. An ELLIPSE has an eccentricity between 0 and 1, a PARABOLA has an eccentricity equal to 1, whereas HYPERBOLAE have eccentricities exceeding 1.

**eclipse** The total or partial concealment of one celestial body by another. In an eclipse of the sun, it is the light of the sun that is totally or partially cut off from the earth by the moon coming between the two bodies.

**eclipsing binary** A BINARY STAR in which one component, in orbiting about the other, is totally or partially ECLIPSED as seen from earth.

**ecliptic** The circle traced out by the sun's apparent path over the CELESTIAL SPHERE in the course of a year.

**effective temperature** The temperature a black body would have if it radiated the same amount of radiation from the same volume as the object being considered.

**electromagnetic radiation** Waves of energy which consist of a combination of electric and magnetic fields at right angles to each other. Such radiation results commonly from the acceleration of an electric charge, and is propagated in a vacuum at the speed of light.

**electromagnetic spectrum** The range of WAVELENGTHS (or FREQUENCIES) over which ELECTROMAGNETIC RADIATION is propagated. The longest wavelengths (lowest frequencies) are those of RADIO WAVES, and the shortest wavelengths are those of gamma rays.

**electron** An elementary particle, having one unit of (negative) electric charge, and a mass of $9.1 \times 10^{-31}$ kg.

**ellipse** A CONIC SECTION. To a good approximation, all the planets (and their satellites) follow elliptical ORBITS, with the sun (or the planet) at one focus.

**ellipticity** The variation of a regular planar or solid shape from a perfect circle or sphere. The departure of the earth, which has a smaller polar than equatorial diameter, from a perfect sphere is more usually described as its OBLATENESS. Elliptical planetary orbits are more usually described in terms of their ECCENTRICITY.

**emission nebula** A NEBULA which, as a result of ionized gas within it, shines by its own light.

**emission spectrum** The spectrum formed by the emission of ELECTROMAGNETIC RADIATION by a source such as a STAR.

**epicyclic motion** According to the GEOCENTRIC Ptolemaic system, planetary orbits have two components: a circular (deferent) ORBIT around the parent body; and a smaller circular orbit (epicycle) around a point on the deferent orbit.

**equatorial mount** A telescope mount with one AXIS parallel to the earth's rotation axis, and the other at right-angles to it. This enables the telescope, once locked onto a STAR's position, to track (follow) the star using a motor drive to compensate for the earth's rotation. Most large telescopes are mounted in this way, but the ALT-AZIMUTH MOUNT, with its simpler construction, is becoming more popular.

**equinox** One of two points at which the ECLIPTIC cuts the CELESTIAL EQUATOR. The vernal equinox is the point at which the sun, traveling on the ecliptic, crosses the celestial equator from south to north. This crossing occurs about March 21 each year. The autumnal equinox is the point at which the sun crosses the equator from north to south. This occurs about September 23 each year.

**escape velocity** To effectively escape the gravitational field of a STAR, planet, or other celestial body, a projectile must have a velocity of at least $v_e$, the escape velocity, given by $v^2 = 2GM/R$, where G is the universal constant of gravitation ($6.67 \times 19^{-11}$ kg/m³/s²), $M$ is the mass of the planet, star, or other celestial body, and $R$ the initial distance of the projectile from the center of the body (e.g., at a planet's surface, where $R$ would then be the planet's radius).

## F

**facula** A region in the sun's PHOTOSPHERE brighter than its surroundings, related to SUNSPOTS and to the sun's magnetic field. Such regions are at a higher temperature than the surrounding area.

**First Point of Aries** The point at which the sun, traveling from south to north on the ECLIPTIC, crosses the CELESTIAL EQUATOR. Identical to the vernal EQUINOX.

**flare** A sudden, transitory burst of activity in the sun's ATMOSPHERE involving the release of radiation and high-energy particles. The origin of flares is uncertain, although they seem to be related to areas of high magnetic field.

**fragmentation** The breakup of a gas cloud into discrete regions as a result of the gravitational collapse of denser regions in the gas (inhomogeneities).

**frequency** The number of cycles or oscillations of a wave motion per unit time, usually taken to be one second, in which case the unit of frequency is the hertz (Hz).

## G

**galaxy** A collection of dust, gas, and STARS measuring thousands of PARSECS across.

**Galilean satellites** The four satellites of Jupiter first observed by Galileo Galilei, namely Io, Europa, Ganymede, and Callisto.

**gamma radiation** ELECTROMAGNETIC RADIATION with WAVELENGTHS shorter then those of X RAYS, that is, less than $10^{-11}$ meters.

**geocentric theory** Any theory of the SOLAR SYSTEM or the UNIVERSE that places the earth at the center.

**globular cluster** A spherical collection of STARS, the concentration of which increases greatly toward the center. The stars are probably of the same age, and the clusters as a whole move in highly elliptical orbits that take them high above the galactic center.

**gravitation** The mutual attraction existing between all objects with mass. Newton's law of gravitation states that the force of attraction between two bodies varies as the product of the two masses and, inversely, as the square of the distance between them. Einstein's theory of general RELATIVITY views the attraction as due to the curving of space and time by a massive object. Quantum gravity considers the force to be the result of the exchange of particles known as gravitons.

**"greenhouse" effect** The trapping of INFRARED RADIATION from the surface of a planet by a dense atmosphere, opaque to heat radiation. This effect occurs on Venus.

## H

**Hawking process** The emission of particles by a BLACK HOLE, leading to the eventual explosion of the black hole in a burst of GAMMA RADIATION.

**heliocentric theory** A theory for the motion of the planets that has the sun at its correct place in the center of the SOLAR SYSTEM.

**Hertzsprung-Russell diagram** A plot of stellar temperatures (or, equivalently, spectral types or colors) and ABSOLUTE MAGNITUDES (or, equivalently, LUMINOSITIES). Most stars are within a diagonal belt, the MAIN SEQUENCE, with WHITE DWARFS and giants to either side.

**Hubble's law** The relation between the RED SHIFT of a distant GALAXY and its distance from us, the constant of proportionality being Hubble's constant, $H_o$, given by the formula $H_o = v/d$, where $v$ is the recessional velocity of a galaxy at a distance $d$ from us. The reciprocal of Hubble's constant can give an estimate of the age of the UNIVERSE in the BIG BANG THEORY (where $H_o$ varies inversely with time).

**hyperbola** A CONIC SECTION. Some COMETS enter the SOLAR SYSTEM on hyperbolic paths, which imply that they swing around the sun and leave the solar system, never to return.

## I

**inclination** For planets, the angle between the plane of the ECLIPTIC and the plane of the planet's ORBIT or the angle between a line perpendicular to the plane of the ecliptic and the planet's AXIS of rotation. For SATELLITES, orbital inclination is expressed relative to the parent planet's orbital plane.

**inferior planet** Any planet whose ORBIT is smaller than that of the earth. Thus, Venus and Mercury are the two inferior planets of the SOLAR SYSTEM.

**infrared radiation** The part of the ELECTROMAGNETIC SPECTRUM that lies between the microwave and visible WAVELENGTHS.

**interference** The combination of two waves, for example ELECTROMAGNETIC WAVES, producing regions of high intensity (where the waves combine) and low intensity (where they tend to cancel each other).

**interferometry** Technique in which two waves, usually of ELECTROMAGNETIC RADIATION (such as light or radio waves) are combined to produce an INTERFERENCE pattern. Radiation from a distant source can be analyzed by this method, and very small angles can be accurately determined.

**ion** An atom or group of atoms that by either losing or gaining one or more ELECTRONS becomes positively or negatively charged.

**ionosphere** A region above a planet where the breakup of atmospheric gases by sunlight leads to large concentrations of free ELECTRONS and IONS. These are capable of seriously disrupting radio communications on earth.

## J

**Jeans mass** The mass of a region of gas above which its own gravity can cause it to collapse in spite of outward thermal pressure.

## K

**Kepler's laws** Three basic laws of planetary motion. (1) The ORBIT of a planet is an ELLIPSE, with the sun at one focus. (2) The line joining the position of a planet in its orbit to the sun (the radius vector) sweeps out equal areas in equal times. (3) The squares of the orbital periods of the planets are proportional to the cube of their mean distances from the sun.

**Kirkwood gap** One of a series of vacancies in the distribution of the ORBITS of the MINOR PLANETS, marked by the absence of minor planets whose orbits have periods that are simple fractions of the orbital period of Jupiter. The reason for the phenomenon is that in such positions any minor planet would be repeatedly perturbed by Jupiter's gravitational field until it was forced out of the "forbidden" orbit. The gaps are an example of gravitational RESONANCE.

## L

**Lagrangian position** One of a set of five positions at which a small object can maintain a stable ORBIT under the influence of two much more massive objects.

**latitude** The angular distance of a point from the earth's equator, measured upon the earth's surface.

**light curve** A plot of the change in brightness (expressed in APPARENT MAGNITUDES) against time of VARIABLE STARS.

**light-year** A measure of distance equal in length to the distance traveled by light in one year. Approximately equal to 5.9 million million miles.

**line emission** ELECTROMAGNETIC RADIATION emitted or absorbed at discrete FREQUENCIES (or WAVELENGTHS). *See* TWENTY-ONE CENTIMETER RADIATION.

**lithosphere** The upper region of the body of a planet comprising the CRUST and top layers of the MANTLE. This layer is often broken up into TECTONIC plates.

**Local Group** The group of about 30 galaxies of which our GALAXY is a member. The whole group is held together by its mutual gravitational attraction.

**longitude** The angular distance measured along the earth's equator between the MERIDIAN passing through the point and the Greenwich (zero) Meridian.

**luminosity** The total amount of energy radiated by a luminous object per unit time (e.g., one second). Common units are watts.

## M

**magnetosphere** The magnetic field of a planet in space. A planet's magnetosphere is molded by the SOLAR WIND into a teardrop shape, its point directed away from the sun.

**magnitude** A measure of a star's LUMINOSITY, in terms of ABSOLUTE MAGNITUDE or APPARENT MAGNITUDE.

**Main Sequence** The diagonal belt of STARS on the HERTZSPRUNG-RUSSELL DIAGRAM stretching from the high temperature and LUMINOSITY region of the diagram down to the low temperature end. A star's position in the belt depends on its mass, and once on the Main Sequence a star remains there for most of its life.

**mantle** The layer in the body of a planet lying between the CRUST and the CORE.

**mascon** A term abbreviated from mass concentration. Mascons are regions on the moon with a higher than normal gravitational field. They are probably due to abnormally dense material just beneath the lunar surface.

**mass-luminosity relation** An empirical relation between the mass and LUMINOSITY (both usually expressed in solar units) for MAIN SEQUENCE STARS. For sunlike stars, the luminosity varies as the 3.5 power of the mass. The power is smaller for lower mass stars.

**meridian** The circle that passes through both poles on a sphere, cutting the equator at right angles.

**meteor** The streak of light seen in the night sky signifying the burning up in the earth's ATMOSPHERE of interplanetary material. See METEORITE.

**meteorite** Interplanetary material that survives passing through a planet's ATMOSPHERE and lands on its surface.

**meteoroid** The general terms for METEORS and MICROMETEOROIDS, the latter usually having masses of less than a microgram.

**Metonic cycle** A period of 19 years after which the phases of the moon recur on the same days of the year. A series of four of five ECLIPSES also occurs on the same dates after this interval.

**micrometeoroid** Particles of cosmic dust, typically less than 0.1 millimeter in size and a microgram in mass.

**microwave background radiation** The radiation which fills the UNIVERSE uniformly in all directions, with a peak intensity at about 1 millimeter wavelength (in the microwave region). It is interpreted in the BIG BANG THEORY as the remnant of the initial explosion.

**Milky Way** The faint band of luminescence crossing the whole CELESTIAL SPHERE, and made up of STARS lying in the central plane of our GALAXY.

**minor planet** One of a family of stony objects mostly orbiting between the orbits of Mars and Jupiter. They probably represent PLANETESIMALS that failed to form a planet.

**Mira variable** A VARIABLE STAR typified by the red giant Mira Ceti. The LIGHT CURVE is irregular, with a varying range of brightness and of period between peaks of brightness.

**Mohorovičić discontinuity** The interface between the earth's CRUST and the MANTLE.

# N

**neap tide** The tide raised on the earth when the sun and moon are in positions forming a right angle at the earth's center. Thus, neap tides are the high tides, and occur at the half-moon phases. *See also* SPRING TIDE.

**nebula** A cloudlike region of gas and dust that shines either by its own light (EMISSION NEBULA) or by reflected light (REFLECTION NEBULA), if it is a bright nebula, or simply absorbs light falling onto it if it is a dark nebula.

**neutrino** An elementary particle with no charge and a very small, perhaps zero, mass. Produced in nuclear reactions in STARS, the particle has a very weak interaction with matter.

**neutron star** The result of the collapse of the remnant from a SUPERNOVA explosion if its mass exceeds the CHANDRASEKHAR LIMIT, but is less than that required for gravity to continue the collapse down to a BLACK HOLE. Its name derives from the fact that the object is so condensed that most of its material is in the form of neutrons. *See also* PULSAR.

**nova** The sudden increase in brightness of a STAR, probably as a result of its interaction with another, very close, star forming a BINARY SYSTEM. The brightness increase is due to the blowing off of a large amount of hot hydrogen gas from the star's surface, the star probably being a WHITE DWARF.

**nuclear fusion** The process which keeps STARS, like the sun, luminous for billions of years. In general, nuclear fusion involves the "fusing" together of atomic nuclei of low mass to form heavier nuclei. A vast amount of energy is released in the process.

**nucleosynthesis** The generation of chemical elements by the BIG BANG, and by SUPERNOVA explosions.

# O

**oblateness** A measure of the amount by which a celestial object, such as a planet, differs in shape from a perfect sphere. It is usually calculated from dividing the difference between the equatorial and polar diameters (or radii) by the equatorial diameter (or radius).

**occultation** The total or partial obscuring of a STAR or other celestial object by the moon or a planet.

**Oort cloud** A cloud of COMETS lying about 50,000 to 100,000 ASTRONOMICAL UNITS from the sun. The Oort cloud is postulated as the source of comets entering the SOLAR SYSTEM.

**opacity** A measure of the absorption of incident radiation by a body, being the ratio of the total radiant energy incident upon a body to the amount that

passes through it.

**open cluster** A loose cluster of young STARS of high LUMINOSITY found in or near the plane of the galaxy.

**opposition** An object lying farther from the sun than the earth is said to be at opposition when it lies on a line from the sun passing through the earth to the body in question. The object is then directly behind the earth, and is fully illuminated as seen from the earth.

**orbit** The path followed by one object about another as a result of their mutual GRAVITATIONAL interaction. As a result of the inverse square law of gravitation, planetary orbits are approximately CONIC SECTIONS.

**orbital elements** A set of six parameters that fix uniquely the shape, size, and orientation of a celestial body.

# P

**parabola** A CONIC SECTION. Some COMETS enter the SOLAR SYSTEM on parabolic orbits, and are therefore never seen again. The parabolic shape is also used in telescope mirrors and radio telescope aerials to bring all the radiation gathered from an object to a sharp focus.

**parallax** The angular displacement undergone by the position of a STAR when observed from two different points.

**parsec** A unit of length equal to the distance at which the mean radius of the earth's orbit subtends an angle of one second of arc. Equal to about 3.26 LIGHT-YEARS.

**penumbra** The region of partial shadow on each side of the central UMBRA produced by one body eclipsing another. An observer within the penumbral region will see a partial ECLIPSE. It is also the name given to the outer dark region of a SUNSPOT.

**perihelion** The point in the ORBIT of a planet, COMET, or other celestial body, at which it passes closest to the sun.

**period-luminosity relation** A relation obeyed by CEPHEID VARIABLE stars, and which states that the period of the changes in LUMINOSITY varies directly with the luminosity of the star.

**perturbation** Irregularity in an object's ORBIT caused by the GRAVITATIONAL influence of another object.

**phase** The appearance of the illuminated surface of a celestial body as seen from earth.

**photomultiplier** An electronic device used to amplify low-intensity light signals by converting them into ELECTRONS. The acceleration of these electrons leads to a cascade, and a relatively large output signal for a small input signal.

**photon** A quantum of electromagnetic energy that can be considered as a particle with no mass, no charge, and traveling at the speed of light. As "packets" of light they can be individually counted and used to build up a picture of, say, a distant GALAXY.

**photosphere** The visible surface of the sun.

**pixel** The basic unit of area of illumination on a display or a detection instrument: also known as a "picture element" or "cell."

**planetary nebula** The cloud of expanding gas surrounding a STAR that has blown off its outer layers, possibly in a NOVA stage.

**planetesimals** The generic term for bodies ranging in size from millimeter-sized particles to kilometer-sized MINOR PLANETS, that are believed to have formed the planets by ACCRETION.

**planisphere** A two-dimensional representation of the night sky as it would appear to a specific observer at one particular LATITUDE and time.

**plasma** The so-called "fourth state of matter," consisting of IONS and ELECTRONS in equilibrium. Such a state can be arrived at in regions of very high temperatures, such as exist within STARS.

**polarization** The degree to which the electric and magnetic components of ELECTROMAGNETIC RADIATION are confined to one configuration.

**Population I** One of two groups that STARS and stellar clusters can be divided into, according to age, position in space, and chemical composition. Population I stars are relatively young, very luminous stars belonging to the spiral arms of GALAXIES. Typical members are O-type stars, Delta Cephei stars, and OPEN CLUSTERS.

**Population II** One of two groups that STARS and other celestial bodies can be divided into. Population II stars are typically old, metal-deficient stars found in the center of the GALAXY, and also following highly elliptical ORBITS that take them far from the galactic disk. Typical Population II members are long-period variable stars, GLOBULAR CLUSTERS, and type II CEPHEID VARIABLES.

**prominence** A cloud of gas in the sun's ATMOSPHERE at a lower temperature than its surroundings; probably CORONAL material under the influence of the sun's magnetic field.

**proper motion** The movement of a STAR in the CELESTIAL SPHERE, which is more noticeable in near stars than in distant stars—in practice, the movement of the latter is negligible.

**proton** An elementary particle with a mass about 1,836 times that of the ELECTRON and a positive charge (equal and opposite to that of the electron).

**protostar** The stage in the evolution of a star between fragmentation and the ZERO AGE MAIN SEQUENCE stage, where nuclear reactions begin.

**pulsar** A neutron STAR which produces regular pulses of ELECTROMAGNETIC RADIATION. The pulses are very short, and are probably due to SYNCHROTRON EMISSION from a beam produced by the object's magnetic field sweeping around like a lighthouse beam.

## Q

**quantum** The smallest unit of electromagnetic energy at a given frequency. A PHOTON is a quantum of light.

**quasar** An exceptionally powerful, yet very compact extragalactic object, whose exact nature is still uncertain. Observations suggest that quasars may be the hyperactive nuclei of GALAXIES, while theory indicates that the high luminosity (100 to 1,000 times that of normal galaxies) could be associated with a supermassive BLACK HOLE.

## R

**radiant** The apparent point on the CELESTIAL SPHERE from which meteors making up a shower seem to emerge, owing to a perspective effect.

**radio telescope** An instrument used to make observations of celestial bodies at radio WAVELENGTHS. The equipment usually comprises an aerial which collects the radiation and feeds it to a processing computer. *See also* VERY LONG BASELINE INTERFEROMETRY.

**radio waves** A form of ELECTROMAGNETIC RADIATION traveling at the speed of light whose frequency lies between about 10 kilohertz and about 100,000 megahertz.

**recession** In astronomy, movement of a celestial object away from the observer, or from another celestial object.

**red giant** A STAR with a relatively low surface temperature (a few thousand degrees at most) and radius between 10 and 100 times that of the sun. Such objects are representative of stars at the end of their evolutionary life.

**red shift** The observed shift of the characteristic spectral lines of, for example, a GALAXY, toward the red, longer-WAVELENGTH, end of the SPECTRUM as a result of the galaxy's RECESSION from us.

**reflection nebula** A NEBULA which shines as the result of the scattering of the light of a STAR or group of stars nearby. Such scattering is usually caused by dust within the nebula.

**refractor telescope** A telescope that uses lenses to gather light from faint objects. The front, objective, lens is usually made of two or more components, with the eyepiece at the other end being the point at which the observer sees the image of the object.

**regolith** The topmost layer of the moon and earth-like planets, which has been broken up by meteoric bombardment.

**relative density** The density of a substance relative to that of water. Thus, a material with a relative density of 5.5 has a density of about 343 pounds per cubic foot (5,500 kilogram per cubic meter).

**relativity** The Special Theory of Relativity was developed by Albert Einstein in 1905 to explain the influence of the relative motion and position of an observer on his own observations. It proposes that an object traveling through space has its own space-time continuum; but, also, that light travels at a constant speed (the speed of light—defined as the ultimate speed) regardless of the speed or direction of travel of the light source or the observer. The General Theory of Relativity, published in 1916, defined gravitation as a function of four-dimensional space-time.

**resolving power** The ability of a telescope to separate two closely spaced sources of radiation, such as STARS.

**resonance** A body is said to be in resonance when it is affected by a force applied with a certain frequency (the resonant frequency) at which the body is seriously perturbed from equilibrium. An example of resonance in astronomy is provided by the KIRKWOOD GAPS.

**retrograde motion** The clockwise, or east to west, motion of a body, and hence the reverse of direct motion. As the majority of bodies in the SOLAR SYSTEM ORBIT about their governing bodies (e.g., the sun or planet) in direct motion, the occurrence of retrograde motion usually indicates some peculiarity.

**right ascension** The angular distance, measured eastward along the CELESTIAL EQUATOR, between a celestial object and the FIRST POINT OF ARIES. Symbol $\alpha$ (alpha), this coordinate is usually expressed in units of time.

**Roche limit** The minimum distance between the center of one body and another orbiting about it at which the second can withstand TIDAL FORCES generated by the first.

**RR Lyrae star** One of a family of pulsating giant STARS, with periods of less than one day. The period of particular examples does show changes, both abrupt and slow. Such stars are commonly found in GLOBULAR CLUSTERS.

## S

**Saros** A period of about 18 years and 10 days after which a sequence of solar and lunar ECLIPSES recurs.

**satellite** An object in ORBIT round a parent body. For clarity, natural satellites are commonly described as moons to distinguish them from man-made or artificial satellites.

**Schmidt camera** A telescope-camera able to take pictures covering a wide area of the sky without optical problems by virtue of having a specially shaped corrector plate near its upper-end.

**Schönberg-Chandrasekhar limit** A limit on the mass of a MAIN SEQUENCE STAR's core above which the star will leave the Main Sequence to become a RED GIANT. This occurs when the helium core makes up 10 to 15 per cent of the star's mass.

**scintillation** The "twinkling" of a point source of light as a result of the turbulence of the atmosphere through which the source's light passes.

**semi-major axis** Half of the larger diameter of an ELLIPSE;

half of the smaller diameter is the semi-minor axis.

**Seyfert galaxy** A GALAXY with an unusually bright central nucleus, often emitting strongly in the INFRARED region of the ELECTROMAGNETIC SPECTRUM, as the result of hot dust within it; X RAYS are also emitted in short bursts. About 2 per cent of all galaxies are Seyferts.

**sidereal period** The time taken for a body to ORBIT once about its primary body. Thus, the sidereal period for the earth is the time taken for one complete orbit about the sun, 365.256 days.

**siderite** The class of iron METEORITES, which includes those with about 90 per cent iron and 10 per cent nickel.

**siderolite** The class of stony-iron METEORITES, which includes those with about 50 per cent silicates and 50 per cent iron and nickel.

**singularity** A point in space at which an infinitely strong gravitational field exists. Such a concept is predicted by general RELATIVITY to exist at the center of a BLACK HOLE.

**solar system** The collective name for the sun and all the bodies that ORBIT about it, including the nine major planets, their satellites, periodic COMETS, and the ASTEROIDS. Its boundary could be taken as the outermost point reached by Pluto—about 50 ASTRONOMICAL UNITS from the sun.

**solar wind** The stream of charged particles "blown" by the thermal pressure of the sun out from its CORONA, which it cannot retain by gravity. In the vicinity of the earth, these particles have a velocity of about 300 miles (500 kilometers) per second.

**solstice** The point at which the sun reaches its greatest positive and negative DECLINATIONS. The northern summer solstice occurs about June 22 each year, and the sun then has its maximum declination of about $+23\frac{1}{2}°$. The northern winter solstice occurs about December 22, when the sun's declination is $-23\frac{1}{2}°$. These dates are also the longest and shortest days of the year, respectively.

**Special Theory of Relativity** *See* RELATIVITY.

**speckle interferometry** A technique for obtaining better images of celestial bodies by taking a series of rapid photographic exposures of the object. This enables the effect of SCINTILLATION to be minimized.

**spectrohelioscope** An instrument for studying an image of the sun taken at one particular WAVELENGTH, instead of the usual mixture of wavelengths.

**spectroscope** An instrument that allows quantitative measurements of SPECTRA to be made.

**spectrum** The splitting up of ELECTROMAGNETIC RADIATIONS into the constituent WAVELENGTHS.

**sporadic** A METEOR not associated with a major meteor shower.

**Spörer's law** The tendency of SUNSPOTS to appear at the start of the sun's 11-year sunspot cycle at high solar latitudes, and for later sunspots to appear at successively lower solar latitudes, before starting the next cycle at the higher latitudes again.

**spring tide** The tide on the earth's surface when the effect of the moon and sun is greatest, i.e., when the two bodies are in line. This occurs at new and full moon. *See also* NEAP TIDE.

**star** A body, such as the sun, that produces energy by means of nuclear reactions taking place within it. The star is held in a stable state by balancing the outward radiation pressure by the inward gravitational force.

**Steady State theory** A theory of the evolution of the UNIVERSE that states that the universe has always been in the state it is now, which leads to the implication that the universe had no origin, but has always existed.

**stellar wind** The stream of particles "blown" by the radiative pressure of a STAR away into space.

**sunspot** A dark path on the sun's surface (PHOTOSPHERE) marking the position of a region of intense magnetic field. A sunspot can be divided into two regions, the central UMBRA, which has a typical temperature of about 4000° F. (2200° C), and the outer PENUMBRA, at about 5500° F. (3000° C); the relative coolness of these regions compared to their surroundings produces the dark contrast. Sunspots usually occur in groups, with typical lifetimes of about two weeks.

**supergiant** The largest and brightest type of all STARS, of which Antares in Scorpius is an example.

**superior planet** Any planet that lies farther from the sun than the earth. Thus the superior planets are Mars, Jupiter, Saturn, Uranus, Neptune, and Pluto.

**superluminal** Any object whose apparent speed exceeds the speed of light.

**supernova** The sudden, temporary and enormous increase in brightness of a STAR, resulting from the blowing off of most of its constituent material in its death-throes. Such an event occurs for stars only about six times more massive than the sun, the result being a WHITE DWARF.

**synchronous orbit** A SATELLITE whose orbital period about the central body is the same as the rotation period of the central body has a synchronous orbit.

**synchronous rotation** The axial rotation of a planetary SATELLITE is said to be synchronous when its period of rotation is exactly the same as that for the satellite to ORBIT once about the central body.

**synchrotron radiation** A form of ELECTROMAGNETIC RADIATION emitted by an electric charge moving RELATIVISTICALLY through a magnetic field. It is characterized by being POLARIZED.

**synodic period** The mean interval between successive OPPOSITIONS, or identical PHASES, of a body in the SOLAR SYSTEM.

# T

**tectonics** The movement of plates that make up the LITHOSPHERE of a planet. Such movement produces fold mountains and other features on the surface of the planet.

**thermal emission** The type of ELECTROMAGNETIC RADIATION emitted when ELECTRONS and atoms forming part of a hot gas interact by collisions; the resulting radiation is CONTINUOUS, as opposed to discrete, LINE EMISSION.

**thermonuclear reaction** NUCLEAR FUSION that occurs at extremely high temperatures.

**tidal force** The force arising from differences in the strength of gravity experienced over different parts of an object. Such a force is responsible for the TIDES, and for the breakup of a body straying within the ROCHE LIMIT of a planet.

**tide** The effect arising from the differential gravitational effect of one body on another. This usually manifests itself in the distortion of the shape of the body, especially the surface layers. *See also* NEAP TIDE; SPRING TIDE.

**Titius-Bode law** An empirical law that generates the distances of planets and position of the minor planet belt from the sun in ASTRONOMICAL UNITS. A derivation based on a theory of the origin of the SOLAR SYSTEM may be possible eventually. The distance in astronomical units $d$ is given by the formula $d = 0.4 + 0.3 \times 2^n$, where $n = -\infty$ for Mercury, 0 for Venus, 1 for Earth, and so on.

**torus** An object formed by joining the two ends of a cylinder producing a doughnut shape with circular cross-section.

**totality** The moment during a total solar ECLIPSE during which the sun completely disappears from view.

**transit** The passage across the observer's MERIDIAN of a celestial body, or the crossing of the face of one body (e.g., the sun) by the path of another (e.g., Mercury or Venus), from the observer's viewpoint.

**trigonometry** A branch of mathematics that deals with the relationships between angles and lengths of sides of right-angled triangles. Knowing the length of one side of the triangle and one angle (apart from the right angle) enables all the other lengths and angles to be calculated. The technique can also be applied to other triangles.

**Trojan group** A group of MINOR PLANETS which are clustered about two of the LAGRANGIAN POSITIONS of the Jupiter-sun system. The first Trojan was Achilles, discovered in 1906.

**T Tauri star** One of a group of STARS which have irregular LIGHT CURVES, and which are believed to represent the stage in a star's evolution shortly before it appears on the MAIN SEQUENCE. The stars characteristically have rapid rotation and throw off much material in STELLAR WINDS.

**twenty-one centimeter radiation** The common name given to RADIO WAVES emitted at 1,420 megahertz as the result of the "flipping over" of the ELECTRON in a hydrogen atom in order to oppose the spin direction of the central proton. The radiation is an example of LINE EMISSION.

## U

**ultraviolet radiation** The region of the ELECTROMAGNETIC SPECTRUM that lies between visible light and X RAYS, with WAVELENGTHS in the range of about $4 \times 10^{-7}$ and $5 \times 10^{-9}$ meters.

**umbra** The main dark inner cone of shadow cast by one body onto another during an ECLIPSE. Any point lying within the umbra will observe a total eclipse of the object. The umbra is also the name given to the darkest part of a SUNSPOT.

**universe** The totality of space, matter, and radiation that is potentially comprehensible.

**universe, expansion of** A feature of our UNIVERSE deduced from the observation that the distant galaxies' light is RED-SHIFTED. *See* HUBBLE'S LAW.

## V

**Van Allen belt** One of two regions, lying at about 1,900 miles (3,000 kilometers) and 12,500 miles (20,000 kilometers) above the equator, in which charged particles, trapped in the earth's MAGNETOSPHERE, oscillate between the magnetic poles. The particles are caught from the SOLAR WIND or produced by collisions between air molecules and COSMIC RAYS.

**variable star** A STAR whose luminous output varies significantly with time. Such variation may be regular, e.g., eclipsing variable stars, or irregular, as with flare stars. In addition, the variation can be intrinsic, due to changes within the star itself, or extrinsic, as the result of the interaction of one star with another.

**Very Long Baseline Interferometry (VLBI)** The technique of linking together several RADIO TELESCOPES spaced by hundreds and even thousands of miles to achieve very high resolution observations of distant objects such as QUASARS. *See also* INTERFEROMETRY.

## W

**wavelength** The distance between successive peaks (or troughs) of a wave. Symbol $\lambda$ (lambda), and related to frequency $f$ by $\lambda$ ($\lambda = v/f$, where $v$ is the velocity of the wave).

**Weichert (Gutenberg) discontinuity** The interface between the mantle of the earth and the outer core. It lies about 1,800 miles (2,900 kilometers) beneath the earth's surface.

**white dwarf** A dense, small low-LUMINOSITY STAR of mass less than the CHANDRASEKHAR LIMIT (1.4 solar masses) left as the remnant of a SUPERNOVA explosion.

**Wilson effect** The foreshortening of a SUNSPOT lying close to the edge of the sun's visible disk.

**Wolf-Rayet star** A member of a class of STARS undergoing rapid mass loss, and having peculiar SPECTRA. Most Wolf-Rayet stars have companions in BINARY SYSTEMS.

## X

**X rays** A form of ELECTROMAGNETIC RADIATION with typical WAVELENGTHS between $5 \times 10^{-9}$ and $6 \times 10^{-12}$ meters, corresponding to FREQUENCIES between about $10^{16}$ and $10^{20}$ Hz.

## Z

**zenith** The point on the CELESTIAL SPHERE that is directly above the observer, i.e., at an ALTITUDE of 90°.

**Zero Age Main Sequence (ZAMS)** The point on the HERTZSPRUNG-RUSSELL DIAGRAM occupied by a STAR that has a core temperature high enough for nuclear reactions.

**zodiac** The band of 12 CONSTELLATIONS through which the ECLIPTIC passes.

# Index

# Credits